www.wadsworth.com

wadsworth.com is the World Wide Web site for Wadsworth and is your direct source to dozens of online resources.

At *wadsworth.com* you can find out about supplements, demonstration software, and student resources. You can also send email to many of our authors and preview new publications and exciting new technologies.

wadsworth.com
Changing the way the world learns®

About the Author

Carolynn A. Lindeman (B.M., Oberlin College, D.M.A., Stanford University) is Professor of Music at San Francisco State University and past president of MENC—The National Association for Music Education. She currently serves on the Board of Directors for the International Society for Music Education. Active as a speaker and clinician, she has given presentations throughout the United States and in Canada, Europe, Southeast Asia, Mexico, Israel, and South Africa. Lindeman is coauthor of *The Musical Classroom: Backgrounds, Models, and Skills for Elementary Teaching* and the compiler of *Women Composers of Ragtime* (a piano folio). She has published more than 50 articles in professional journals and served as series editor for 16 publications (MENC, 1995–2003) related to implementing and assessing the National Standards for Music Education.

fifth edition with CD

PianoLab
An Introduction to Class Piano

Carolynn A. Lindeman

San Francisco State University

THOMSON

SCHIRMER

Australia · Canada · Mexico · Singapore · Spain · United Kingdom · United States

THOMSON
™
SCHIRMER

Publisher, Music: Clark Baxter
Assistant Editor: Julie Yardley
Editorial Assistant: Eno Sarris
Technology Project Manager: Jennifer Ellis
Marketing Manager: Mark D. Orr
Marketing Assistant: Kristi Bostock
Advertising Project Manager: Brian Chaffee
Project Manager, Editorial Production: Emily Smith
Print/Media Buyer: Rebecca Cross
Permissions Editor: Bob Kauser

Production Service: Greg Hubit Bookworks
Text Designer: Kelly Shoemaker
Photo Researcher: Terri Wright
Copy Editor: Carole Crouse
Autographer: Mansfield Music-Graphics
Compositor: TBH Typecast, Inc.
Text Printer: Quebecor World/Dubuque
Cover Designer: Ark Stein
Cover Printer: The Lehigh Press, Inc.

Printed in the United States of America
1 2 3 4 5 6 7 07 06 05 04 03

For more information about our products, contact us at:
Thomson Learning Academic Resource Center
1-800-423-0563
For permission to use material from this text, contact us by:
Phone: 1-800-730-2214
Fax: 1-800-730-2215
Web: http://www.thomsonrights.com

Wadsworth Group/Thomson Learning
10 Davis Drive
Belmont, CA 94002-3098
USA

Asia
Thomson Learning
5 Shenton Way #01-01
UIC Building
Singapore 068808

Australia/New Zealand
Thomson Learning
102 Dodds Street
Southbank, Victoria 3006
Australia

Canada
Nelson
1120 Birchmount Road
Toronto, Ontario M1K 5G4
Canada

Europe/Middle East/Africa
Thomson Learning
High Holborn House
50/51 Bedford Row
London WC1R 4LR
United Kingdom

Latin America
Thomson Learning
Seneca, 53
Colonia Polanco
11560 Mexico D.F.
Mexico

Spain/Portugal
Paraninfo
Calle/Magallanes, 25
28015 Madrid, Spain

Library of Congress Control Number: 2003102372

ISBN 0-534-60354-8

Contents

chapter six — Performing Major Scales and I and V7 Chords   113

A Couple of Reading Tips   140

chapter seven — The Primary Chords and 12-Bar Blues   141

chapter ten   *Other Scales, Modes, and Tonalities*   226

Supplementary Music   *251*

Appendixes

Note to Students

ABOUT *PIANOLAB*

PianoLab, fifth edition, is designed for you, the beginning student. It assumes no background in music but does assume you have a genuine interest in learning to play the piano and learning about music. All the music, exercises, learning and playing tips, and reference and resource materials are aimed at helping you realize your goal of learning to play the piano and develop basic understandings about music.

PianoLab is organized into ten chapters, and each chapter is divided into three units. Objectives are presented at the beginning of each chapter to familiarize you with the expectations for developing keyboard skills and musical understandings. End-of-Chapter Evaluations help you assess what you have learned.

As you learn to read and play, you will discover that reading notes and playing scales and chord progressions are not enough. You must also develop an understanding of how music is put together, how it "works," and how rhythm, melody, and harmony interrelate to form musical compositions. This musical understanding evolves mainly through performing but also through analyzing, improvising, transposing, harmonizing, and composing. Helping you develop keyboard skills and music concepts simultaneously is the goal of PianoLab.

WIDE VARIETY OF MUSIC

PianoLab includes more than two hundred pieces of music; ninety-four are recorded on the accompanying CD. A wide variety of music is included—everything from classical music of the eighteenth through the twentieth centuries to folk, jazz, and popular music. Some of the music will be familiar and much will be new. It is not necessary to learn every piece of music in the book to acquire essential concepts and skills.

Twenty of the musical selections are arranged to be played as ensemble pieces with one or two students per piano or with students playing one part and the instructor the other. For individual practice, you can perform the student part and use the accompanying CD to play the instructor's part.

RESOURCE MATERIALS

You will find Playing Tips, Key Facts, Key Terms and Signs, and Notes about Composers highlighted throughout the book. These are intended to provide you with important information as you progress with your piano study. Illustrations of keyboard positions and visuals to help with learning about the keyboard and music appear frequently. You will discover tips for practicing the piano, memorizing music, sight-reading, and pedaling.

The accompanying CD should serve as one of your main resource materials for *PianoLab*. This CD offers you the opportunity to hear some of the varied repertoire presented in the book and gives you a playing partner when your instructor or fellow piano students are not around.

The appendixes in the back of the book present additional reference materials that are helpful to have all in one place, such as musical terms and signs, scales, chords, and a Timeline of Western Art Music and the Development of Keyboard Instruments. A complete glossary follows the appendixes defining terms referred to throughout the text. The handy pull-out Keyboard and Grand Staff Chart, attached to the inside back cover, can be propped up on your piano and used to help you learn to associate the key names with the staff notation.

Visit the *PianoLab* Web site (http://music.wadsworth.com) for additional information and resources.

THE PIANO AND YOU

Beginning pianists progress at different rates of speed. Some of you will develop eye and hand coordination quickly and almost effortlessly. Others will work diligently and slowly to achieve the same results in a longer period of time. Do not become frustrated by this phenomenon—whenever you learn a new technical skill, whether it be a sport or piano playing, individual differences always come into play.

Remember that your progress and pleasure in piano study depend on *you*. *You* must make the personal commitment and accept the challenge of learning a new skill. Yes, and that means setting aside time for practice, preferably a little each day! Use the Practice Worksheet and Practice Journal to help you set goals and accomplish them. It is hoped that the many components of *PianoLab* and the assistance of your instructor will help you meet the many challenges of keyboard playing and, most important, turn you on to the exciting world of music.

Preface to the Fifth Edition

PianoLab: An Introduction to Class Piano, fifth edition, like the editions that preceded it, was created mindful of the challenges faced by students and their instructors in most class piano courses. Students want to play the piano as quickly as possible and often become frustrated when their physical skills do not keep pace with their conceptual skills. Their varying backgrounds, motivation, and cognitive and psychomotor skills make it impossible for everyone to learn at the same rate. Even with the best facilities, the instructor faces a limited time frame in which to teach the piano basics. It may take one or two quarters or semesters for students to learn their "keyboard geography" and become comfortable at the piano. Add to that the desire to give students more than just a brush with music concepts, and there is indeed a great deal to accomplish in a short time.

These challenges, however, are not insurmountable. Assuming that students have no prior background in music, *PianoLab,* fifth edition, focuses on teaching them to *perform.* And it goes a step further: It gives students an *understanding* of music that they can take with them, whether or not they continue to play the piano. Each chapter includes brief materials to develop understanding of the elements of music: melody, rhythm, harmony, and form. Students are then encouraged to apply that knowledge through performing, analyzing, improvising, transposing, harmonizing, and composing.

ORGANIZATION OF THE BOOK

PianoLab is organized into ten chapters, and new in this edition is the division of each chapter into three units. The main focus of each unit and chapter is the development of skills and technique. Chapter 1 invites students to explore the keyboard by *making music and creating music* before learning to read it. Subsequent chapters build on that initial exploration through the following:

- A wide variety of *playing materials* (over two hundred), representing art music of the eighteenth through the twentieth centuries by male and female composers, indeterminate music, folk songs, piano blues, boogie-woogie, ragtime, jazz, and popular music

- *Ensemble pieces* integrated throughout the text and arranged for two or more players

- Careful *grading of selections* from the simplest to the more challenging

- *Development of music-reading and playing skills simultaneously* through exercises and playing materials

- *Composing and improvising projects* to encourage and develop creativity

- *Technique exercises* covering skills encountered within each chapter and those to come in subsequent chapters
- *Learning objectives* clearly stated at the beginning of each chapter
- *End-of-chapter* evaluations for students and instructors to evaluate skill development and progress in musical understanding before moving ahead to the next chapter.

ADDITIONAL FEATURES

- A new and important feature of this fifth edition is the addition of an **accompanying CD**. The CD includes ninety-four pieces of music. Solo repertoire pieces from each chapter and ensemble pieces are the core components of the CD.
- Instructors will receive free MIDI disks of the ninety-four selections on the CD by requesting the bundle ISBN 0-534-60358-0.
- *PianoLab,* fifth edition, also includes a **Supplementary Music** section with sixty selections of solo piano pieces; traditional folk and patriotic songs with piano accompaniment; and folk and popular melodies.
- Several **appendixes** on such topics as musical terms and signs, fingerings for selected major and minor scales, primary chords in root position and in I–IV$^6_4$–V$^6_5$ position, accompaniment patterns, and **a Timeline of Western Art Music and the Development of Keyboard Instruments** help to answer student questions and provide references for study, practice, and review. Following the appendixes is a **Glossary** of musical terms.
- In addition to the general index, *PianoLab,* fifth edition, has several **specialized indexes** to provide flexibility and ease of use.
- *PianoLab* stresses **strong student orientation**, from the Note to Students through each chapter, where a variety of music is offered to help students acquire needed skills and concepts. A practice worksheet and a practice journal are provided for students to duplicate and use in keeping track of their progress. The handy pullout Keyboard and Grand Staff Chart, attached to the inside back cover of the text, will help students learn to associate the key names with staff notation.
- **Root-position chords** are stressed to solidify student understanding of chord building. Although only the primary chords (in root position and all inversions) are presented throughout the text, several examples in the Supplementary Songs sections include secondary chords. Appendix H identifies primary chords in selected major and minor keys.
- **Eighteenth-century music** appears primarily in original (*Urtext*) edition with only fingerings added. Since few dynamic, tempo, or articulation markings were included in music of this period, performance notes are often provided, but little editing is added by the author. It would be helpful to remind students to follow these simple performance guidelines for eighteenth-century pieces: play *non legato* (not connected), *mezzo forte* (medium loud), and *moderato* (moderate tempo).
- An **Instructor's Resource Guide** is available online at http://music.wadsworth.com. It includes answer keys for End-of-Chapter Evaluations, supplementary worksheets, and ideas and strategies for teaching specific topics.

ACKNOWLEDGMENTS

Creating *PianoLab* required the help and support of many people. I am particularly grateful to:

My colleagues and students in the San Francisco State University School of Music and Dance for their help in developing, improving, and critiquing *PianoLab* in its various stages.

Composers and friends Nancy Van de Vate, Herbert Bielawa, and Emma Lou Diemer for contributing pieces to *PianoLab*.

Keyboard and performance practices specialist Sandra Soderlund for her critical assessment and review of the Technique Exercises and musical examples and her expert advice on eighteenth-century keyboard performance practices.

The following reviewers for their thoughtful and critical comments: Tanya Gille, University of Colorado at Boulder; Ellen Grolman Schlegel, Frostburg State University; Dee Spencer, College of Creative Arts, San Francisco State University; and Lisa Zdechlik, University of Arizona.

Finally, my husband, Al, for his expert editorial help in making *PianoLab,* fifth edition, become a reality.

Introduction

THE PIANO

Historical Development

Bartolomeo Cristofori (1655–1732) is credited with inventing the piano about 1709 in Florence, Italy. The piano differed from two earlier keyboard instruments, the **clavichord** and the **harpsichord,** in that its hammer action could provide continuous gradations of loud and soft tones. Cristofori's name for his invention was *gravicembalo col piano e forte* ("harpsichord with soft and loud"). The instrument, however, came to be known as the *pianoforte* or the abbreviated name *piano.* (A Timeline of Western Art Music and Keyboard Instruments is located

Grand piano by Johann Schmidt, Salzburg, Austria, 1788

in Appendix K.) For more on the history of the piano, log on to the Web site www.piano300.org.

Although the piano was invented in the early part of the eighteenth century, it did not become widely used until the latter part of that century. In the nineteenth century, it went through numerous improvements that ultimately resulted in our present-day grand piano.

Grand piano

Courtesy of Yamaha Corporation of America, California, and Yamaha Corporation, Japan

The upright piano was an innovation of the nineteenth century, and with this smaller and more economical instrument, pianos became a fixture in many American and European homes. In fact, it is said that in the 1850s there were more pianos than bathtubs in the United States, and in the early 1900s more pianos than telephones in the home.

Today pianos still come in the two eighteenth- and nineteenth-century shapes—the grand and the upright; also in recent years electronic pianos and various electronic keyboards have been developed. Because the sound can be

Upright piano

channeled through headphones, the electronic pianos are often used in a group piano setting.

Acoustic Pianos

An acoustic piano produces its sound by strings being struck by hammers, which are put into action by the keys. The complex mechanism connecting this key–hammer motion is called the piano's *action*. The small but long pieces of felt-covered wood that lie above the strings are called the *dampers*. They move up and down with the action via connecting wires. The dampers allow the strings to vibrate freely the moment the hammer strikes and stop the vibration when the key is released.

A standard-size piano *keyboard* has eighty-eight keys: fifty-two white and thirty-six black keys. Some electronic pianos have shorter keyboards.

The modern piano has two or three foot-operated **pedals:** the **soft pedal** to the left, the **sostenuto pedal** in the middle, and the **damper pedal** to the right. Some upright pianos have only the soft and damper pedals. The damper pedal is used to connect and sustain tones, whereas the soft pedal, called **una corda** ("one string") **pedal,** is used to reduce the volume of sound. The sostenuto pedal (on a grand piano) permits the sustaining of a chord or a single note with the pedal while the hand is free to play other notes.

Courtesy of Soundtree, A Division of Korg USA

Electronic Keyboards

Electronic keyboards may be grouped into three categories: *basic keyboards, digital pianos,* and *synthesizers.*

Basic Keyboards

Basic keyboards are the most commonly purchased (and the least costly) non-professional electronic keyboards. Their most attractive features, outside of price, are battery operation, portability, and self-contained speaker systems. In addition, all basic keyboards include preprogrammed rhythmic accompaniments and automatic chordal accompaniments.

Digital Pianos

Unlike basic keyboards and synthesizers, digital pianos are distinguishable because they have the look and, more important, the feel (weighted keys) of a conventional acoustic piano. One of the important differences is a digital piano's MIDI (Musical Instrument Digital Interface) capabilities, which allow it to be used as a controller keyboard for other MIDI instruments, allow a performer to "record" a melody and then "play" it back at the touch of a button (called *sequencing*—essentially digital tape recording), and offer choices of preprogrammed timbres. The timbre choices may include the distinctive sounds of specific brands of pianos, organ sounds, or string sounds. Some instruments play stored music from disks, similar to the operation of early player pianos. Others offer the capability to make the instrument sound as though it is being played in a room, on a stage, or in a large concert hall.

Performance techniques for digital pianos, when employing an acoustic piano sound, are the same as for any acoustic piano.

Synthesizers

The most electronically sophisticated of the three groups of instruments, synthesizers offer far more options for programmability than either basic keyboards or digital pianos. They also come in many styles, types, and sizes.

Generally, synthesizers do not include preprogrammed rhythmic accompaniments, self-contained speaker systems, or automatic chording. Some do specialize in sampling (a digital "recording" of any acoustic sound), and others include onboard sequencers, as opposed to a separate electronic sequencing device like a computer. Performance techniques for synthesizers are quite different from those used for acoustic and digital pianos, mostly because of the lighter, organlike action. Ultimately, instrument or timbre selection will dictate performance technique.

Recent synthesizer and basic keyboard models include internal sequencers that can be programmed. The sequencing process involves the layering of two or more sound patterns or tracks—the part entered one at a time. Each track contains a specific instrument performance that is stored. When many tracks are layered and stored, a sequence program is created. Some *sequencers* allow for additional fine tuning of pitches and tempi.

THE ELEMENTS OF MUSIC

Although a pianist must develop skills in playing and reading music, he or she must also learn how music is put together, how music "works," and how the various elements of music combine and interrelate to form musical compositions. Most Western music includes the elements melody, rhythm, harmony, form, dynamics, tempo, and tone color. An individual element may be studied by itself; however, the elements seldom occur singularly in music.

> **Melody** is a succession of sounds (pitches) and silences moving through time—the horizontal structure of music. Each melody is a unique combination of sounds and silences, which, when organized in a series, creates a sense of line or a meaningful musical shape.

> **Rhythm** refers to all the durations of sounds and silences that occur in music as well as the organization of those sounds and silences in time. Perhaps the most fundamental ingredient of rhythm is the beat—the underlying pulsation that one feels recurring steadily as music moves through time. Sounds and silences in a melody move through time with a beat or, more often, in longer or shorter durations than the beat.

> **Harmony** is the simultaneous sounding of two or more tones—the vertical structure of music that moves through time and supports the melody. Chords are the principal building blocks of harmony. Chords are often indicated by an uppercase letter above the staff.

> **Form** refers to the overall design, plan, or order of a musical composition. Musical ideas expressed with pitches and rhythms are organized by the composer in various ways to create artistic balance. Usually, smaller units of musical ideas are put together to create larger ones until finally an overall form or total piece of music emerges. Music, as well as other art forms, utilizes unity and variety to achieve aesthetic balance.

Dynamics refers to the degree and range of loudness of musical sound.

Tempo refers to the speed of the musical sounds and silences.

Tone color or **timbre** refers to the characteristic or unique quality or color of sound of each voice, instrument, or sound source.

SUMMARY

To play the piano intelligently and sensitively, one must develop basic keyboard skills and understand basic concepts about melody, rhythm, harmony, form, dynamics, tempo, and tone color. This preliminary discussion is an introduction to the elements of music. Each chapter in *PianoLab* focuses on these elements.

chapter one

Exploring the Piano

Unit 1. Getting Ready! Learning Piano Basics
- Keyboard Position
- Finger Numbers
- Exploring the Black Keys and the White Keys
- The Pedals
- Exploring and Creating at the Keyboard

Unit 2. Exploring the White Keys
- Names of the White Keys

Unit 3. Exploring the Black Keys
- Sharps and Flats
- Names of the Black Keys—Enharmonics
- Improvisation—Black Keys

Composing Projects

End-of-Chapter Evaluation

OBJECTIVES

After completing this chapter, you will be able to

- ✔ Demonstrate correct hand, arm, and body positions for piano playing, and accurate finger numbers
- ✔ Identify, locate, and name the white and the black keys
- ✔ Demonstrate use of the damper pedal
- ✔ Perform a folk song, an indeterminate piece, a blues progression
- ✔ Improvise on the black keys
- ✔ Perform chord roots and drones as accompaniments
- ✔ Compose a descriptive miniature and a black-key piece

KEYBOARD POSITION

- Sit directly in front of the middle of the keyboard, with feet flat on the floor and knees barely under the keyboard.
- Sit far enough back from the keyboard that your arms and elbows can move freely.
- Sit erect, but lean slightly forward at the waist—maintain a good posture.

Correct Playing Position

To assume the correct playing position at the keyboard, follow these three steps:

Step 1. Drop your arms to your sides in a dangling position. Let your arms hang loosely from the shoulders.

Step 2. Lift your hands to the keyboard keeping that same relaxed position.

Step 3. Rest your fingers on the keys. Notice that

- your hands are slightly arched
- your fingers are gently curved
- your wrists are straight but flexible (and level with the keys)

Correct hand position

Correct Hand Position

As you position your hands at the keyboard, remember to

- Maintain a natural rounded hand shape and keep your fingers as close to the keys as possible.

- Play each key with the fleshy part of the finger. Keys should be "struck," not pressed. Fingernails must be short.

- Strike (do not push) the keys, making sure your hands do not move up and down with the fingers. Your hands should stay as motionless as possible.

- Watch that your wrists do not collapse. Think of a straight line going along your forearms to the knuckle of your middle finger.

Playing Tip Relax! Check and recheck your posture and playing position for any signs of tension. Stop from time to time and dangle your arms to your sides to relax the arms and hands. Strive for no tension in your arms and hands.

FINGER NUMBERS

The numbers 1–5 are assigned to specific fingers of both hands. These numbers (usually written very small) appear above or below the notes in piano music to indicate the preferred fingering.

Finger numbers in music

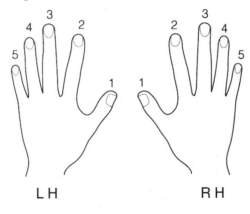

L H   R H

Finger-Number Practice

1. Practice saying the finger numbers aloud and moving the correct finger of each hand up and down.

2. As finger numbers are called out, play the correct fingers "in the air." Practice first with separate hands, then hands together.

EXPLORING THE BLACK KEYS AND THE WHITE KEYS

- Pitches go *higher* or *up* as your fingers move to the right on the keyboard.

- Pitches go *lower* or *down* as you move to the left on the keyboard.

- The black keys alternate in groups of twos and threes up and down the keyboard.

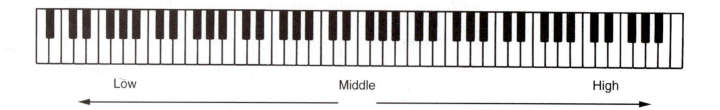

Low   Middle   High

Keyboard Practice—Groups of Black Keys

1. Find two black keys together in the middle of the keyboard. Using your right-hand (RH) index finger (2) and middle finger (3), play these two keys (both keys at once), moving up the keyboard.

2. Using your left-hand (LH) index finger (2) and middle finger (3), find two black keys together in the middle of the keyboard. Play these two keys (both keys at once), moving down the keyboard.

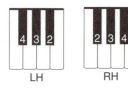

3. Find three black keys together in the lowest part of the keyboard. Play these three keys with your LH index (2), middle (3), and ring (4) fingers (one key at a time), moving up to the middle of the keyboard. With your RH, begin with the three black keys at the highest part of the keyboard and play these keys (one key at a time), moving down to the middle.

THE PEDALS

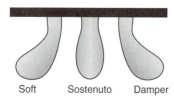

Soft   Sostenuto   Damper

The modern piano has two or three foot-operated pedals: the soft pedal, the sostenuto pedal, and the damper pedal. Some upright pianos have only the soft and damper pedals.

The damper pedal (far right) connects and sustains tones. To use the damper pedal, rest your foot lightly on the pedal, keeping your heel on the floor. When you press the damper pedal down, any tone you sound will be sustained—even after you have taken your finger (s) off the key. Play a black key, depress the damper pedal, then remove your finger from the key. Listen to the continuing sound.

Keyboard Practice—Exploring the Damper Pedal

Locate the two marked black keys (play them at the same time). Depress the damper pedal as you play the LH black keys together and keep the pedal depressed while you play the RH black keys. Continue alternating hands slowly, never releasing the damper pedal until you are ready to conclude your exploration. For a nice finish, end with your LH crossing over your RH to the same keys up higher.

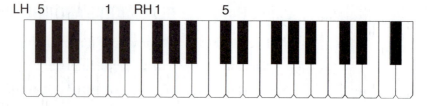

EXPLORING AND CREATING AT THE KEYBOARD

Follow the written directions of composer Tom Johnson to create your first piano composition—just read the words and doodle as he suggests. "Doodling" is an example of indeterminate music (music in which the outcome or result is unpredictable and no two performances are the same). Have fun!

Doodling

Tom Johnson (b. 1939)

Begin some very soft doodling with your right hand in the upper part of the keyboard. Continue the doodling as you read. Do not let your playing distract you from your reading, and do not let your reading distract you from your playing. The two must accompany each other. Now, without stopping the right-hand doodling, play a loud low note with your left hand, and sustain it for a moment. Continue the doodling and, whenever you feel the time is right, play another loud bass note. Do not wait too long between the loud low notes, but do not play them too close together either. Try not to worry about when you should or should not play another loud low note. If you become too involved with thinking about that, you will not be able to carry out your other tasks as well. Your attention should always be about equally divided between the three things: the reading, the right-hand doodling and the loud low notes.

Of course, you are quite limited in what you are permitted to play at the moment, and the music might become tedious after a while to someone who was only listening. But that is immaterial since these are *Private Pieces,* and are only for your own entertainment. The piece will not be tedious to you since it is not easy to do three things at once. The only way you can do all three well is by dividing your attention equally between them, so that you never ignore one of them. If you forget about the doodling, it will not sound the way you want it to sound. If you forget about the loud low notes, there will be a long awkward gap in the music. If you forget about the reading, you may miss some instruction or idea.

After another paragraph, you will be asked to play something else, but in the meantime continue playing and reading as you have been. If you find that you have been paying more attention to one of your tasks than to the other two, try to balance your attention more equally. Although no more instructions are necessary at the moment, the text is continuing in order to give you time to achieve a sense of balance between the three things, so that they seem to accompany one another. You have three more sentences in which to try to achieve this balance before going on to a new section of the piece. Now only two sentences, including this one, remain before the paragraph will end and you will be asked to do something else. This is the last sentence of this part of the piece.

Now stop playing, but continue reading. At some point during this paragraph, play a single note and sustain it. It may be loud or soft, high or low, black or white, but it must be a single note, and must be played only once. You may choose to play it early in the paragraph, or you may wish to play it toward the end of the paragraph. Perhaps you will want to read more of the text before making your decision. You must, however, remain within the limits of the paragraph. So if you have not played your note by this time, you must do so soon, as the paragraph is almost finished. You may wish to pause a moment before proceeding to the next paragraph, which will be quite demanding.

Resume the doodling with your right hand, as you did in the beginning of the piece, but this time let it gradually become more energetic. For a while it can be played by the right hand only, and should sound as it did at the beginning, but soon it should become faster. As it accelerates, you will probably want to use the left hand too, so that you can play more and more notes in less and less time. As the doodling becomes faster, you should also let it move into a wider range. By now the doodling should be noticeably more energetic than when you began this section. Do not let it increase too quickly, however, as there is still quite a ways to go before it reaches a peak. Gradually begin to use more and more of the keyboard and let the intensity increase until it is quite furious. Do not let the tension subside, even for a moment, and continue building until you are playing as wildly as you can. You may play anything necessary to maintain the high energy level. By now you should be playing as loud and fast as you can. You will perhaps find it more difficult to concentrate on the text now than when you were not playing so vigorously, but try to read the text as carefully as you have been, without making any sacrifices in your playing. Continue playing as wildly as you can, and look for ways that will enable you to play even more wildly. Do not be afraid to make booming or crashing sounds, if they will fit in with what you are already doing. When you find yourself running out of ideas or energy and want to end the piece, play one enormous crash and stop. Then listen for a moment to the silence.

TOM JOHNSON ● *(b. 1939), composer, pianist, writer, and music critic. Much of his music, which reflects a "minimalist" attitude, explores visual and verbal, as well as musical, media.*

Exploring the White Keys

NAMES OF THE WHITE KEYS

The first seven letters of the alphabet are used to identify the white keys. This alphabetical pattern proceeds from left to right.

Keyboard Landmarks

Two keys, C and F, may be used as landmarks for identifying and learning the names of keys. **Middle C**, the C closest to the middle of the keyboard, is a focal point for beginning piano instruction.

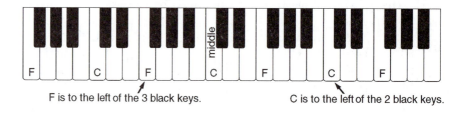

F is to the left of the 3 black keys.   C is to the left of the 2 black keys.

Keyboard Practice—White Keys

1. Locate and play every C on the keyboard; then play every F.

2. Start with the lowest white key and play up the keyboard, saying the names as you play. Change fingers so that you use them all. Reverse the naming by start-ing with the highest white key and playing downward, again saying the names of the keys as you play.

Playing Tip   Saying the key names aloud helps you learn the names more quickly!

3. Locate and play the following pitches as quickly as you can.

a high D	the lowest A	middle C
a low G	the highest F	the A above middle C
an E in the middle	a B in the middle	the G below middle C

4. Play "Suo Gan" (white keys C-D-E).

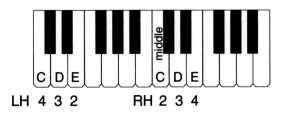

Using the C-D-E keys (note that they surround the two black keys), play the first part of "Suo Gan" with your RH and the second half with your LH. Use the designated fingers written above the letter names. The horizontal lines below the key names indicate which keys should be held longer and which shorter. When you are comfortable playing the melody, try performing with different dynamic levels: (1) Play all soft; (2) play all loud; (3) play the RH part loud followed by the LH part soft.

Suo Gan

Traditional Welsh Folk Melody

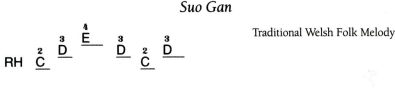

5. Play "Suo Gan" (white keys F-G-A).

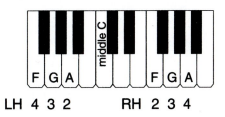

Now use the F-G-A keys to play "Suo Gan." Note that the LH begins this time and the RH follows.

Suo Gan

Traditional Welsh Folk Melody

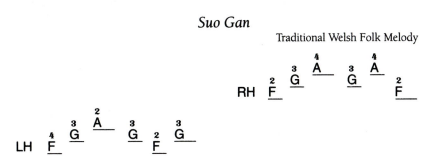

Playing the Blues Progression

Key Term **Blues** is a type of music developed in the late 1800s by African Americans in the South. It is the foundation of much popular music and had a profound influence on the development of all styles of jazz. Blues has its own special harmonies (three chords), musical form (twelve bars), and lyrics.

The blues are based on a particular **progression** of basically three chords. To get you started playing the blues, an ensemble piece follows. Your part is to play just a single note of each chord—C, F, and G (chords include at least three notes)—while your instructor plays Duke Ellington's "C Jam Blues" with you.

With your LH, practice the blues progression for "C Jam Blues" with correct fingering (see keyboard chart). Hold each key for four steady beats as you read from left to right. When you are secure with the progression, your instructor (or CD Track 1) can perform "C Jam Blues" with you. Next, switch to playing the progression with your RH (see keyboard chart), and hold for four steady beats. Again, once you are secure with these notes, your instructor (or CD Track 1) can perform "C Jam Blues" with you.

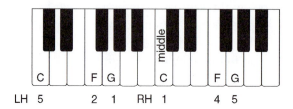

Student, Piano 1

Blues Progression for "C Jam Blues"

	C	C	C	C
Count:	1 2 3 4	1 2 3 4	1 2 3 4	1 2 3 4
	F	F	C	C
	1 2 3 4	1 2 3 4	1 2 3 4	1 2 3 4
	G	F	C	C
	1 2 3 4	1 2 3 4	1 2 3 4	1 2 3 4

 TRACK 1

Instructor, Piano 2

C Jam Blues *(excerpt)*

"Duke" Ellington (United States, 1899–1974)

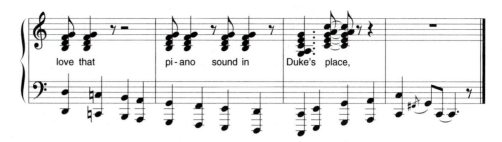

EDWARD KENNEDY "DUKE" ELLINGTON ● *(United States, 1899–1974), pianist, composer, bandleader, and one of the most important figures in jazz history. With over two thousand pieces to his composing credit, he also had the distinction of being one of the creators of the big-band sound. His Duke Ellington Orchestra entertained audiences in the United States and abroad for over fifty years.*

unit three ● *Exploring the Black Keys*

SHARPS AND FLATS

The keys immediately to the left and right of the white keys are identified as **sharps** (♯) and **flats** (♭).

Sharps: Move one key up (right) to the nearest black or white key.

Flats: Move one key down (left) to the nearest black or white key.

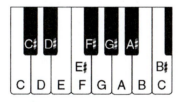

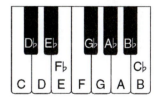

NAMES OF THE BLACK KEYS—ENHARMONICS

Each black key has two names. For example, the black key between A and B is called A-sharp (A♯) or B-flat (B♭). A♯ and B♭ are referred to as *enharmonics*, as are C and B♯.

K e y   T e r m   **Enharmonics** are tones sounding the same pitch or key on the keyboard but identified by different letter names.

Enharmonics

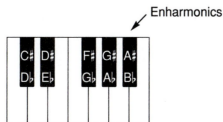

Keyboard Practice—Black Keys

1. Locate the black keys by touch. Find black-key groupings; then play and name individual black keys.

2. Start with the lowest black key and play the black keys up the keyboard, saying the sharp names as you play. Repeat, saying the flat names for each key.

3. Locate and play the following pitches as quickly as you can.

a high D♯	the highest E♭	the F♯ above middle C
a low G♭	the lowest C♯	a high A♭
an A♯ in the middle	a D♭ in the middle	the B♭ below middle C

Keyboard Practice—Sharps and Flats

1. Locate and play the black-key sharps; then play the white-key sharps.

2. Locate and play the black-key flats; then play the white-key flats.

Playing a Flat

Play the following accompaniment line of F, B♭, and C with correct fingering. Hold each pitch for three steady beats and observe the repeat signs. This part will fit with the Minuet by Leopold Mozart below, which either your instructor or CD Track 2 can perform.

Key Sign **Repeat sign.** Two dots before a double bar (:‖) indicate that you should go back to the beginning and perform again. When repeat signs appear in pairs, ‖:   :‖, return to the first repeat sign and perform again.

Student,
Piano 1   *Accompaniment Line for Mozart Minuet*

RH ‖: F	F	B♭	B♭
Count: 1 2 3	1 2 3	1 2 3	1 2 3
F	F	C	F :‖
1 2 3	1 2 3	1 2 3	1 2 3
LH ‖: C	C	C	C
1 2 3	1 2 3	2 3	1 2 3
F	F	C	F :‖
1 2 3	1 2 3	1 2 3	1 2 3

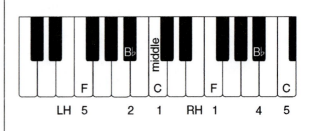

TRACK 2

Instructor, Piano 2

Minuet

Leopold Mozart (Austria, 1719–1787)

Key Fact This **minuet** is one of the keyboard pieces included in the music book compiled by Leopold Mozart for his eight-year-old daughter, Nannerl. As a child, Nannerl concertized throughout Europe with her younger brother, Wolfgang, and won praise for her extraordinary keyboard skills.

IMPROVISATION—BLACK KEYS

The black keys are an excellent place to begin **improvisation,** or music performed extemporaneously. As you create different melodies and accompaniments, you will find that practically everything blends well.

Improvisation No. 1. Solo Melody with Drone Accompaniment

Key Term A **drone** consists of two tones, often five notes apart, sounded together and repeated over and over, as an accompaniment.

1. With your LH, play F♯ and C♯ simultaneously on the lower part of the keyboard. Repeat this drone over and over in a steady rhythm.

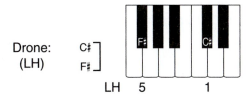

2. Play the F♯-C♯ drone with your LH and improvise on any of the black keys with your RH. Keep the LH part steady. In the beginning, if you have trouble playing two different things, try matching the RH playing with the LH steady-rhythm part. Then gradually experiment with your RH moving more freely on the black keys. Finally, try the drone with the RH and improvise with the LH.

Improvisation No. 2. Ensemble Boogie-Woogie

Key Term **Boogie-woogie** is a jazz piano style (fast blues) in which the LH repeats a fast-moving bass while the RH improvises a melody part.

1. One pianist or a group of pianists should set up the following boogie-woogie bass in the lower register. The pitches can be distributed between the two hands. "Walk" up and down the keys without stopping.

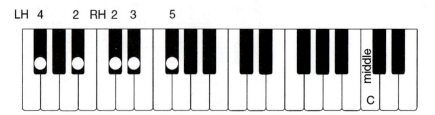

2. When the walking bass is secure, a second pianist or group of pianists should join in playing the same black keys but in the middle register and simultaneously in a slower rhythm. One idea would be to play the pitches at the beginning of each walking-bass pattern.

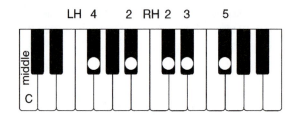

3. When these two parts are secure, a third pianist can improvise on the same black keys but in the middle to upper register of the piano.

4. To end the improvisation, the third pianist(s) should drop out, then the second, and finally the first.

COMPOSING PROJECTS

Composing or making up your own music is very exciting and challenging. You can create all kinds of compositions to express your musical ideas. Here are two composing projects to get you started as a composer.

Project 1. Descriptive Miniature

Step 1. Think of something that would be interesting and exciting to describe in a miniature piece: a thunderstorm, a dripping faucet, space travel, scary soundscape.

Step 2. After choosing your topic, experiment (improvise) at the keyboard using either black keys or white keys, or both, to describe your idea. Explore dynamics—soft, loud, very soft, and so on. Also, try tempo changes—fast, slow, gradually slower, suddenly fast, and so on.

Step 3. When you are ready, ask a friend to listen to your descriptive miniature and guess its title.

Project 2. Black-Key Piece

Create a piano piece using only the black keys.

Step 1. Using the five black keys, experiment with playing a drone in one hand. This repetitive part should establish the steady rhythmic background for the melody.

Step 2. The other hand should explore any of the black keys. Experiment with many ideas until you decide on something that you like.

Step 3. If you wish to notate the pitches in your piece, write down the letter names of the notes. Lines can show shorter and longer durations. See the example.

Example:

RH	F♯	F♯	C♯	D♯
LH	C♯			
	F♯			

Step 4. With a classmate, take turns playing your pieces for each other. Assess your work for accuracy and creativity.

END-OF-CHAPTER EVALUATION

1. Demonstrate the correct hand, arm, and body positions for piano playing.

2. Play and name any pitch on black or white keys.

3. Improvise a simple black-key melody. Either alternate the hands or play a drone with one hand and the melody with the other.

4. The piano was invented about _____. It is a unique keyboard instrument because it can play both _____ and _____.

5. Write the numbers (1–5) assigned to each finger of both hands on the diagram below.

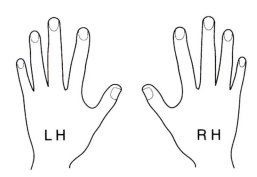

6. Describe the function of the damper pedal.

7. Write the letter name for each white key on the keyboard below and the letter name for each black key above the keyboard.

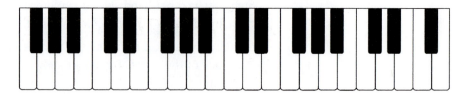

8. Identify the following musical symbols:

   a. ‖:   :‖

   b. ♭

   c. ♯

9. Write the enharmonic spelling for the following keys:

   a. C♯ _____   f. D♭ _____

   b. G♭ _____   g. A♭ _____

   c. E♭ _____   h. D♯ _____

   d. G♯ _____   i. B♭ _____

   e. A♯ _____   j. F♯ _____

10. Describe the following terms:

    a. Enharmonics

    b. Improvisation

    c. Blues

    d. Drone

    e. Boogie-woogie

An Introduction to Music Reading and the Major Five-Finger Pattern

OBJECTIVES

After completing this chapter, you will be able to

✔ Identify whole steps and half steps and demonstrate these distances at the keyboard

✔ Spell and locate at the keyboard the major five-finger pattern on any given tonic and play the C, G, D, A, and F major patterns

✔ Demonstrate keyboard recognition of pitches notated in the treble and bass clefs

✔ Clap, chant, or play the rhythm of any melody or rhythmic example in this chapter

✔ Perform melodies in the chapter with pitch and rhythmic accuracy

✔ Compose and notate the rhythm of an eight-measure black-key melody

✔ Demonstrate legato playing

Major Five-Finger Pattern

HALF STEPS AND WHOLE STEPS

The distance from one pitch to another (**interval**) may be measured in whole steps and half steps.

Key Terms   A **half step** is the distance from one key (black or white) to the very next key above or below. No keys in between! Two pairs of white keys are naturally a half step apart—B to C and E to F.

half steps

A **whole step** includes two half steps or involves skipping one key in between (black or white)—for example, C to D or D♭ to E♭.

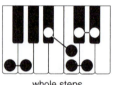

whole steps

All adjacent keys on the keyboard are a half step apart. The **chromatic scale**, a twelve-tone scale, proceeds entirely in half steps. One fingering approach for playing up or down in half steps is to use finger 3 on black keys and fingers 1 and 2 on white keys (2 only on consecutive white keys). Notice that the LH fingering going down is the same as the RH going up and vice versa. Begin on any key and play up every black and white key.

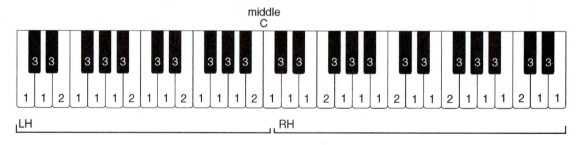

THE MAJOR FIVE-FINGER PATTERN

The *major five-finger pattern* (the first five notes of a major scale) is one of the familiar piano hand positions—all five fingers rest on adjacent keys. The whole-step–half-step arrangement of the major five-finger pattern is as follows:

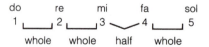

The five notes in the pattern are spelled with consecutive letter names. The first pitch of the pattern is called the *tonic* or *do*. Any key or pitch can be used as the tonic.

Playing the C Major Five-Finger Pattern

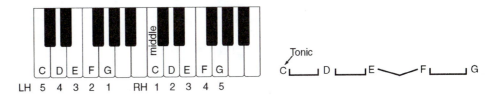

1. Play each key of the C major five-finger pattern, first up and then down, one hand at a time. Say or sing the pitch names as you play.

2. Say the whole-step–half-step arrangement as you play the C major five-finger pattern: tonic, whole step, whole step, half step, whole step.

3. Play the C major five-finger pattern, one hand at a time, calling out the correct finger numbers.

4. Play the following exercise using the C major five-finger pattern. Play hands separately and hands together. Try playing in a smooth, connected manner (legato playing).

Playing Tip To play in a smooth and connected manner (*legato playing* or *legato touch*), hold down each key, lifting as you play the next key. The second key must go down as the first is coming up. Try not to let keys carry over into the sound of the next.

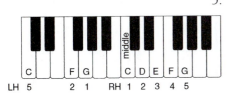

5. Play this familiar song with the C major five-finger pattern. Note that your RH plays the melody while your LH adds an accompaniment. A *Piano 2* part for your instructor to perform (or play CD Track 4) turns this into a jazzy ensemble piece.

When the Saints Go Marching In

TRACK 3

Student, Piano 1

African American Spiritual

RH	C E F	G (hold) C E F	G— C E F	G E C E	D—
	Oh, when the	saints go march-ing	in, Oh, when the	saints go march-ing	in,
LH		C (hold)	C	C	G—

	E E D	C C E G G	G F E F	G E C D	C—
	Oh, Lord, I	want to be in that	num-ber, When the	saints go march-ing	in.
		C	F	C	C

When the Saints Go Marching In

Instructor, Piano 2   *Introduction*   Arranged by Eric Tamm

Spelling Major Five-Finger Patterns

1. Spell and play the following major five-finger patterns on the given tonic. Use a different letter name for each note.

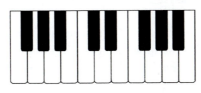

Major Five-Finger Pattern

tonic
1 ⌞____⌟ 2 ⌞____⌟ 3 ⌵ 4 ⌞____⌟ 5
  whole   whole   half   whole

a. __C__ _____ _____ _____ _____

b. __G__ _____ _____ _____ _____

c. __D__ _____ _____ _____ _____

d. __A__ _____ _____ _____ _____

e. __E__ _____ _____ _____ _____

f. __B__ _____ _____ _____ _____

g. __F__ _____ _____ _____ _____

h. __B♭__ _____ _____ _____ _____

i. __E♭__ _____ _____ _____ _____

j. __A♭__ _____ _____ _____ _____

2. Practice the major five-finger exercise on page 23 in the G, D, and A major five-finger patterns.

---

unit two●   *Rhythmic Reading*

Key Terms   **Rhythm** refers to all the **durations** (long and short tones) of sounds and silences that occur in music. **Notes** are the symbols used to represent durational sounds. **Rests** are used to notate silences.

NOTES AND RESTS

Note parts

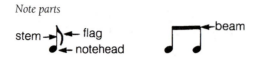

A *notehead* can be open (longer-duration notes) or solid (shorter-duration notes). The *stems* extend upward from the right or downward from the left of the notehead. *Flags* on both upward and downward stems always curl to the right. Notes with flags are frequently *beamed* together in groups.

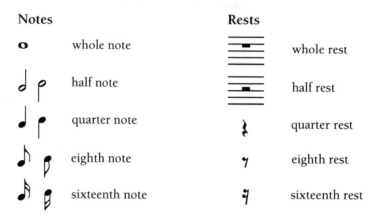

Notes		Rests	
𝅝	whole note	▬	whole rest
𝅗𝅥	half note	▬	half rest
♩	quarter note	𝄽	quarter rest
♪	eighth note	𝄾	eighth rest
𝅘𝅥𝅯	sixteenth note	𝄿	sixteenth rest

Relative Note Durations

Notes are of relative duration, one to the other.

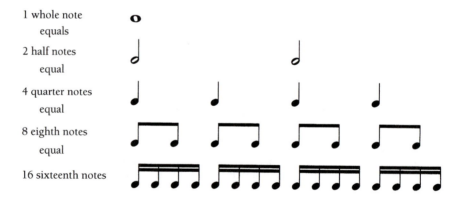

1 whole note equals

2 half notes equal

4 quarter notes equal

8 eighth notes equal

16 sixteenth notes

BEAT AND METER

Most music has a steady **beat** or pulse. Beats are organized into groups or **meter**. Some beats are stressed more than others, and the result is beat groupings of twos (**duple meter**), threes (**triple meter**), or fours (**quadruple meter**). The first beat in each meter is a strong beat and is followed by weaker, unaccented beats. Vertical **bar lines** are used to indicate the meter or beat grouping and divide the music into **measures.** A double bar line is used at the end of a composition or section.

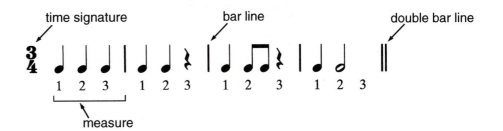

Time Signature

The two numbers, one above the other, that appear at the beginning of a piece of music are the **meter signature** or **time signature.** Example:

4 The top number specifies the number of beats per measure (4).

4 The bottom number specifies the note that gets one beat or count (♩).

Frequently Used Time Signatures (Simple Meter)

The following meters are referred to as **simple** because the beat in each divides into two equal parts.

Duple Meter: **2/4**

Triple Meter: **3/4**

Quadruple Meter: **4/4** or **C** (common time)

Rhythm Exercise 1. 2/4, 4/4, c (♩, ♩, o, ♩)

Clap, chant, or play the following rhythmic lines on any key. The numbers under the notes refer to each consecutive beat in the measure, and these numbers are often spoken to aid in reading rhythms. (The numbers in parentheses are not clapped or played, but are counted.) Use the number counting system or any counting method recommended by your instructor.

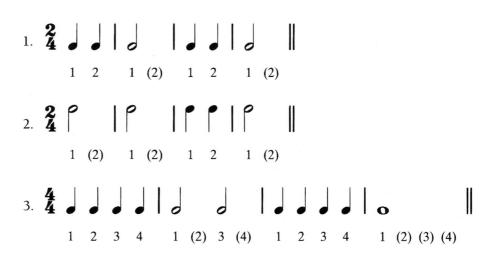

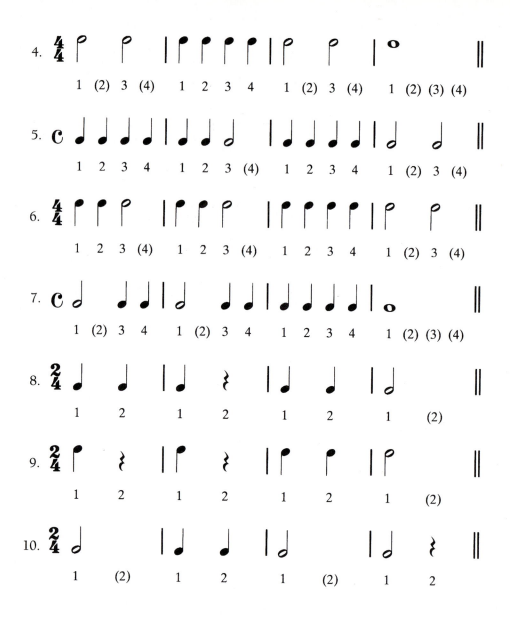

4. 𝄴 ♩ ♩ | ♩ ♩ ♩ ♩ | ♩ ♩ | 𝅝 ‖
   1 (2) 3 (4)   1 2 3 4   1 (2) 3 (4)   1 (2) (3) (4)

5. 𝄴 ♩ ♩ ♩ ♩ | ♩ ♩ ♩ | ♩ ♩ ♩ ♩ | ♩ ♩ ‖
   1 2 3 4   1 2 3 (4)   1 2 3 4   1 (2) 3 (4)

6. 𝄴 ♩ ♩ ♩ | ♩ ♩ ♩ | ♩ ♩ ♩ ♩ | ♩ ♩ ‖
   1 2 3 (4)   1 2 3 (4)   1 2 3 4   1 (2) 3 (4)

7. 𝄴 ♩ ♩ ♩ | ♩ ♩ ♩ | ♩ ♩ ♩ ♩ | 𝅝 ‖
   1 (2) 3 4   1 (2) 3 4   1 2 3 4   1 (2) (3) (4)

8. 𝟤𝟦 ♩ ♩ | ♩ 𝄽 | ♩ ♩ | ♩ ♩ ‖
   1   2   1 2   1   2   1   (2)

9. 𝟤𝟦 ♩ 𝄽 | ♩ 𝄽 | ♩ ♩ | ♩ ‖
   1   2   1   2   1   2   1   (2)

10. 𝟤𝟦 ♩ | ♩ ♩ | ♩ | ♩ 𝄽 ‖
    1   (2)   1   2   1   (2)   1   2

Rhythm Exercise 2. Two-Part Rhythms

When playing the piano, one must often perform two rhythms simultaneously—one with the RH and one with the LH. These examples should be performed by tapping or playing on any key the notes on the bottom line with one hand and the notes on the top line with the other hand. Perform each line separately, then hands together.

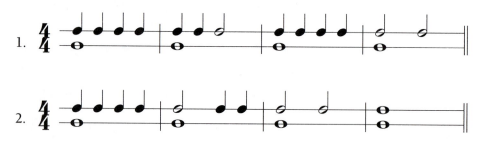

Reading and Performing Melodies

1. Determine the number of beats each note receives in "Aura Lee." Count the beats as you clap the rhythm. Play the melody using the C major five-finger pattern. Play the entire melody with your RH, then with your LH, and continue alternating hands. Try playing the first line with one hand and the second line with the other. Try to play as expressively as you can.

C major five-finger pattern

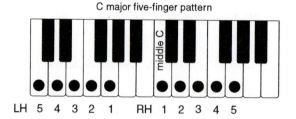

LH 5 4 3 2 1   RH 1 2 3 4 5

Aura Lee

American Folk Song

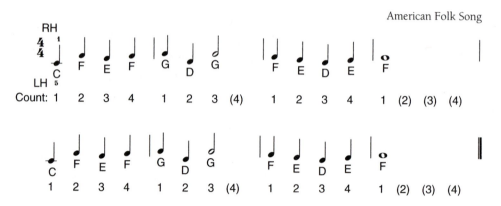

RH
4/4
C F E F G D G   F E D E F
LH 5
Count: 1 2 3 4   1 2 3 (4)   1 2 3 4   1 (2) (3) (4)

C F E F G D G   F E D E F
1 2 3 4   1 2 3 (4)   1 2 3 4   1 (2) (3) (4)

Key Fact   "Aura Lee," an American folk song, was made into a popular song—"Love Me Tender"—and sung by Elvis Presley. The staff notation for "Aura Lee" is on page 302.

2.   Determine the number of beats each note receives in "Chorale Melody." Clap and count the rhythm of the melody before playing it with the G major five-finger pattern, hands separately and hands together.

G major five-finger pattern

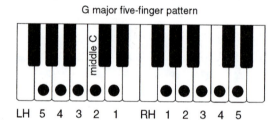

LH 5 4 3 2 1   RH 1 2 3 4 5

Chorale Melody

RH 3
4/4
B A A D B G A   G G G G A B A   G
LH 3
Count: 1 2 3 4   1 2 3 (4)   1 2 3 4   1 2 3 (4)   1 (2) (3) (4)

Key Term   A **chorale** is a hymn tune of the German Protestant church. Many compositions (especially in the seventeenth and eighteenth centuries) have been based on chorale melodies.

Pitch Reading

TREBLE-CLEF AND BASS-CLEF NOTATION

Pitches are notated on a *staff*. Those at the top sound higher than those at the bottom. Notes are placed *on* the five lines or *in* the four spaces.

Staff

staff

line notes   space notes

Clefs: Treble and Bass

The letters A, B, C, D, E, F, and G are used to name pitches. These seven letters are repeated over and over to designate the entire range of pitches. A **clef sign** must be placed on the staff to locate a particular pitch. The *treble clef* is used for higher pitches, and the *bass clef* is used for lower pitches.

Key Sign   The **treble clef** (or **G clef**) curls around the second line (G) of the staff. Usually, pitches written on the treble-clef staff are played with the RH.

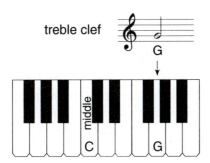

treble clef

Key Sign   The **bass clef** (or **F clef**) is written with a dot above and a dot below the fourth line (F) of the staff. Usually, pitches written on the bass-clef staff are played with the LH.

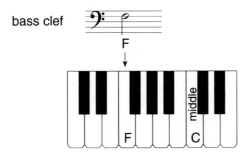

bass clef

The Grand Staff

The **grand staff** consists of two staves bracketed together, one with a treble clef and one with a bass clef. In piano music, the upper staff is usually played by the RH, and the lower staff is usually played by the LH. Notice that middle C is located between the two staves and that some pitches may be notated in both clefs. **Leger lines,** short lines added above or below the staff, are used to extend the pitch range. The following grand staff includes the notation for white keys of the piano. *Notice that stems go up on notes below the middle line and down on notes above the middle line of the staff.*

Grand Staff (white keys are notated)

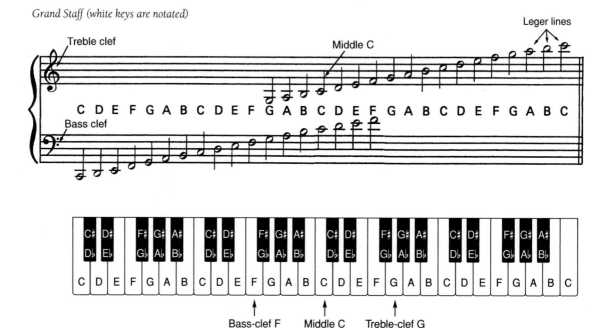

When black keys are indicated, sharps and flats are placed before the note on the same line or space as the notehead or after the clef sign as a key signature on each staff of music. (See Appendix C for a grand staff with notation for both white and black keys.)

Pitch-Reading Exercises

1. Beginning with the lowest C on the bass-clef staff above, play and name aloud the bass-clef notes up to middle C (with your LH), and then play the notes going back down.

2. Beginning with middle C on the treble-clef staff, play and name the treble-clef notes up to high C (with your RH), and then reverse the naming and playing back to middle C. Memorize the names and their staff positions.

Learning Tip Pull out the Piano Keyboard and Grand Staff Chart at the back of your book and stand it on the top of your keyboard. Use this chart to help with learning the staff positions of notes.

3. Sing the letter names and play the following exercises in the C and G major five-finger patterns. Play hands separately and hands together.

Playing Tip Notice that all the notes in the C and G major five-finger patterns are on white keys.

C major

C major five-finger pattern

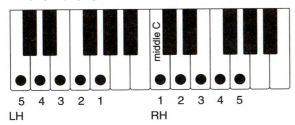

G major

G major five-finger pattern

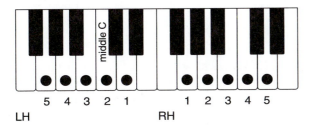

4. Sing the letter names and play the following exercises in the D and A major five-finger patterns. Play hands separately and hands together.

Playing Tip Notice that your middle finger is on a black key in the D and A major five-finger patterns.

D major

D major five-finger pattern

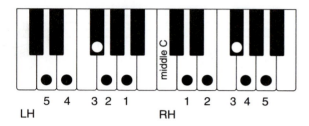

A major

A major five-finger pattern

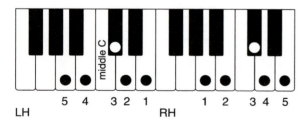

K e y S i g n A **key signature,** placed after the clef sign on each staff, is the grouping of sharps or flats to be played throughout a piece. For example, if there is a sharp on the F line, all Fs in the music should be performed as F-sharp rather than F-**natural** (♮). *Key signature*

Performing Melodies

The following melodies are in the C, G, D, and A major five-finger patterns. Remember, the key signature will indicate sharps. For each, do the following:

1. Count and clap the rhythm.

2. Review the pitch names, noting any sharps in the key signature.

3. Place your hand in the correct five-finger pattern and "finger" the melody without producing any sound.

4. Play the melody with pitch and rhythmic accuracy.

Au Clair de la Lune (C major)

French Folk Melody

French Folk Melody (C major)

Russian Folk Melody (G major)

Folk Melody 1 (D major)

Love Somebody (A major)

American Folk Song

Playing Tip   Look at the music, not at your hands, to develop confidence in your sense of touch!

Au Clair de la Lune (C major)

French Folk Melody

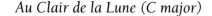

French Folk Melody (C major)

Russian Folk Melody (G major)

Folk Melody 1 (D major)

Love Somebody (A major)

American Folk Song

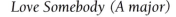

COMPOSING PROJECT

Black-Key Melody

Create a melody using only the black keys.

Step 1. As you play the following eight-measure rhythm, experiment with the five black keys. Try various pitches until you decide on something that you like.

Step 2. Notate the letter names of the pitches in your melody above the rhythm (or on a staff). Use either all sharps or all flats; do not mix the two. Try a drone with your melody.

Step 3. Play the melody, reading from the notation. Then, exchange your piece with a classmate's. Play your pieces for each other, and assess your work for accuracy and creativity.

SOLO REPERTOIRE

Beginning with this chapter, solo piano pieces are included under the heading of Solo Repertoire. Most pieces in this section are classical piano selections commonly performed by beginning keyboard players. Brief notes on the composer(s) are provided.

Bartók's "Unison Melody" should be performed *legato* (in a smooth, connected manner), often indicated by a curved line (**slur**) above or below the pitches. Review Technique Exercise 1 in this chapter. Then practice hands separately and hands together. Notice that the two hands move in the same direction (**parallel motion**). Observe the tempo and dynamic markings—perform expressively!

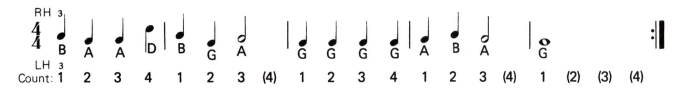

Key Term   *Moderato* is the Italian **tempo** term meaning to perform in a moderate tempo.

Key Sign   The sign *f* is the dynamic symbol for *forte*, an Italian term meaning to perform loud.

TRACK 5

Unison Melody
(No. 1 from *First Term at the Piano*)

Moderato

Béla Bartók (Hungary, 1881–1945)

BÉLA BARTÓK ● *(Hungary, 1881–1945), one of Hungary's greatest composers. He collected folk music of his native land and incorporated these folk elements into his music. His works include string quartets, orchestral works, operas, and piano-teaching pieces such as "Unison Melody."*

Beyer's Etudes No. 12 and No. 13 should also be performed *legato*. Practice hands separately and hands together. Notice that the two hands move independently in the two etudes, not parallel as in "Unison Melody."

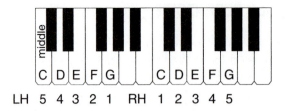

Etude No. 12

Moderato   Ferdinand Beyer (1803–1863)

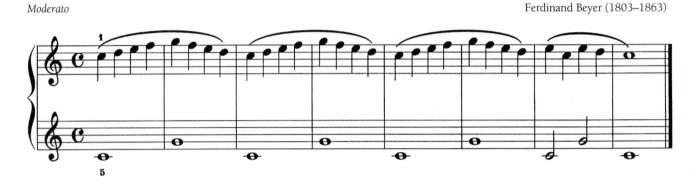

Etude No. 13

Moderato   Ferdinand Beyer (1803–1863)

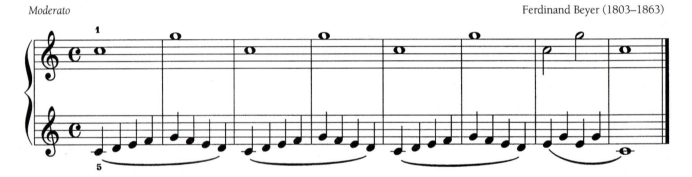

TECHNIQUE EXERCISES

Technical development is an important part of piano playing. In addition to studying and playing the musical examples in each chapter, you need to practice specific exercises to increase your technical facility and tonal control. In fact, each time you sit down to play the piano, make it a habit to warm up with a technical exercise or two.

Before practicing any of these technique exercises, check your hand position at the keyboard.

- Are your hands slightly arched?

- Are your fingers gently curved? Is the fleshy part of your fingers striking the keys?

- Are your fingernails short?

- Are your wrists and arms straight but flexible?

Technique Exercise 1. Legato Touch

Legato touch requires playing in a smooth, connected manner. You must hold down each key, lifting as you play the next key without a break between them. The second key must go down as the first is coming up. Let the weight of your arms shift from one finger to the next while you keep a good hand position and a flexible wrist.

The following examples can be played with any major five-finger pattern, hands separately and hands together.

Part A

Part B

Part C

Technique Exercise 2. Independent Finger Action

Your fingers must become independent and strong. Practice this exercise very slowly. Begin with a good hand position. Play legato (hold each key, lifting as you play the next key). Play the following patterns, beginning on any note.

Part A

Part B

END-OF-CHAPTER EVALUATION

1. Demonstrate whole-step and half-step distances at the keyboard.

2. Play a major five-finger pattern on the following tonics: C, G, D, and A.

3. Clap, chant, or play the rhythm of any melody or rhythm example in this chapter.

4. Demonstrate keyboard recognition of pitches notated in the treble and bass clefs.

5. Perform one of the melodies in this chapter with pitch and rhythmic accuracy and using correct fingering.

6. Demonstrate legato playing by performing an example from Technique Exercise 1 in this chapter.

7. Identify each interval as a half step or a whole step.

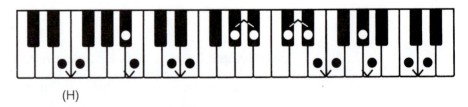

(H)

8. Identify the whole-step–half-step arrangement of the major five-finger pattern:

1 (whole) 2 _____ 3 _____ 4 _____ 5

9. Using capital letters, write the letter name for each note below the staff.

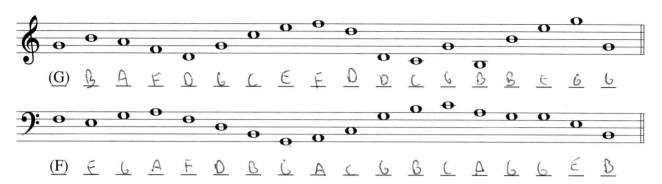

(G) B A F D G C E F D D C G B B E G G

(F) E G A F D B C A C G B C A G G E B

10. Notate "Aura Lee" (p. 30) and "Chorale Melody" (p. 30) in treble- and bass-clef notation.

Aura Lee

Chorale Melody

11. Notate the following major five-finger patterns on the staff and on the keyboard chart. Circle the tonic pitch for each. When accidentals are needed, write the sharps or the flats on the staff *before* the pitches on the *same* line or in the *same* space.

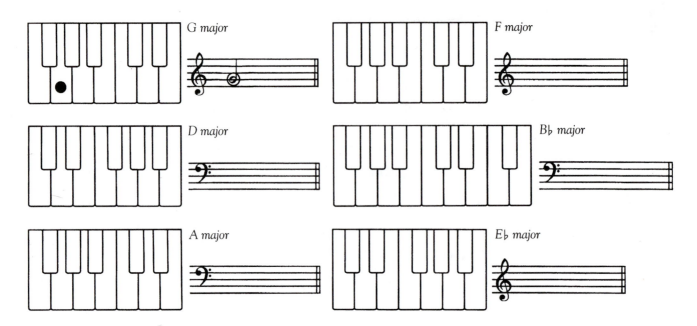

12. Write numbers under the notes to refer to each consecutive beat in the measure.

13. Create and notate four measures of rhythm for each of the following time signatures.

14. Describe the following musical terms:

a. Whole step

b. Half step

c. Time signature

d. Measure

e. Legato touch

f. Leger line

g. Tonic

15. Identify the following musical symbols:

a. 𝄞

b. 𝄢

c. ‖

d. 𝅝

e. ♩

f. 𝄽

g. 𝅗𝅥

h. *f*

Practicing the Piano

Your progress and pleasure in learning to play the piano depends on *you*. In making the commitment to and accepting the challenge of learning this new skill, you will need to set aside time to practice and study. Establishing a practice plan, preparing a practice worksheet, and keeping a practice journal will help you meet the challenge!

SUGGESTED PRACTICE PLAN

✔ Set goals for each practice session. Decide what you need to accomplish. Duplicate the Practice Worksheet and the Practice Journal that follow, and use them to plan and record your work.

✔ Begin each session with several warm-up exercises to limber up your fingers, work on seeing and feeling correct hand and finger positions, and listen for good tone production.

✔ Work on new music and exercises at each session, but be sure to review music you have played before.

✔ Set aside a little time in each practice session to try out some of your own musical ideas by improvising and composing.

✔ Always conclude each practice session by assessing what you have accomplished and deciding what you want to accomplish in the next session.

$\mathcal{P}$RACTICE WORKSHEET

_____   _____
(Name)   *(Week, e.g., January 7, 2004)*

	MON	TUE	WED	THU	FRI	SAT	SUN
Warm-Ups *(Write page numbers of exercises)*							
1.							
2.							
3.							
New Repertoire *(Write titles and page numbers)*							
1.							
2.							
3.							
Previously Learned Repertoire *(Write titles and page numbers)*							
1.							
2.							
3.							

PRACTICE JOURNAL

_____   _____
(Name)   (Week, e.g., January 7, 2004)

	MON	TUE	WED	THU	FRI	SAT	SUN
Total Practice Time for each day							

What I accomplished this week:

1.

2.

3.

4.

5.

What I want to accomplish next week:

1.

2.

3.

4.

5.

chapter three

Interval Reading, Transposing, and Accompanying with Chord Roots

OBJECTIVES

After completing this chapter, you will be able to

✔ Demonstrate recognition of intervals (P1, M2, M3, P4, P5) at the keyboard and in writing

✔ Transpose major five-finger patterns and melodies at the keyboard and in writing

✔ Clap, chant, or play the rhythm of any melody or rhythmic example in this chapter

✔ Perform musical pieces in the chapter with pitch and rhythmic accuracy

✔ Perform chord-root accompaniments to melodies

✔ Compose and notate a major five-finger melody

✔ Demonstrate hand coordination in contrary motion

INTERVALS

Learning to recognize musical distances (*intervals*) is important in reading and performing music. You need to identify the intervals in music notation, then develop a feel for the keyboard distances of those intervals. For example, when notes are on adjacent lines and spaces, you move from one key to the next (and from one letter name to the next—e.g., C to D) and the interval distance is a *second*. When notes skip from one space to the next space or from one line to the next line, you skip one piano key (and one letter name—e.g., C to E) and the interval distance is a *third*.

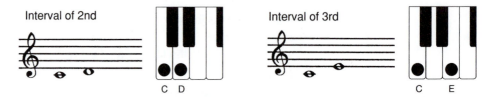

Key Term   An **interval** is the pitch distance between two tones. An interval can be written or performed with the two pitches occurring successively (a *melodic interval*) or with the two pitches sounding simultaneously (a *harmonic interval*).   Melodic interval of 3rd   Harmonic interval of 3rd

Interval-Number Exercises

1. Beginning with the lowest C on your keyboard, move up in thirds, saying the letter names and playing the notes. Use finger 2 in each hand—alternating hands to play each interval. For example, C–E, E–G.

2. Beginning with the lowest F on your keyboard, move up in seconds, saying the letter names and playing the notes. Use finger 2 in each hand—alternating hands to play each interval. For example, F–G, G–A.

3. Beginning with the highest A on your keyboard, move down in thirds, saying the letter names and playing the notes. Use finger 2 in each hand—alternating hands to play each interval. For example, A–F, F–D.

4. Beginning with the highest B on your keyboard, move down in seconds, saying the letter names and playing the notes. Use finger 2 in each hand—alternating hands to play each interval. For example, B–A, A–G.

INTERVALS IN THE MAJOR FIVE-FINGER PATTERN

The following intervals are commonly used in major five-finger melodies. Notice that the intervals are identified by *number* and by *quality* (perfect, major, etc.). The number represents the number of letter names covered by the two notes. For example, C to E is called a third because there are three letter names covered (C, D, E). The quality is determined by the precise number of half steps between the two notes. For example, C to E includes four half steps and is classified as a major third (M3). (All intervals are presented in Appendix G.)

C major

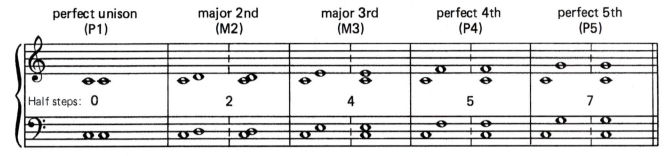

perfect unison (P1)	major 2nd (M2)	major 3rd (M3)	perfect 4th (P4)	perfect 5th (P5)

Half steps: 0   2   4   5   7

Notice these five intervals in the following musical excerpt.

One Moment in Time (excerpt)

Words and music by Albert Hammond and John Bettis

I want— one mo-ment— in time   when I'm more than— I thought I—could be

Interval-Playing Exercises

Playing Tip Try to develop a feel for the keyboard distances in each of the intervals. For example, note the feel of a 5th as compared with that of a 2nd.

1. Play the harmonic intervals of M2, M3, P4, and P5 in the following five-finger exercise. Listen to the sound of each interval. Practice one hand at a time.

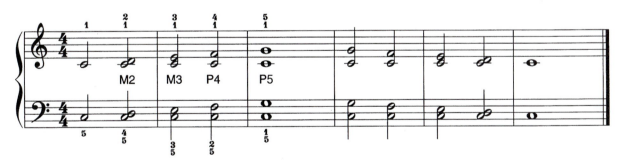

2. Practice the melodic intervals in the major five-finger pattern in Technique Exercise 3 in this chapter.

Performing Melodies—Interval Reading

As you perform this etude using the C major five-finger pattern, first *look* at the notation and try to identify the interval distances (numbers!) between pitches by sight. Then try to *feel* the keyboard distances of those intervals as you play.

Etude No. 14

Moderato

Ferdinand Beyer (1803–1863)

As you perform "Clothespin Boogie," notice that your LH hand covers the five white keys F to C and your RH the five white keys D to A.

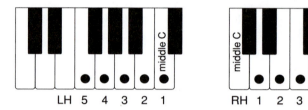

Look at the notation and identify the interval distances (numbers!) between pitches by sight. Try to *feel* the keyboard distances of those intervals as you play with your instructor or CD Track 7. How would you interpret the composer's recommendation to perform "cheerfully, with a bounce" and at a *mezzo forte* dynamic level?

Key Sign   The sign *mf* is the dynamic symbol for *mezzo forte*, which means to perform medium loud.

TRACK 6

Student, Piano 1

Clothespin Boogie

Cheerfully, with a bounce

Lee Evans (United States, b. 1933)

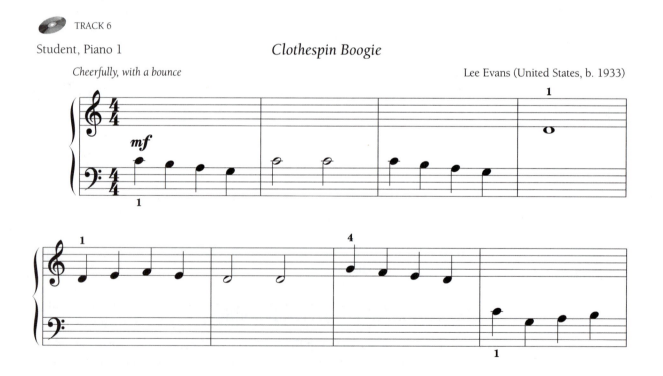

TRACK 7

Instructor, Piano 2

LEE EVANS ● *(United States, b. 1933), pianist, composer, and teacher. Evans specializes in teaching a "classical approach" to jazz and contributes significantly to the jazz repertoire for beginning and intermediate pianists.*

unit two ● *Transposing*

Changing a melody from one **key** (scale) or five-finger pattern to another is called **transposition.** For example, if you play "The Old Oak Tree" in the G major pattern and then play it in the D major pattern, you have transposed the song from the key of G to the key of D. Because all the intervals are parallel, the two versions should sound exactly the same—only higher or lower.

The Old Oak Tree

G major (original)

English Folk Melody

do re mi fa sol
1 2 3 4 5

mf

D major (transposed)

do re mi fa sol
1 2 3 4 5

mf

THE SCALE AND INTERVAL APPROACHES TO TRANSPOSITION

There are several approaches to transposition. Guidelines for the scale and interval approaches follow.

GUIDELINES FOR TRANSPOSITION

Approach 1. Scale Position

Step 1. Determine the scale or the five-finger pattern of the piece to be transposed. Identify each pitch in the piece by its number in the five-finger pattern or scale.

Step 2. Decide what scale or five-finger pattern you will use for the transposed version. Number each pitch. Then change each pitch number in the original piece to the letter name of the pitch in the new scale or five-finger pattern.

Approach 2. Intervals

Step 1. Determine the scale or the five-finger pattern of the piece to be transposed. Decide what scale or five-finger pattern you will use for the transposed version.

Step 2. Calculate the interval distances between the pitches in the original scale or five-finger pattern and in the pattern to which it will be transposed. (For example, G major to F major results in shifting every pitch down a M2, or a whole step.) Then change each pitch to the correct pitch in the new scale or five-finger pattern.

Transposition Practice

1. Perform the two versions of "The Old Oak Tree" above. Feel the similarity in keyboard distances.

2. On the blank staff provided below, notate another transposition of "The Old Oak Tree." Transpose to the A major five-finger pattern. Use either of the transposition approaches described above. Play your transposition and check for accuracy.

The Old Oak Tree

A major *(transposed)*

3. At the keyboard, transpose some or all of the following pieces.

   "Suo Gan," p. 13, to G major

   Russian Folk Melody, p. 35, to C major

   "Unison Melody," p. 37, to D major

   Etude No. 12, p. 38, to G major

More Rhythm Reading

Rhythm Exercise 1. $\frac{2}{4}$, $\frac{4}{4}$, $\frac{2}{2}$, 𝄴, 𝄵, 𝅝, 𝅗𝅥, 𝅘𝅥, 𝅘𝅥𝅮𝅘𝅥𝅮, 𝄾, 𝄼

Clap, chant, or play the following rhythmic lines on any key(s). Use the number counting system or any counting method recommended by your instructor.

(continued)

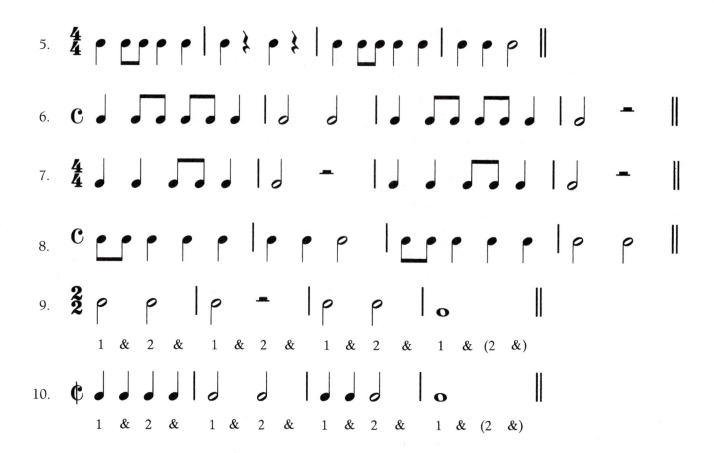

Rhythm Exercise 2. Two-Part Rhythms

Perform by tapping or playing on any key(s) the notes on the bottom line with one hand and the notes on the top line with the other hand. Perform each line hands separately and then hands together.

unit three • *Chord-Root Accompaniments*

CHORDS

The building blocks of harmony are *chords*. Chords are often played with the LH to provide an **accompaniment** for a melody.

Key Term   A **chord** consists of three or more pitches a third apart, sounded simultaneously. Of the chord tones, the **chord root** (bottom note) is the strongest.

Chord Symbols

In jazz and in popular and folk music, the chord names are used in a symbol system called *lead sheet notation*. Uppercase letters are written above the staff, specifying what chords should be used and when they should be played. The single pitch indicated by the chord symbol is the chord root. (When a number appears next to a capital letter, a four-note chord is indicated.)

Since playing three or more notes simultaneously may be a challenge to beginning pianists, chord accompaniments can be simplified by playing only one or two tones of the chord. To add an accompaniment to a melody using just chord roots, play with your LH the single pitch indicated by the chord symbol. Play the roots eight notes (an octave) lower than the melody and on the strong beats of the measure. Play the same chord root until a new symbol is given.

J'ai du bon tabac

French Folk Song

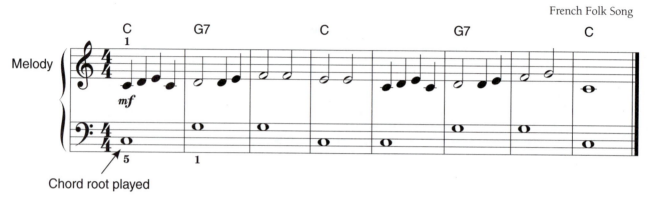

Chord root played

PERFORMING MELODIES WITH CHORD-ROOT ACCOMPANIMENT

GUIDELINES FOR PERFORMING CHORD-ROOT ACCOMPANIMENT

Step 1. Locate the chord symbols for each melody. Notice that in the following melodies the chord roots for each are the first (I) and fifth (V) tones of the major five-finger pattern. Remember that the I is called the *tonic* and the V is called the *dominant*.

Step 2. When playing the chord roots in the LH, you may use the little finger for the tonic (I) and the thumb for the dominant (V). Or you may play the tonic (I) with your thumb and the dominant (V) *below* the tonic by using your little finger. Try both the *dominant-above* and the *dominant-below* positions and decide which sounds better for each melody.

Step 3. When playing the chord roots in the RH, use the thumb for the tonic (I) and the little finger for the dominant (V).

Step 4. Play a chord root on beat 1 of each measure.

Little River

German Folk Melody

Jim-Along Josie

English Folk Melody 1

Exercise

At the keyboard, transpose one or two of the preceding folk melodies to other major patterns. To transpose the chord-root accompaniment, remember that the chord roots will be the first and fifth pitches of the major pattern.

PERFORMING CHORD ROOTS FROM STAFF NOTATION

Chord roots for the following five melodies are written out in the bass and treble clefs. Strive for a good balance between hands. Notice that Hungarian Folk Melody 1 and American Folk Melody 1 are written in the F major five-finger pattern while Danish Folk Melody is in the familiar G major pattern. Transpose one or more of these melodies to familiar major patterns such as C, G, D, and A.

F major five-finger pattern

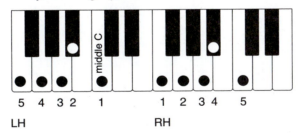

Hungarian Folk Melody 1

American Folk Melody 1

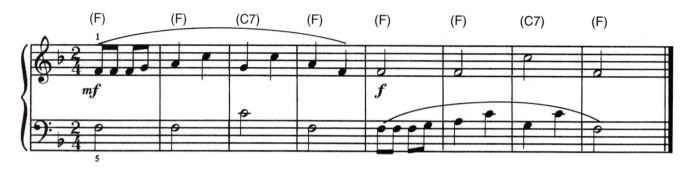

Danish Folk Melody

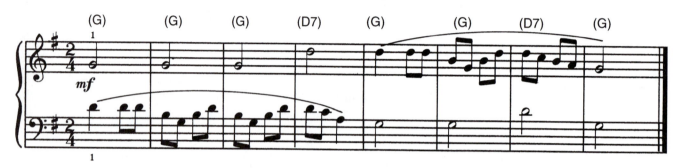

"Love Somebody" (C major five-finger pattern) and "J'ai du bon tabac" (F major five-finger pattern) are both arranged for two pianos. One person or half of a piano class can perform one part while another person (or the other half of the class) performs the other part. For practicing on your own, use the CD to play the accompanying part.

TRACK 8

Love Somebody

Student, Piano 1

American Folk Song

Student, Piano 2

Love Somebody

American Folk Song

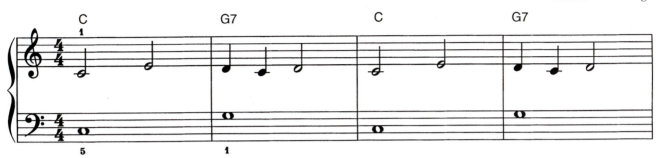

Student, Piano 1

J'ai du bon tabac

French Folk Song

Student, Piano 2

J'ai du bon tabac

French Folk Song

COMPOSING PROJECT

Major Five-Finger Melody

Create a melody based on a selected major five-finger pattern.

Step 1. Choose a major five-finger pattern that you can play comfortably.

Step 2. Experiment with those five pitches as you perform the following eight-measure rhythm. Try various pitches until you decide on something that you like. Be sure to conclude your melody on the tonic.

Step 3. Notate your melody on the staff below, and then play, reading from staff notation. Exchange your melody with a classmate's. Play your pieces for each other, and assess your work for accuracy and creativity.

SOLO REPERTOIRE

Visually analyze each of the following pieces, determining the tonic, the time signature, and the hand position for each. Research the historical period of each piece by reviewing the Timeline of Western Art Music (Appendix K).

Playing Tip   Keep your eyes on the music, not on your hands. *Feel* the interval distances between notes.

To play Olson's "Swing Tune," the RH is in the C major five-finger pattern while the LH plays only the pitches G and A (M2 interval). Notice other intervals and the introduction of the whole rest (—). Enjoy how the RH and the LH take turns making this tune swing, and show what an "easygoing" tempo means to you.

TRACK 12

Swing Tune

Lynn Freeman Olson (United States, 1938–1987)

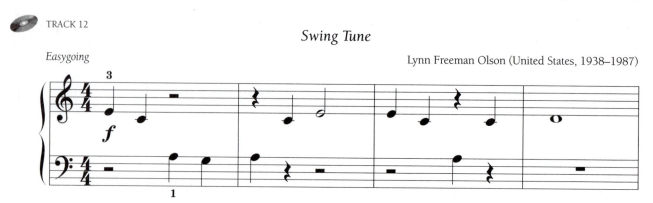

LYNN FREEMAN OLSON ● *(United States, 1938–1987), composer, author of many piano books, and music educator. His work has appeared on several highly successful children's television shows.*

In Gurlitt's Op. 117, No. 5, *both* the RH and the LH parts are notated in the treble clef. Make sure that you place your hands in the correct location on the keyboard! Perform expressively, following the tempo and dynamic markings.

Key Term   *Allegretto* is the tempo term meaning to perform moderately fast.

Key Sign   The sign *p* is the dynamic symbol for *piano*, meaning to perform soft.

TRACK 13

Op. 117, No. 5

Cornelius Gurlitt (Germany, 1820–1901)

Allegretto

CORNELIUS GURLITT ● *(Germany, 1820–1901), keyboardist, composer, and teacher. He wrote operas, orchestral and choral works, chamber music, song cycles, and numerous educational piano pieces.*

Türk's March falls within the G major five-finger pattern for both hands. Notice the C time signature (⁴/₄). Although the composer gave no dynamic or tempo ideas, it would be safe to interpret music of this period by performing in a moderate tempo and a medium-loud dynamic level.

March

Daniel Gottlob Türk (Germany, 1756–1813)

DANIEL GOTTLOB TÜRK ● *(Germany, 1756–1813), composer, violinist, organist, and teacher of the Classical period. (Mozart and Haydn were his contemporaries.) He was known for his keyboard pieces and the method book* Klavierschule.

TECHNIQUE EXERCISES

Before playing any of these exercises, check your hand position. Make sure you are comfortably seated at the piano.

Technique Exercise 1. Contrary Motion

Pianists must learn to coordinate their two hands playing together. When two hands move in opposite directions, the motion is called **contrary.**

Practice the following contrary-motion exercise, keeping the wrists flexible and the arms moving in a gentle outward and upward movement for each two-measure pattern in Part A. In Part B, the movements will be reversed. Transpose this exercise to the major five-finger patterns of G, D, A, and F.

Part A

Part B

Technique Exercise 2. Independent Hands and Hand Coordination

This exercise should be practiced in two parts. The first (Part A) focuses on the RH moving in quarter notes while the LH moves in whole notes. Part B reverses this rhythmic movement. Transpose to other major patterns.

Part A

Part B

Technique Exercise 3. Intervals (Major Five-Finger Pattern)

Play these melodic intervals in the following pattern. Feel the keyboard distance for each interval. Stress independent finger action, and work for a legato sound.

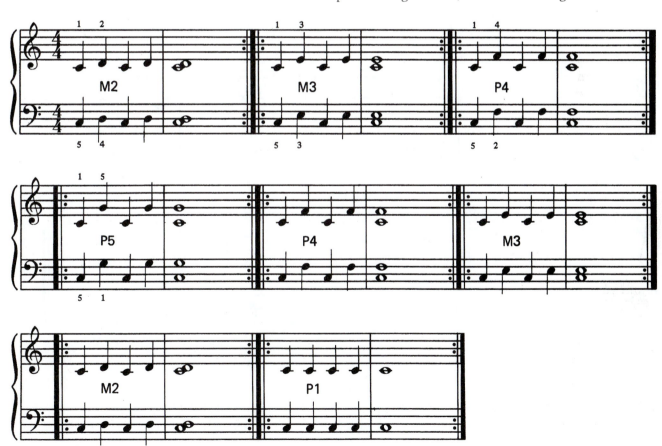

Technique Exercise 4. Register Change

Try to move as smoothly as possible as you change from one register to another. First play the five-finger pattern up the keyboard in C, and then play the five-finger pattern down the keyboard. Then transpose to other major patterns.

Key Sign The musical sign *8va--------⌐* stands for *ottava bassa*, which means to perform eight notes (an octave) lower than written.

Part A

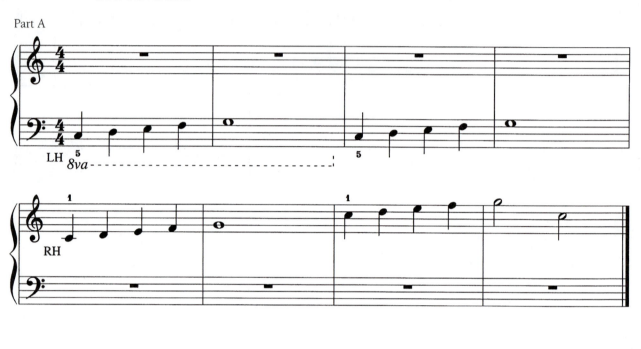

Part B

END-OF-CHAPTER EVALUATION

1. At the keyboard, demonstrate these intervals: perfect unisons (P1), major seconds (M2), major thirds (M3), perfect fourths (P4), and perfect fifths (P5).

2. At the keyboard, transpose Folk Melody 1, on p. 57, from the D major five-finger pattern to the G major pattern.

3. Perform a chord-root accompaniment for "Jim-Along Josie," p. 57.

4. Demonstrate hand coordination in *contrary motion* by performing Technique Exercise 1 in this chapter.

5. Label the following intervals by quality and number, such as P5. Using the keyboard chart, count the number of half steps between the two notes. Remember: P1 = 0, M2 = 2, M3 = 4, P4 = 5, P5 = 7.

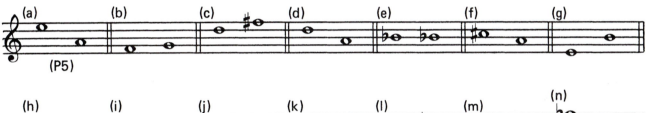

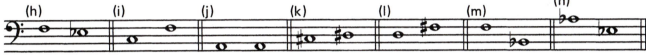

6. Complete the specified intervals by notating the second pitch above (↑) or below (↓) the given pitch (as in melodic intervals). Use the preceding keyboard chart to count the needed half steps for each.

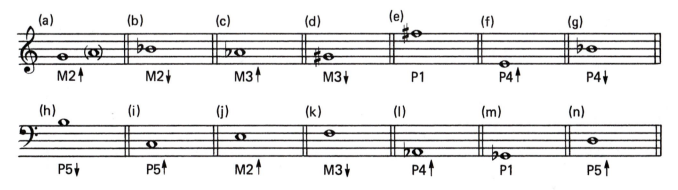

7. Transpose Op. 117, No. 5, on p. 61, to the D major five-finger pattern. Notate the transposition. When accidentals are needed, write the sharps or the flats on the staff *before* the notes on the *same* line or in the *same* space.

8. Notate the chord roots (in the bass clef) for each chord in "Little River," p. 56 and "Jim-Along Josie," p. 57.

9. Describe the following musical terms:

   a. Interval

   b. Transposing

   c. Chord

   d. Chord root

   e. Lead sheet notation

10. Identify the following musical symbols:

   a. P1   e. M2

   b. *mf*   f. M3

   c. *allegretto*   g. P5

   d. ━   h. P4

Performing Dotted Notes, Upbeats, and Major Triads

OBJECTIVES

After completing this chapter, you will be able to

✔ Demonstrate understanding of dotted notes, upbeats, and triple meter

✔ Transpose any melody in this chapter to another major five-finger pattern

✔ Play and construct major triads in block-chord and arpeggio forms

✔ Perform musical pieces in the chapter with pitch and rhythmic accuracy and with expression

✔ Compose parallel- and contrasting-phrase melodies

✔ Demonstrate expanded hand positions and hand-position shift

unit one • *Dotted Notes*

A dot placed to the right of a notehead increases the duration of the note by one-half. For example, a dotted half note is equal to the duration of three quarter notes (or one half note plus a quarter note).

$$\text{𝅗𝅥. } = \text{♩ ♩ ♩}$$

Dotted rests are also possible. Appendix B presents a chart of dotted rests.

Dotted Notes

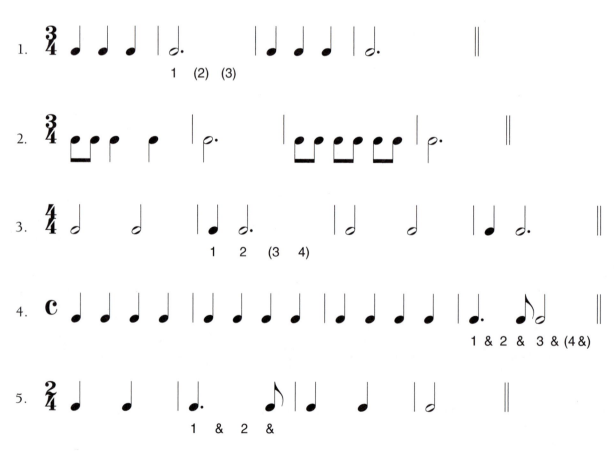

Rhythm Exercise 1. Dotted Notes, $\frac{3}{4}$.

Clap, chant, or play the following rhythmic lines on any key(s). Determine the number of counts each dotted note receives.

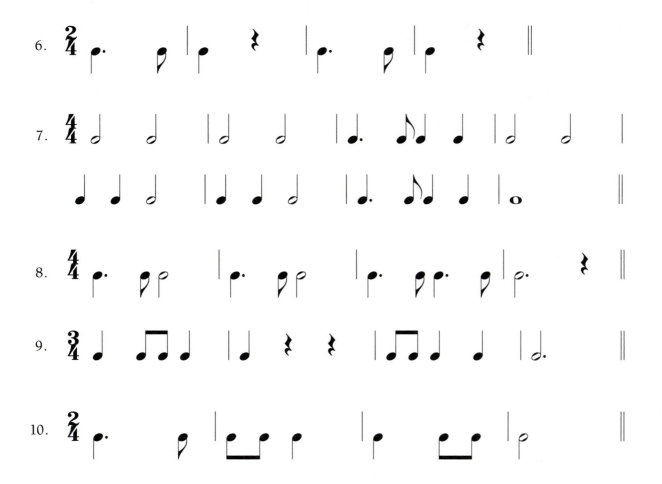

PERFORMING MELODIES WITH DOTTED NOTES

- Visually analyze each melody and decide which hand position is used for each.
- Determine the number of beats each dotted note receives, and mark the beats for each measure.
- Count and clap the rhythm of each piece.
- Observe dynamic markings and perform pieces expressively.

Westminster Chimes

English Melody

Key Sign The sign *mp* is the dynamic symbol for *mezzo piano*, which means to perform medium-soft.

Key Terms   **Phrases** are musical clauses or sentences. Pianists often punctuate the end of a phrase by a momentary lift or "breath." When two phrases begin with the same pitches and include almost identical material, the paired phrases are said to be *parallel*. When a second phrase (especially its beginning) includes musical materials that are different from those of the first phrase, the phrases are *contrasting*. Often one feels a question-and-answer type of dialogue in paired contrasting phrases. Beethoven's "Ode to Joy" consists of four phrases—three parallel (phrases 1, 2, and 4) and one contrasting (phrase 3).

Ode to Joy
(excerpt from the fourth movement, Symphony No. 9, Op. 125)

Ludwig van Beethoven (Germany, 1770–1827)

Key Fact   Beethoven, one of the greatest composers of all time, had lost his hearing by the time he composed Symphony No. 9 with its "Ode to Joy." At its first performance, he had to be turned to *face* the audience to see their enthusiastic reaction.

Jingle Bells
(excerpt)

James Pierpont (United States, 1822–1893)

Cradle Hymn

J. S. Bach (Germany, 1685–1750)

JOHANN SEBASTIAN BACH ● *(Germany, 1685–1750), outstanding composer of the late Baroque period. He wrote cantatas, passions, and other choral works; organ, harpsichord, and clavichord works; and **chamber** and orchestral music. Bach also harmonized hundreds of chorales.*

America

Samuel F. Smith (United States, 1808–1895)
Henry Carey (England, 1685–1743)

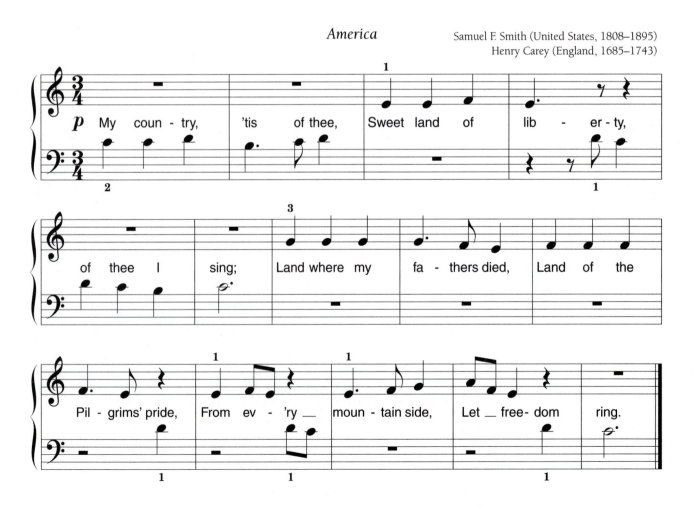

In Beyer's "Duet Exercise 32," note the G major five-finger pattern—the fingerings are not given. Decide what the starting fingering should be and mark on your copy. Note the $\frac{3}{4}$ time signature and the special markings. Play as expressively as you can. Can you discover which of the three large phrases are parallel phrases and which one is contrasting? (In this ensemble piece, either your instructor or CD Track 16 can perform the *Piano 2* part.)

Key Terms   *Andante* is the Italian tempo term indicating a moderate tempo. *8va sempre* indicates that the notes should always be performed eight notes (an octave) higher. *Dolce* is the Italian term for performing sweetly and softly.

TRACK 15

Student, Piano 1*
Andante

Duet Exercise 32

Ferdinand Beyer (1803–1863)

TRACK 16

Instructor, Piano 2

(continued)

*If two students are to perform at one piano, one student plays the part as written, and the other plays it tw octaves lower.

DOTTED NOTES

unit two • *Upbeats*

The notes in the incomplete measure found at the beginning of many pieces are called the **upbeat** or the **anacrusis.** Often the upbeat (or "pickup" notes) and an incomplete last measure combine to make one complete measure. The notes in the upbeat are unaccented and actually anticipate the accent of the first beat in the first full measure.

Happy Birthday
(excerpt)

Mildred and Patty Hill

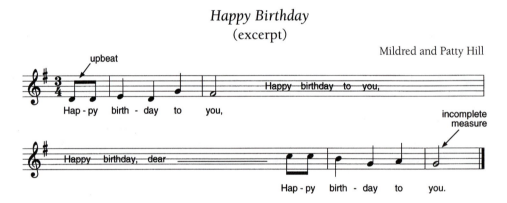

Rhythm Exercise 2. Upbeat, $\frac{3}{4}$

Clap, chant, or play the following rhythmic lines on any key(s). To perform the rhythmic lines that include an upbeat, count a full measure of beats first; then count the beat that precedes the upbeat. Be sure you know on which beat the upbeat falls.

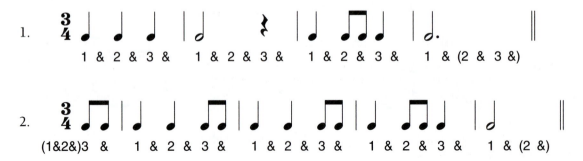

3. $\frac{3}{4}$

4. $\frac{4}{4}$

5. $\frac{4}{4}$

(1&2&3&)4 &   1 & 2 & 3 & 4 &   1 & 2 & 3 & (4 &)   1 & 2 & 3 & 4 &   1 & 2 & 3 &

6. $\frac{4}{4}$

7. $\frac{2}{4}$

8. $\frac{2}{4}$

9. $\frac{2}{4}$

(1&2)&   1 & 2 &   1 & 2 &   1 & 2 &   1 & 2

10. **c**

Rhythm Exercise 3. Two-Part Rhythms (2 hands)

Analyze, then perform these examples by tapping or playing on any key the notes on the bottom line with your LH and the notes on the top line with your RH. Perform each line separately, and then perform the lines together.

1. $\frac{3}{4}$

2. $\frac{2}{4}$

Performing Melodies with Upbeats

For the following pieces:

* Determine on which beat the upbeat falls.

* Count a full measure of beats first; then count the beat or beats that precede the upbeat.

* Transpose each piece to another major pattern.

O Tannenbaum
(excerpt)

Traditional German Carol

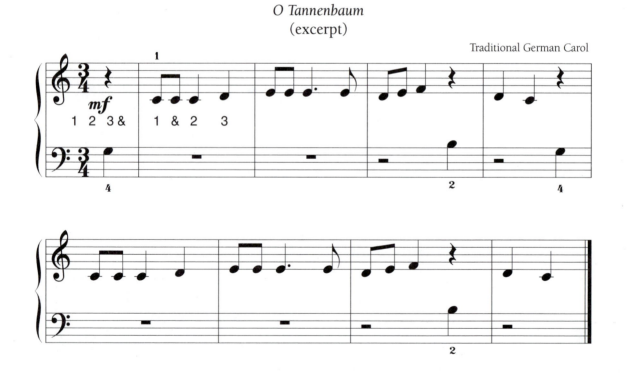

Key Sign   A **tie** (a curved line over or under the notes) connects two notes of the same pitch. Play the first note only, and hold it through the time value of the second note.

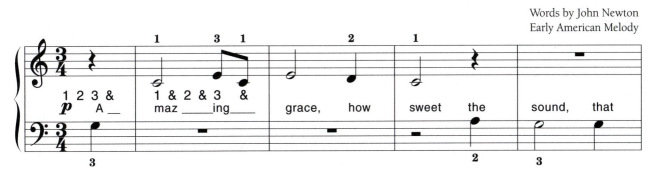

Amazing Grace

Words by John Newton
Early American Melody

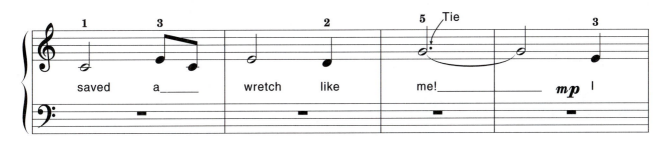

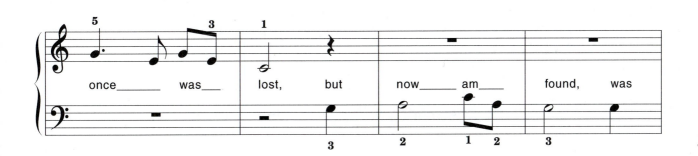

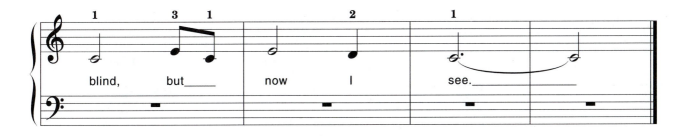

Standin' in the Need of Prayer

African American Spiritual

Triads

The most common chords are built by arranging intervals of thirds one above the other. The most basic chord of tonal music is the *triad*.

Key Term   A **triad** is a three-note chord with pitches a third apart. The three pitches of any triad are identified by the terms *root, third,* and *fifth*. The root gives the triad its name, for example, C is the root of, and gives its name to, the C triad.

TRIADS IN ROOT POSITION AND INVERSIONS

A triad can be performed with the root on the bottom (called *root position*), or the pitches in the triad may be rearranged into **inversions.** However, the root also gives the triad its name.

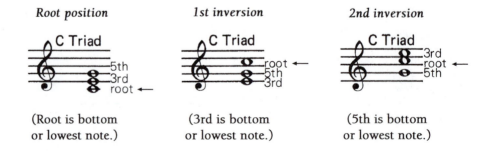

Root position	*1st inversion*	*2nd inversion*
(Root is bottom or lowest note.)	(3rd is bottom or lowest note.)	(5th is bottom or lowest note.)

THE MAJOR TRIAD

By combining the *first, third,* and *fifth* pitches of the major five-finger pattern, one forms a **major triad.** The major triad always includes a *major third* (four half steps) between the root and the third, a *minor third* (three half steps) between the third and the fifth, and a *perfect fifth* (seven half steps) between the root and the fifth.

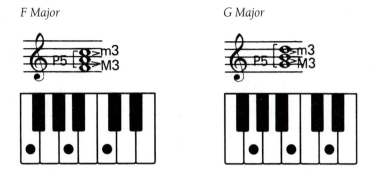

F Major   G Major

Performing Major Triads in Block-Chord and Arpeggio Forms

Block-Chord Exercise. Major Triad

Practice the major triad in *block-chord form* (**chord tones** played simultaneously) in the following positions at the keyboard.

- Sit centered at the keyboard and far enough back to allow freedom of movement.

- To play the chords, push keys down simultaneously, with equal weight on each key. Try to connect playings of the chord as smoothly as possible. Be careful not to overlap the chords when hands cross.

- Transpose this exercise to G, F, D, A, and E major triads.

Part A

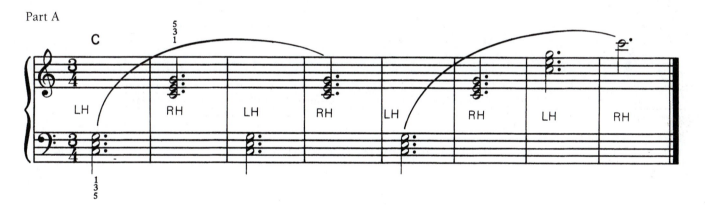

Part B

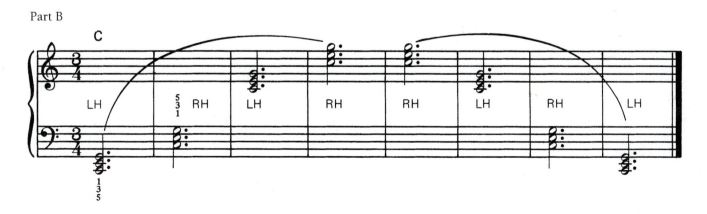

Arpeggio Exercise. Major Triad

This exercise uses the major triad in *broken-chord,* or **arpeggio**, *form* (chord tones played one after the other).

- Connect chord tones as smoothly as you can and use the hand-over-hand technique when specified.
- Transpose to the major triads of F, G; D, A, E; and D♭, A♭, E♭. Learn the feel of these chords grouped by color of keys.

Playing Tip Hold the chord shape in the hand and touch each new key's location just before playing.

Part A

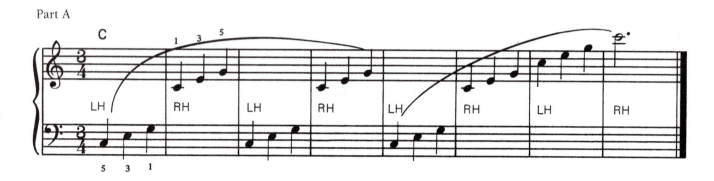

Part B

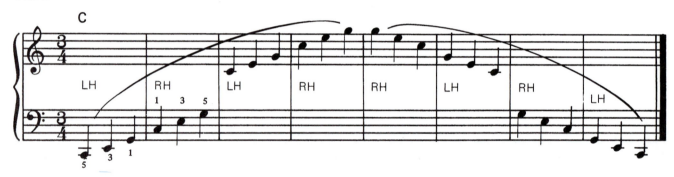

Performing a Major Triad Melody

"Reveille" is based on the F major triad (FAC). Notice that the LH plays C and the RH performs F and A (this is an inversion of the F major triad).

Reveille

U.S. Army Bugle Call

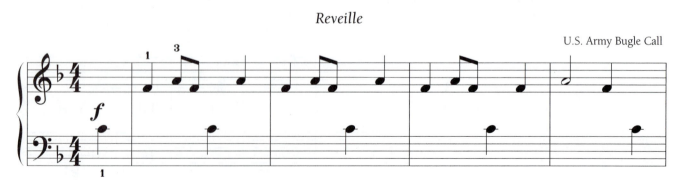

THE TONIC CHORD (MAJOR)

The first pitch of the major five-finger pattern is called the **tonic**, and the chord built on the first step is called the *tonic chord* or the I chord. The tonic chord for the major pattern is a major triad.

C major five-finger pattern—
Tonic chord

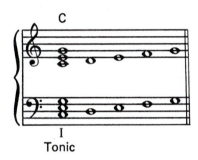

The Tonic Chord and the Major Five-Finger Pattern

Locate the major triad built on the tonic for each major five-finger pattern. Play the following example in these major five-finger patterns: C, G; D, A; F; and E.

C major

Performing Melodies with Tonic Chord Accompaniments

The first three melodies are accompanied with the tonic chord of the major pattern. Perform with a good balance of sound between the melody and the chord (melody should dominate). Note the dynamic markings. Transpose to other major patterns.

Whistle, Daughter

American Folk Song

Dressed in Blue

American Folk Song

Umptum Lady

American Folk Song

The next three melodies have the tonic chord as part of their accompaniment.

Little River

German Folk Melody

American Folk Melody 2

Folk Melody 2

COMPOSING PROJECTS

Compose two melodies, one illustrating *parallel phrases* and one illustrating *contrasting phrases*.

- Follow the Guidelines provided and review the sample melody for each.

- The first phrase for each melody is given; write a second phrase of the same length.

- Use the F major five-finger pattern, and make sure you conclude on the tonic F.

Project 1. Parallel-Phrase Melody

↑ tonic

GUIDELINES FOR COMPOSING A PARALLEL PHRASE

Step 1. For the first two measures of your second phrase (measures 5–6), notate the exact pitches used for the beginning of phrase 1 (measures 1–2).

Step 2. For measures 7–8, be creative. Use the same pitches of the five-finger pattern, but in a different combination or rhythm from what was used for the concluding measures (3–4) of phrase 1. Be sure to end on the tonic pitch.

Step 3. Play both phrases. Check to see that they look and sound parallel. (The two begin the same and include almost identical pitches and rhythm; they are the same length.) Exchange your notated melody with another student. Play your melodies for each other and and assess your work for accuracy and creativity.

Sample Parallel-Phrase Melody

Israeli Folk Melody 1

Project 2. Contrasting-Phrase Melody

↑ tonic

GUIDELINES FOR COMPOSING A CONTRASTING PHRASE

Step 1. Play phrase 1 and be attentive to the exact pitches and rhythm.

Step 2. To create a contrasting phrase to pair with the first phrase, use the same pitches of the five-finger pattern but in a different combination. Experiment until you compose a phrase that is contrasting to phrase 1, but not so different that it does not seem to pair well enough to make a complete melody. (Using similar rhythmic patterns in the two phrases helps to unify the entire melody!) Be sure to conclude on the tonic.

Step 3. Play both phrases. Check to see that they look and sound contrasting (the two phrases begin and end with different pitches; they are the same length). Exchange your notated melody with another student. Play your melodies for each other and and assess your work for accuracy and creativity

Sample Contrasting-Phrase Melody

Folk Melody 3

SOLO REPERTOIRE

Visually analyze each of the repertoire pieces before playing. Determine the tonic and the hand position. Review the rhythmic considerations, and note all dynamic and tempo markings.

In the Kabalevsky piece, both the LH and the RH parts are notated in the treble clef. (The LH part extends beyond the five-finger pattern.) Observe the phrasing, and work for a legato touch, playing as expressively as you can.

Key Signs The short horizontal line above or below a note ($\bar{\Gamma}$ $\bar{\downarrow}$) indicates that the note should be performed with a slight stress (*tenuto*) and that the tone should be sustained. The sign $\underset{}{\diagup\!\!\!\diagdown}$ is the dynamic symbol for *crescendo* (abbreviated *cresc.*), meaning to gradually get louder.

TRACK 17

Melody, Op. 39, No. 1
(from *24 Little Pieces*)

Moderato   Dmitri Kabalevsky (Russia, 1904–1987)

DMITRI KABALEVSKY ● *(Russia, 1904–1987), composer of operas, ballets, symphonies, incidental music for plays and films, and numerous piano pieces. In addition to composing, he became an important spokesperson for Soviet cultural policy, a teacher, and an administrator.*

In Türk's Allegro, the RH stays within the C major five-finger pattern (an octave above middle C). The LH, however, covers the range of an octave. Practice the LH fingering and range before playing the piece with hands together.

Allegro

Daniel Gottlob Türk (Germany, 1756–1813)

"Seeds" has several unique features: one pitch (C) throughout, but in different registers, and the pedal depressed. Olson's directions suggest that the pedal is depressed from the first note and held for the entire piece. Note the tempo and dynamic markings!

Seeds

Lynn Freeman Olson (United States, 1938–1987)

Slowly

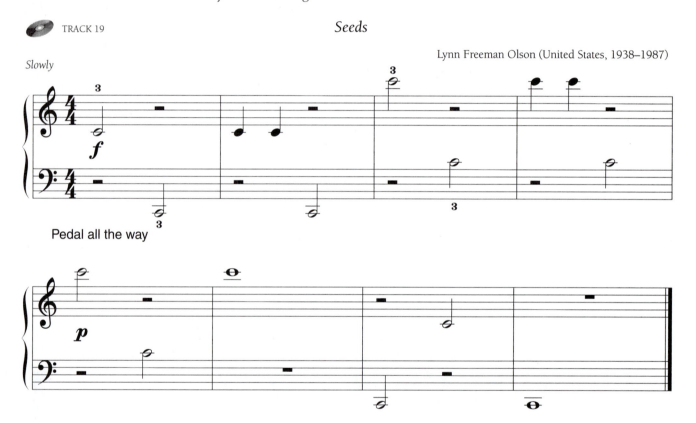

Pedal all the way

"Seeds" from *Beginnings* by Lynn Freeman Olson. Copyright © 1997 by Carl Fischer LLC. All Rights Reserved. Reprinted By Permission.

TECHNIQUE EXERCISES

Play all the exercises in the major patterns of C, G, D, A, F, E, and B.

Technique Exercise 1. Independent Hands and Hand Coordination

Review Technique Exercise 2 on page 63 before playing this one. This exercise, like the one on page 63, is in two parts. Part A features the RH rhythmically moving in shorter durations against the longer durations of the LH. Part B reverses this rhythmic movement. Practice hands together and with each hand separately. Work on a legato touch.

Playing Tip   For legato playing, strive to allow only one note to sound at a time. Let the weight of your arm shift from one finger to the next while you keep a good hand position and a flexible wrist.

Part A

Part B

Technique Exercise 2. Hand-Position Shift

In this Bartók study, you will shift from the G major five-finger pattern to the D major pattern and then return to the G pattern. Practice this hand-position shift, trying not to look down at the keys.

Study: Changing Hand Position
(from *First Term at the Piano*)

Moderato

Béla Bartók (Hungary, 1881–1945)

END-OF-CHAPTER EVALUATION

1. Perform with rhythmic accuracy the following pieces, which include anacrusis, dotted notes, or both: "Amazing Grace," p. 77, and "O Tannenbaum," p. 76. Play major triads constructed on the tonic of the following major five-finger patterns: C, F, D, A, B♭, E♭. Perform in block-chord and broken-chord forms.

3. Transpose any melody in this chapter to another major five-finger pattern.

4. Demonstrate hand-position shift by performing Bartók's "Study: Changing Hand Position" on p. 88.

5. Circle the upbeat in the following example. Indicate on what beat the upbeat begins.

America the Beautiful
(excerpt)

Katherine Lee Bates (United States, 1859–1929)
Samuel A. Ward (United States, 1847–1903)

O beau - ti - ful for spa - cious skies, For am - ber waves of grain,

6. For each dotted note, write the equivalent notes.

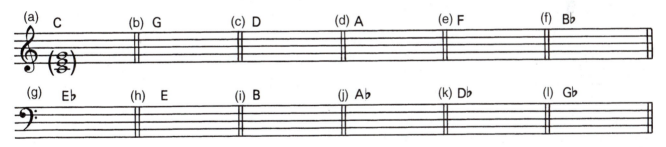

7. Write the designated major triads. When accidentals are needed, write the sharps or the flats on the staff *before* the notes.

(a) C   (b) G   (c) D   (d) A   (e) F   (f) B♭

(g) E♭   (h) E   (i) B   (j) A♭   (k) D♭   (l) G♭

8. On the staff below, notate the A major five-finger pattern in the treble and bass clefs and the tonic (I) chord.

9. Describe the following musical terms:

a. Arpeggio

b. Parallel phrases

c. Contrasting phrases

d. Tonic chord

e. Triad

f. Major triad

g. Upbeat

10. Identify the following musical symbols:

a.

b.

c.

d. *mp*

e.

Memorizing Music

Memorizing music requires several kinds of skills. It is not enough to keep repeating a piece until your fingers can play it automatically. Your mind needs to guide your fingers for a lasting memorization.

First, a thorough understanding of what's happening in the music is necessary for recalling the total "picture" of the piece under study. That means knowing what is special about the rhythm, the melody, the harmony, and any dynamics or tempo features, and how the piece is organized—its form.

Second, after you have performed a piece many times and studied the technical aspects, your fingers should know the physical movements.

Third, you must be able to remember aurally the pitches and their rhythmic values. Here are some guidelines to help with memorizing music.

GUIDELINES FOR MEMORIZING PIECES

Step 1. You are ready to memorize when you can play a piece expressively with pitch and rhythmic accuracy and correct fingering (hands separately and hands together). In addition, you should have a sound knowledge of the characteristics of melody, rhythm, form, dynamics, and tempo.

Step 2. Next, work on aurally recalling the pitches and the rhythm. Begin by dividing the piece into smaller parts. (In short compositions, these parts are phrases.) Learn to play these smaller parts from memory with each hand separately. When you can do that easily, try playing each hand alone but using just one finger (index). This is a good test to see if you know the notes aurally without the aid of physical involvement.

Step 3. Play the smaller parts hands together from memory. Try playing with your eyes closed.

Step 4. Combine the smaller parts until you have memorized the whole piece. Then try playing the piece with your eyes closed.

chapter five

An Introduction to the Minor Five-Finger Pattern and Minor Triads

OBJECTIVES

After completing this chapter, you will be able to

✔ Construct and play a minor five-finger pattern

✔ Transpose minor five-finger patterns and melodies at the keyboard and in writing

✔ Play and construct minor triads and perform in block-chord and arpeggio forms

✔ Perform musical pieces in the chapter with pitch and rhythmic accuracy and with expression

✔ Compose a composition with parallel phrases based on the minor triad

✔ Demonstrate extension fingerings

Minor Five-Finger Pattern

COMPARISON OF MAJOR AND MINOR PATTERNS

The whole-step–half-step arrangement of the *minor five-finger pattern* (the first five notes of a minor scale) features the half step between pitches 2 and 3, whereas the major five-finger pattern includes the half step between pitches 3 and 4.

Major five-finger pattern

1 ⌐ 2 ⌐ 3 ⌐ 4 ⌐ 5
whole   whole   half   whole

Minor five-finger pattern

1 ⌐ 2 ⌐ 3 ⌐ 4 ⌐ 5
whole   half   whole   whole

The minor five-finger pattern, like the major one, uses consecutive letter names and can be built on any of the twelve keys or pitches. The whole-step–half-step patterns for C major and C minor are illustrated below. Notice that the third pitch is the only one that is different.

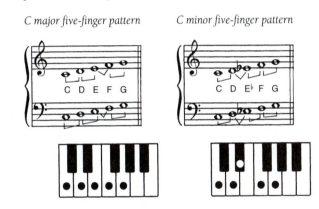

C major five-finger pattern   *C minor five-finger pattern*

C D E F G   C D E♭ F G

Playing Major and Minor Patterns

To hear, understand, and feel the contrast between the major and minor patterns, play the following exercise. Listen for the unique "color" of minor compared with major. Transpose the exercise to the five-finger patterns of G, D, and A.

C major / C minor

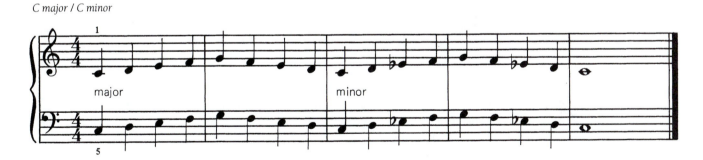

major

minor

In "Duet Exercise 42," note the A minor five-finger position and the special musical markings. Play as expressively as you can. Of the four phrases in the Piano 1 part, determine which are parallel phrases and which are contrasting. The instructor (or CD Track 21) plays the *Piano 2* part.

TRACK 20

Student, Piano 1

Andante

Duet Exercise 42

Ferdinand Beyer (1803–1863)

TRACK 21

Instructor, Piano 2

Andante

Composer Lee Evans mixes a bit of major and minor together in "It's Natural to Have a Flat." Note the E-flat and the E-natural! Determine the hand setup for each hand. Play this bluesy piece in an "easy swing" tempo; the instructor (or CD Track 23) adds the *Piano 2* part.

Student, Piano 1
Easy swing

It's Natural to Have a Flat

Lee Evans (United States, b. 1933)

Instructor, Piano 2

Easy swing

INTERVALS IN THE MINOR FIVE-FINGER PATTERN

The only interval that is different in the major and minor five-finger patterns is the interval of the third. This new interval—the *minor third*—is a half step smaller than the major third.

Major 3rd (M3) = 4 half steps

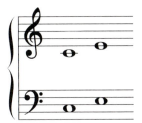

Minor 3rd (m3) = 3 half steps

Arpeggio Exercise. Minor Triad

Practice the minor triad in the broken-chord, or *arpeggio,* form. Again, connect chord tones as smoothly as you can. Try these positions with different minor triads.

Part A

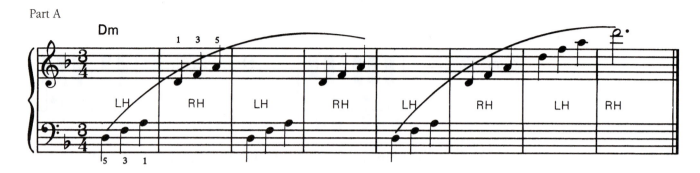

Part B

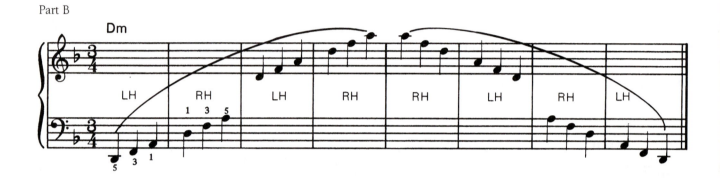

THE TONIC CHORD (MINOR)

The first pitch of the minor five-finger pattern is called the tonic, and the chord built on the first pitch is called the *tonic chord* or i. The tonic chord for the minor pattern is a minor triad. (Lowercase roman numerals are often used for minor triads.)

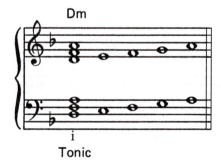

Tonic

Tonic Chord and Minor Five-Finger Pattern

Locate the tonic triad for each minor five-finger pattern. Play the following exercise in these minor five-finger patterns: D, A, E; and C, G, F.

D minor

Performing Melodies with Minor Triad Accompaniment

The following minor melodies are accompanied with the minor triad or use the minor triad as part of the accompaniment. Analyze each before playing. Determine the minor pattern and triad; then play both. Notice the interval relationship between notes. Be sure to keep your eyes on the music. Transpose to other minor patterns.

Key Term *Allegro* is the Italian tempo term indicating a fast and lively tempo.

Bulgarian Folk Melody

Allegro

Folk Melody 4

Adagio

Israeli Folk Melody 2

Moderato

Polish Folk Melody

Moderato

COMPOSING PROJECT

Minor Triad Composition

Create a parallel-phrase melody based on a minor triad.

Step 1. Choose a minor triad on which to base your piece. Identify the three pitches in the triad. Play those pitches with both hands.

Step 2. Using those three pitches, create an eight-measure melody that includes two parallel phrases. (Refer to Chapter 4 to review parallel phrases.) Experiment with various pitches and rhythms until you decide on something that pleases you. You may divide the melody equally between the two hands or play the melody in one hand and add a triad accompaniment in the other. Be sure to conclude your melody on the root of the triad.

Step 3. Notate your composition on the staff that follows, and then play, reading from staff notation. Exchange your melody with a classmate's and assess each other's work for accuracy and creativity.

SOLO REPERTOIRE

Visually analyze the following pieces.

- What can you say about the intervals between pitches?

- Are there definite phrases? If so, are they parallel, contrasting, or something different?

- What about the tempo and the dynamics?

Choose one of the pieces to memorize.

Van de Vate's "A Quiet Exchange" falls within an E-to-B white-note five-finger position, which is part of the Phrygian mode (see Chapter 10). Notice how the material in the first four measures appears in opposite hands in the second four measures (called *invertible counterpoint*).

Playing Tip   The composer suggests that when repeating "A Quiet Exchange," you move your RH up one octave and play as softly as possible.

Key Term   The word *ritardando* (abbreviated *rit.*) is the Italian tempo term meaning to gradually get slower and slower.

TRACK 24

A Quiet Exchange

Moderato   Nancy Van de Vate (United States, b. 1930)

NANCY VAN DE VATE   ● *(United States, b. 1930), composer of orchestral, chamber, vocal, and keyboard works. Her music has been performed in eighteen countries on four continents. She is the founder of the International League of Women Composers.*

In Konrad Künz's "Canon," notice the imitation of the RH melody in the LH. This piece falls within the E minor five-finger pattern. Practice hands separately and then hands together.

Key Term   A **canon** is a composition in which all parts have the same melody but start at different times.

Canon

Konrad Max Künz (Germany, 1812–1875)

TECHNIQUE EXERCISES

Check your keyboard position and your hand position.

Technique Exercise 1. Contrary Motion

Keep your wrists flexible and your arms moving in a gentle outward and upward movement for each two-measure pattern in Part A. When you arrive at the whole note, look ahead to what comes next so you'll be ready. In Part B, the arm movements will be reversed. Transpose this exercise to the minor patterns of G, A, D, E, B, and F.

Part A

Part B

Technique Exercise 2. Intervals (Minor Five-Finger Pattern)

Play these intervals in the following pattern. Stress independent finger action, and work for a legato sound. Transpose to other minor five-finger patterns.

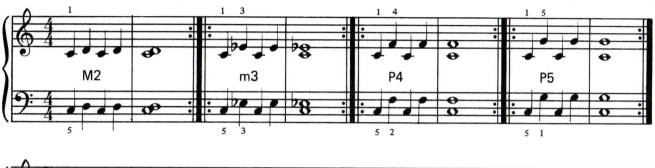

Technique Exercise 3. Consecutive Thirds

Practice this exercise slowly with each hand separately and with hands together. Connect the thirds as smoothly as possible. Change to other major and minor patterns.

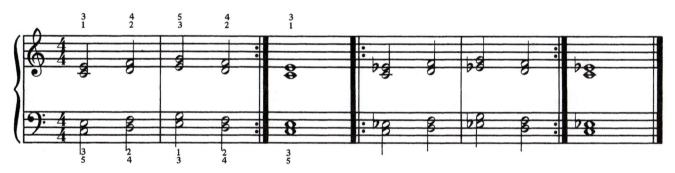

Technique Exercise 4. Parallel Motion

The major and minor five-finger patterns and major and minor triads are explored in this exercise. Be attentive to independent finger action on the major and minor patterns. Transpose to the major and parallel minor patterns of G, A, D, E, B, and F.

Technique Exercise 5. Extension Fingering

The five-finger pattern is extended to cover six pitches instead of five in this major and minor exercise. Play without accidentals (in parentheses) for the C major pattern and with accidentals for the C minor pattern. Practice for clarity and accuracy. Transpose to other major and minor patterns.

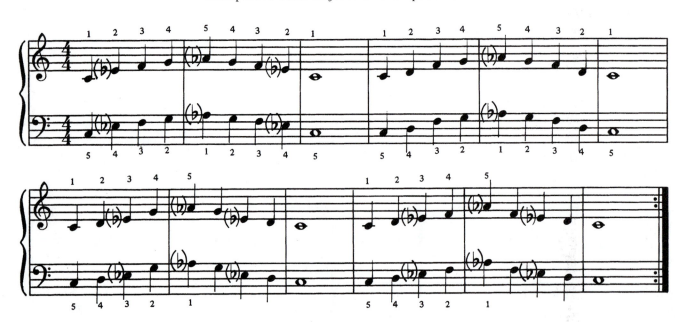

END-OF-CHAPTER EVALUATION

1. Build and play a minor five-finger pattern on the following tonics: C, D, E, F, and G.

2. Using the A minor pattern, play major seconds (M2), minor thirds (m3), and perfect fourths (P4) and fifths (P5).

3. At the keyboard, transpose Czech Folk Melody 1, on p. 98, from D minor to C minor.

4. Demonstrate a minor triad on any given root, and identify the minor third and the perfect fifth. Contrast a major triad with a minor triad at the keyboard.

5. Perform by memory one of the pieces in this chapter.

6. Demonstrate extension fingering by performing Technique Exercise 5 in this chapter.

7. Notate the following minor five-finger patterns on the staff and keyboard chart. When accidentals are needed, write the sharps or the flats on the staff *before* the pitches on the *same* line or in the *same* space.

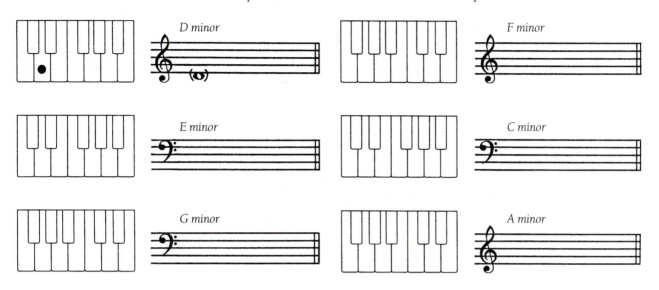

8. Label the following intervals by quality and number (for example, m3). Underneath that identification, specify the number of half steps in each interval. Use the preceding keyboard charts to help in visualizing the half steps.

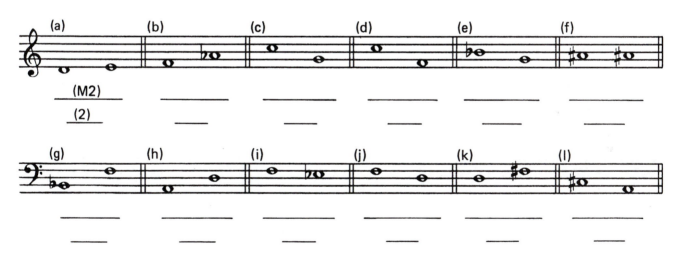

9. Write minor triads on the following roots.

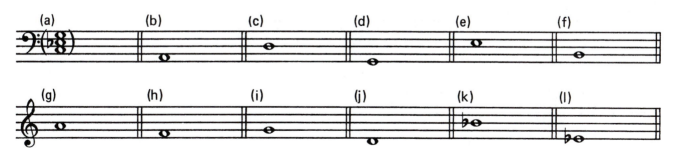

10. Identify and explain the following musical symbols and terms:

a. $\frac{3}{4}$

b. Em

c. m3

d. block chord

e. arpeggio

f. *adagio*

g. *rit.*

Performing Major Scales and I and V7 Chords

Unit 1. The Major Scale
         Identification of Scale Tones
         Intervals
         Major Scale Fingering

Unit 2. Major Key Signatures
         Placement of Sharps and Flats in Key Signatures
         The Circle of Fifths (Major Keys)
         Identifying Major Keys

Unit 3. Tonic and Dominant Chords
         The Dominant Seventh Chord

Composing Project

Solo Repertoire

Technique Exercise

End-of-Chapter Evaluation

OBJECTIVES

After completing this chapter, you will be able to

✔ Construct major scales on given tonics and perform selected major scales demonstrating one-hand fingerings

✔ Transpose major scale melodies at the keyboard and in writing

✔ Demonstrate understanding of major key signatures

✔ Play and construct I and V7 chords

✔ Perform musical pieces in the chapter with pitch and rhythmic accuracy and with expression, performing at least one from memory

✔ Compose a two-phrase melody using the I and V7 chords

✔ Demonstrate cross-over and cross-under fingerings and staccato touch

The Major Scale

The word **scale** comes from the Latin word *scala*, meaning ladder. In music of Western civilization, scales can be identified by particular interval patterns. The two scale forms most familiar to us are the *major* and the *minor scales*, but many other scales and modes also serve as the pitch framework for much of the world's music.

The **major scale** is a series of eight pitches, arranged in alphabetical order with an interval pattern of five whole steps and two half steps. The half steps occur between the third and fourth, and the seventh and eighth pitches. Each scale begins and ends on a note of the same name.

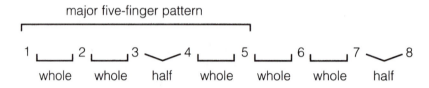

major five-finger pattern

1 whole 2 whole 3 half 4 whole 5 whole 6 whole 7 half 8

The major scale pattern is illustrated by the white keys on the keyboard from C to C.

C major scale

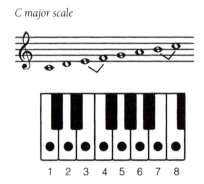

1 2 3 4 5 6 7 8

Performing the C Major Scale

1. Say or sing the letter names as you play the C major scale. Use the *tetrachord* or two-handed fingering. Notice the important pull of the seventh (B) toward the eighth (C).

C major scale

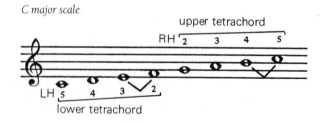

upper tetrachord

RH 2 3 4 5

LH 5 4 3 2

lower tetrachord

Key Term   A **tetrachord** is a series of four pitches with a pattern of whole step, whole step, half step between pitches. A major scale consists of two tetrachords joined by a whole step.

2. Play the descending C major scale at the beginning of "Joy to the World."

Joy to the World
(excerpt)

Words: Isaac Watts (England, 1674–1748)
Music: George Frideric Handel (Germany, 1685–1759)

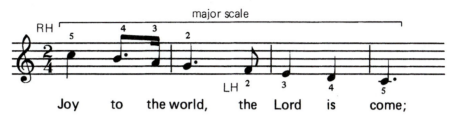

Joy to the world, the Lord is come;

3. Play "St. Paul's Steeple" using the tetrachord fingering.

(Play also as a **round** with up to four groups, each group starting after the first two notes of the previous group.)

St. Paul's Steeple

American Folk Melody

IDENTIFICATION OF SCALE TONES

Scale Degrees

Each pitch, or degree, of the major scale has a name.

Major scale degrees

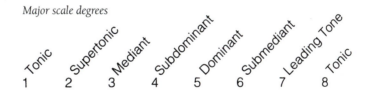

Tonic	Supertonic	Mediant	Subdominant	Dominant	Submediant	Leading Tone	Tonic
1	2	3	4	5	6	7	8

Syllable Names

Pitches may be identified by letters, numbers, degree names, and *syllable names*. Seven syllable names—*do, re, mi, fa, sol, la, ti*—are often used to identify pitches in a scale. (In the song "Do-Re-Mi" from the musical *The Sound of Music*, syllables are used as part of the lyrics.)

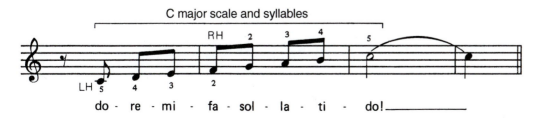

do - re - mi - fa - sol - la - ti - do! _____

INTERVALS

Eight intervals are created between the tonic and the eight ascending degrees of the major scale. The seconds, thirds, sixths, and sevenths are always major intervals; the unisons, fourths, fifths, and octaves are always perfect intervals.

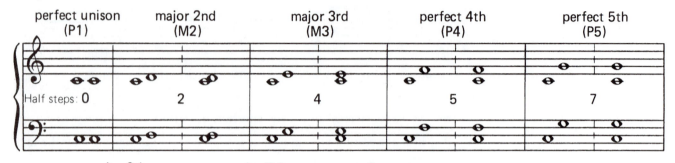

Interval Exercises

1. Read and play each interval in the major scale. Feel the distances and listen to the sound of each interval. Practice hands separately and hands together. Transpose to other major scales.

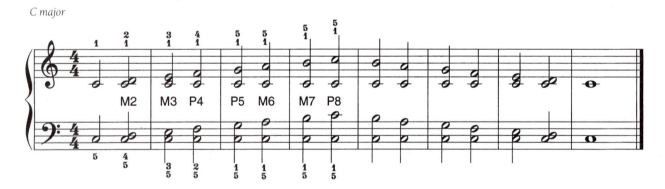

2. Practice these intervals in Technique Exercise 4 in this chapter.

MAJOR SCALE FINGERING

One-Hand Fingering in One Octave

To play a major scale with one hand, you must cross fingers over and under other fingers. One-hand fingerings for all major scales are in Appendix E.

The fingering for the C major scale in one octave (also the same for the G, D, A, and E scales) is as follows:

RH: 1 2 ③ 1 2 ③ 4 5
LH: 5 4 ③ 2 1 ③ 2 1

C major scale

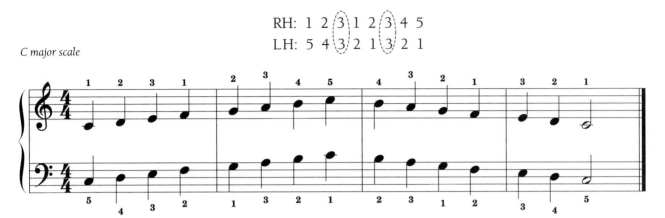

Performing Major Scale Melodies

1. Both Hispanic Folk Melody and American Folk Melody 2 use the pitches in the major scale. Use the one-hand fingering with the RH. What is the range of the LH part?

Hispanic Folk Melody

American Folk Melody 3

2. "Come, Follow" may be played as a round—even a round for up to three groups of pianists. Each group starts four measures after the previous group. Notice that both hands use the one-hand fingering.

TRACK 26

Come, Follow

John Hilton (England, 1599–1657)
Arranged by Linda Mankin

3. "The First Noel" is a more challenging scale melody. Practice the RH one-hand fingering. Look only at the music, even when your thumb moves under. Feel the movement. Perform by yourself or with another pianist. (One pianist can play the RH melody while another plays the bass line. At one piano, a pianist can play the bass line as written with the LH or the RH while another plays the melody an octave higher.)

The First Noel

Carol

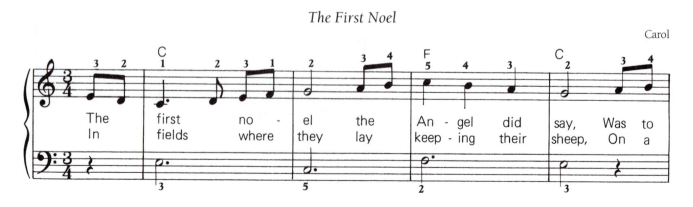

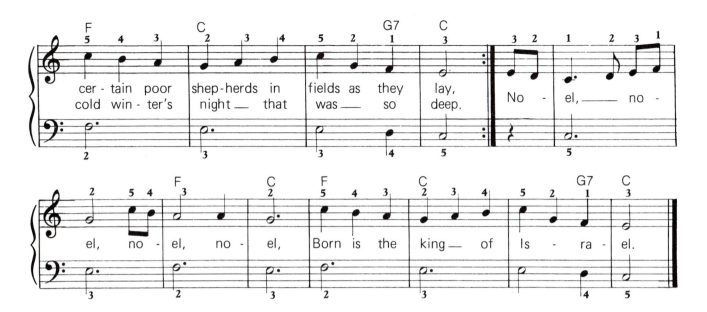

4. For an even more challenging scale melody, try "Joy to the World," p. 296.

One-Hand Fingering in Two Octaves

The fingering for the C major scale in two octaves (also the same for the G, D, A, and E scales) is as follows:

RH: 1 2 ③ 1 2 ③ 4 ① 2 ③ 1 2 ③ 4 5
LH: 5 4 ③ 2 1 ③ 2 ① 4 ③ 2 1 ③ 2 1

C major scale

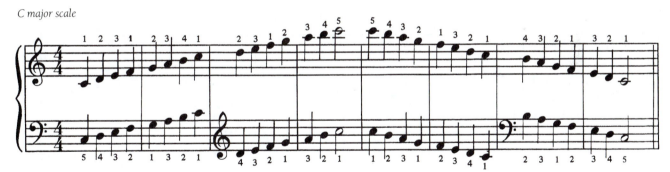

Performing Major Scales in Two Octaves

1. Practice the C major scale with one-hand fingering in two octaves in contrary motion. Practice hands separately, then hands together. Notice that the fingering is the same in the two hands.

C major scale in contrary motion

2. Practice the C major scale with one-hand fingering in two octaves in parallel motion (p. 119). Practice hands separately and, when the fingering is secure, hands together.

3. Once the fingering is secure for the C major scale, try the G and D major scales in contrary motion and in parallel motion.

G major scale in parallel motion

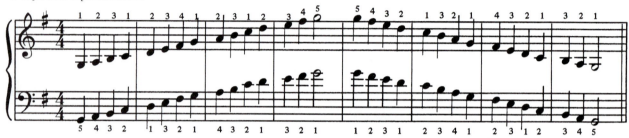

D major scale in parallel motion

4. Practice Technique Exercises 1 and 2 at the end of this chapter.

unit two · ## *Major Key Signatures*

The sharps or the flats needed to create the various major scales are placed at the beginning of each staff of music (right after the clef sign). This grouping of the sharps and flats is called a **key signature.**

Any sharp or flat in the key signature applies to the corresponding note in all octaves. For example, if a B-flat is in the key signature, then all Bs (whether in bass or in treble clef or in any position on the staff) must be performed as B-flats.

Placement of Sharps and Flats in Key Signatures

The sharps and the flats in the key signature are placed in a specific order.

Learning Tip   Notice that the order of flats is the reverse of the order of sharps!

GUIDELINES FOR USING THE KEY SIGNATURE TO DETERMINE THE TONIC OR MAJOR KEY

Step 1. Determine whether the key signature uses sharps or flats. (See key signature tables below.)

Step 2. If the key signature includes *sharps*, locate the sharp farthest to the right. This is the scale tone 7, and the next line or space above (one half step above) is the key or the tonic.

Step 3. If the key signature includes *flats*, there are two ways to determine the tonic or major key. One way is to simply identify the next-to-the-last flat in the key signature—that pitch is the tonic. (With this approach, you need to memorize that the key of F has one flat.) The other way is to locate the flat farthest to the right (scale tone 4) and count down to 1 (the tonic).

Sharp key signatures

Flat key signatures

The Circle of Fifths (Major Keys)

The fifteen major scales and key signatures can be arranged in a sequence called the **circle of fifths.** Moving clockwise *up* the interval of a perfect fifth to the tonic, you can see that each new key adds one more sharp. Moving counterclockwise *down* a perfect fifth, you can see that each key adds one more flat. Three keys are enharmonic: B and C♭, F♯ and G♭, and C♯ and D♭.

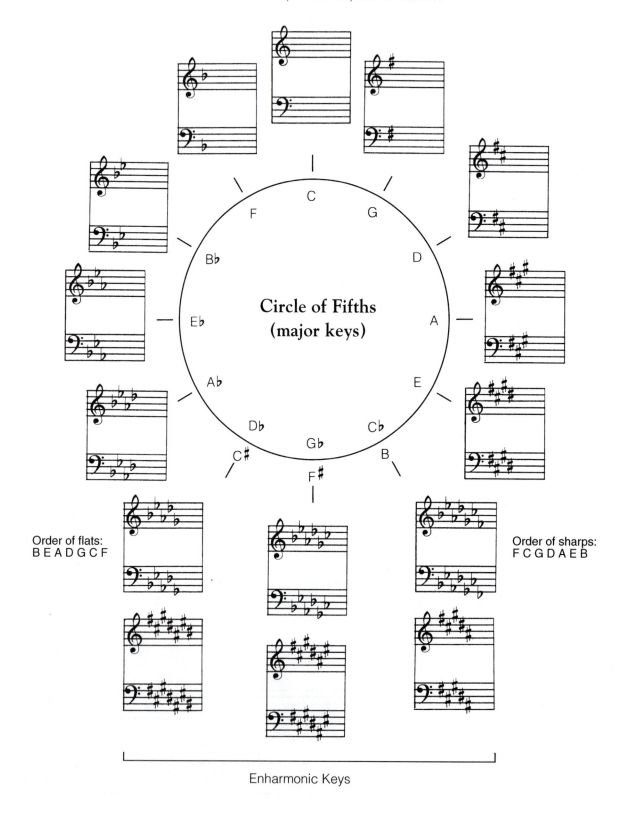

Order of flats:
B E A D G C F

Order of sharps:
F C G D A E B

Enharmonic Keys

IDENTIFYING MAJOR KEYS

Before performing the following pieces, determine the major key for each. To identify the major key,

1. Examine the key signature to determine the tonic or key.

2. Locate the final pitch in the piece. Most often, that pitch will be the tonic.

The results of steps 1 and 2 will most likely be the same, and therefore, the major key has been identified.

America the Beautiful

Katherine Lee Bates (United States, 1859–1929)
Samuel A. Ward (United States, 1847–1903)

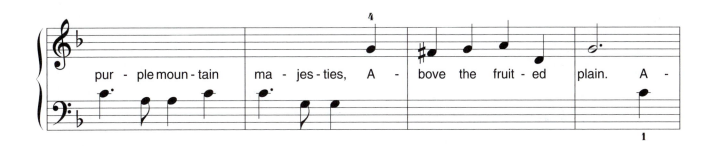

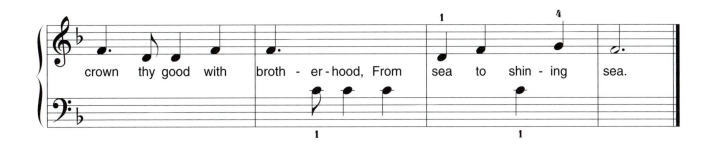

Wiegenlied

Daniel Gottlob Türk (Germany, 1756–1813)

 TRACK 27

Waltz
(from *Melodious Exercises*, Op. 62, No. 3)

Student, Piano 1

Allegro

Hermann Berens (Germany, 1826–1880)

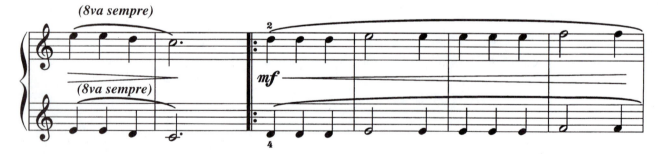

TRACK 28

Instructor, Piano 2

Allegro

unit three ●   *Tonic and Dominant Chords*

The most important chord in the scale is the **tonic** (I), and second in importance is the **dominant,** or V. In a major scale, both the I and the V are major chords. The tonic triad includes pitches 1, 3, and 5 of the major scale, and the dominant triad includes pitches 5, 7, and 2.

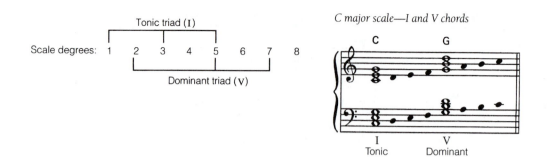

C major scale—I and V chords

K e y   T e r m When a phrase, section, or piece concludes with the V–I progression, the closing, or **cadence,** is called **authentic.** Since I conveys the strongest sense of arrival, most melodies conclude on the tonic pitch or chord. Because two of the pitches (7 and 2 of the major scale) in the V chord have a tendency to "pull" toward the I, the V often precedes the I.

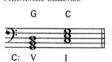

Authentic cadence

Cadence

Notice the authentic cadence in Gurlitt's Op. 117, No. 10.

K e y   S i g n A dot above or below a notehead indicates that the tone should be disconnected and shortened (staccato). See more on staccato touch in Technique Exercise 3 at the end of the chapter.

Op. 117, No. 10

Con moto

Cornelius Gurlitt (Germany, 1820–1901)

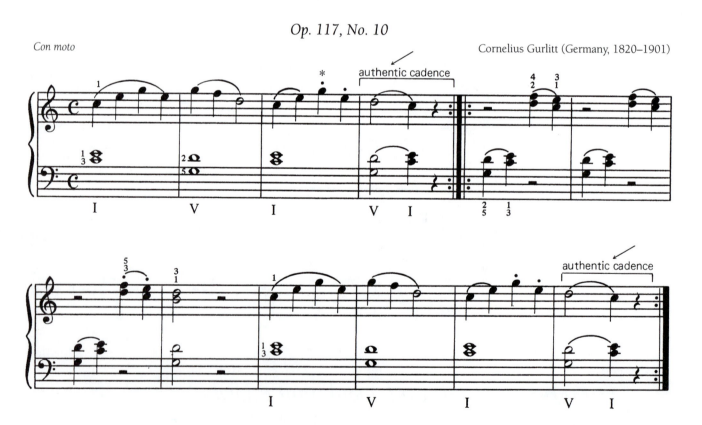

THE DOMINANT SEVENTH CHORD

The dominant (V) chord is not always a triad. Quite often it includes four notes and is called a **dominant seventh chord** (V7). (More information on seventh chords appears in Chapter 8.) The V7 is represented in lead sheet notation by a capital letter plus a 7—for example, C7, G7, F7.

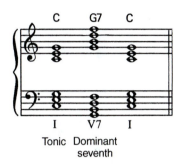

Tonic Dominant
seventh

"Piano Position" for the V7 Chord

When one chord progresses to another, it is important to find tones that are common to both or tones that are closest to one another. This simplifies the fingering, avoids awkward sounds, and allows the chord tones to move smoothly one to another.

To simplify the moves between the I and the V7 chords, the fifth of the V7 chord is sometimes omitted and the other tones are rearranged or inverted. This is often called the "piano position."

The common tone in the I and the V7 chords is the top one, so those pitches in the two chords stay the same. As you move from the I to the V7 chord, the middle note of the I chord moves up a half step and the bottom note moves down a half step, forming the V7 chord inversion.

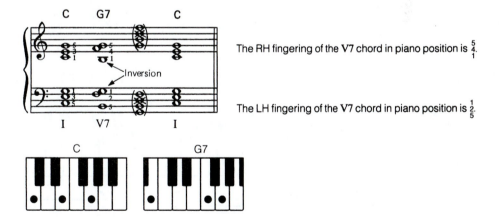

The RH fingering of the **V7** chord in piano position is $\frac{5}{4}$.

The LH fingering of the **V7** chord in piano position is $\frac{1}{2}$.

I and V7 Chords in Selected Major Keys

Practice the I and the V7 chords in the following frequently used major keys. (All chords and fingerings are in Appendix H.) Develop a feel for this progression and be ready to change chords.

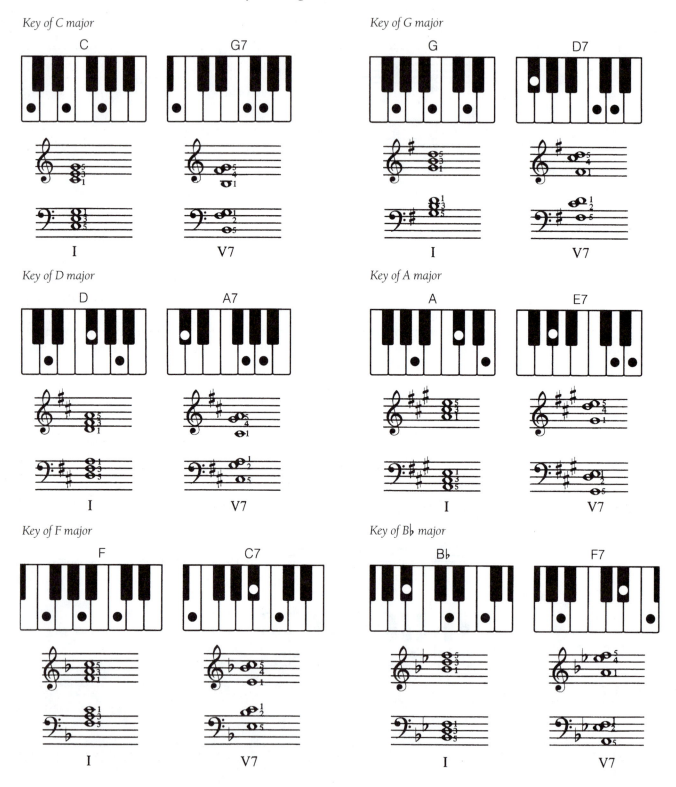

Key of C major

C   G7

I   V7

Key of G major

G   D7

I   V7

Key of D major

D   A7

I   V7

Key of A major

A   E7

I   V7

Key of F major

F   C7

I   V7

Key of B♭ major

B♭   F7

I   V7

Performing I–V7 Chords

1. Perform the following exercise (Parts A–C) to practice the necessary moves between the two chords. Part A prepares the hands for the moves between the two chords in Parts B and C. Transpose this exercise to other major keys.

Part A

Part B

Part C

2. Perform the following pieces based on the I and the V7 chords. Review the rhythm and the melody of each before playing. Transpose to other major keys.

The Cuckoo

German Folk Song

English Folk Melody 2

Andante

August Eberhard Müller (Germany, 1767–1817)

COMPOSING PROJECT

I and V7 Melody

Create a two-phrase melody that uses the pitches in the I and the V7 chords.

Step 1. Select a major key of your choice, and identify the pitches in the I and the V7 chords for that key.

Step 2. Use the following chord progression for the eight-measure melody. Experiment with various rhythms, using the pitches in the designated chords. Unify your composition with repetition, and incorporate contrasting ideas for variety.

Phrase 1: I | V or V7 | I | V or V7 |

Phrase 2: I | V or V7 | V or V7 | I ||

Step 3. Create an accompaniment to go with your melody. You can use chord roots, block chords, broken chords, or any member of the chord.

Step 4. Notate your melody and accompaniment on a staff, and then play, reading from staff notation. Exchange your melody with a classmate's. Play your pieces for each other, and assess your work for accuracy and creativity.

SOLO REPERTOIRE

Analyze each of the following pieces. Choose at least one to memorize.

In Reinagle's Minuet, try for a good contrast between the staccato notes and the slurred ones. Review staccato touch in Technique Exercise 3 in this chapter. Notice the I (tonic) and V (dominant) tones in the LH part.

TRACK 29

Minuet

Allegretto

Alexander Reinagle (England, 1756–1809)

ALEXANDER REINAGLE ● *(England, 1756–1809), English composer and pianist. He moved to the United States in 1786 and became a prominent teacher, concert organizer, and theater musician.*

Gurlitt's "Study for Two" features a dialogue between the RH and the LH. Practice in four-measure segments, hands together.

Study for Two

Cornelius Gurlitt (Germany, 1820–1901)

Con moto

A **duet** is usually a composition to be performed by two people. Bartók's "A Duet" is for just one person; actually, the duet is performed by the player's left and right hands.

A Duet
(No. 2 from *First Term at the Piano*)

Béla Bartók (Hungary, 1881–1945)

Moderato

Kabelevsky's "Funny Dialogue" has three **sections** (A B A). Notice how the rhythmic **motives** (brief musical ideas) ♩ ♫ ♩ and ♫♫ ♩ are manipulated and used to unify. Clap these rhythms first; then practice a section at a time. This piece could also be performed with another player (one on RH and one on LH).

TRACK 32

Funny Dialogue

Allegretto

Dmitri Kabalevsky (Russia, 1904–1987)

TECHNIQUE EXERCISES

Thumb-Under

Technique Exercise 1

This exercise requires the thumb to slide under several fingers. Make the moves as smooth as possible. Keep the hand in position, and the hands and arms relaxed. Make the thumb do all the work! Play in different major patterns.

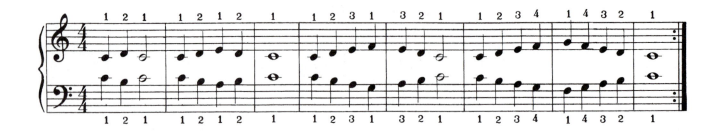

Technique Exercise 2

Practice the following exercise hands separately first and then hands together. Continue the pattern until you reach the upper C.

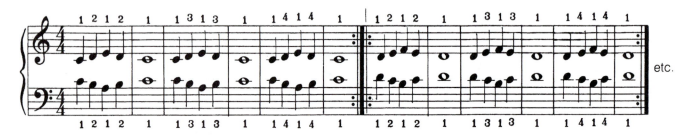

etc.

Staccato Touch

Staccato touch requires playing in a detached style. In notation, the staccato mark (♩ or ♪) appears above or below the notehead to indicate that the tone should be disconnected and shortened. Staccato playing is the opposite of legato playing.

Playing Tip   To get a feel for the wrist action important in staccato touch, knock with your knuckles on the keyboard lid or the top of the piano. Be sure to knock with your wrist loose and your arm not moving. Once this knocking action is secure, tap first with your index finger (2), gradually adding the middle (3) and the ring (4) fingers.

Technique Exercise 3

Transfer this knocking wrist action to the keyboard by playing the following examples, hands separately, with the staccato touch. Strike each key with a precise motion from the wrist only. Release the key immediately. Keep your wrist loose but your arm still.

Part A

Intervals (Major Scale)

Technique Exercise 4

Practice these intervals in the following pattern. Stress independent finger action, and work for a legato sound.

END-OF-CHAPTER EVALUATION

1. At the keyboard, transpose "St. Paul's Steeple" (earlier in this chapter) from C major to D major.

2. Using the C major scale, play and identify these intervals: major second (M2), major third (M3), perfect fourth (P4), perfect fifth (P5), major sixth (M6), major seventh (M7), and perfect octave (P8).

3. Demonstrate the one-hand fingering (two octaves) for the G major scale.

4. Play I and V7 chords (with the V7 rearranged in "piano position") in any major key. Demonstrate smooth hand shifts.

5. Perform one of the pieces in the Solo Repertoire section accurately and musically. Be able to discuss the characteristics of its melody, rhythm, and form.

6. Write the whole-step–half-step arrangement of the major scale:

   1 (whole) 2 _____ 3 _____ 4 _____ 5 _____ 6 _____ 7 _____ 8

7. Construct one-octave major scales, ascending and descending, on the following tonics. When accidentals are needed, write the sharps or the flats *before* the pitches on the *same* line or in the *same* space. Write finger numbers for the right hand above the staff and left-hand finger numbers below the staff.

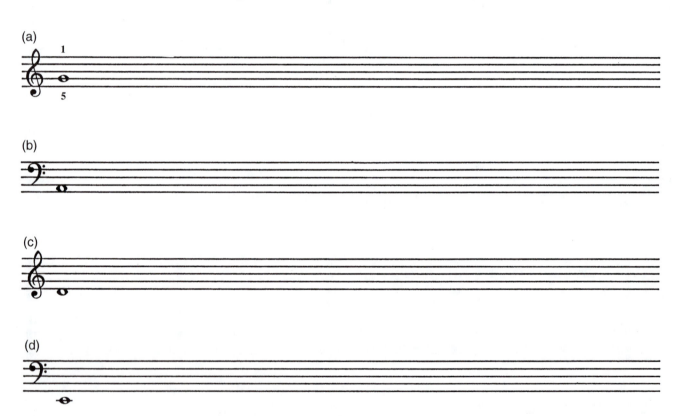

(a)

(b)

(c)

(d)

8. Identify the following scale degrees by letter name.

   a. The tonic of the E♭ major scale is _____.

   b. The dominant of the F major scale is _____.

c. The leading tone of the D major scale is _____.

d. The subdominant of the G major scale is _____.

e. The supertonic of the B♭ major scale is _____.

f. The mediant of the A major scale is _____.

g. The submediant of the C major scale is _____.

9. Notate the tonic for each major key as determined by the key signature.

10. Write the key signatures for the designated keys. Be sure that the flats and the sharps are in the correct order, are in the appropriate lines or spaces, and are not crowded. Refer to the key signature chart on p. 122.

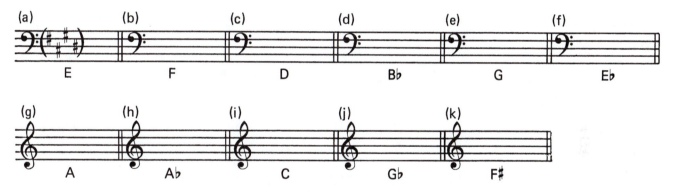

11. Complete the following:

a. The key of F major has _____ flats.

b. The key of D major has _____ sharps.

c. The key of E major has _____ sharps.

d. The key of B♭ major has _____ flats.

e. The key of A major has _____ sharps.

f. The key of E♭ major has _____ flats.

g. The key of G major has _____ sharps.

12. Label the following intervals by quality and number.

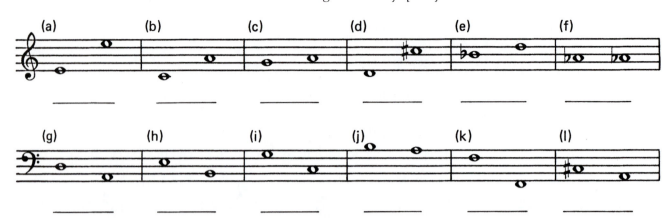

(a)   (b)   (c)   (d)   (e)   (f)

_____   _____   _____   _____   _____   _____

(g)   (h)   (i)   (j)   (k)   (l)

_____   _____   _____   _____   _____   _____

13. Label each marked interval in the "Chopsticks" excerpt.

Chopsticks
(excerpt)

Traditional

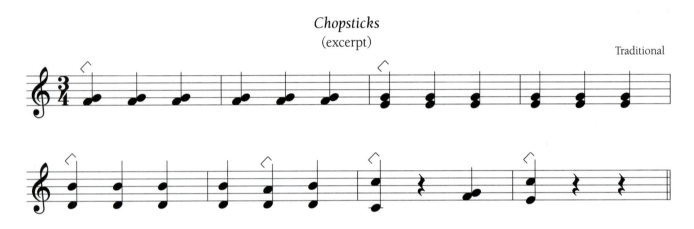

14. Construct the tonic (I) and the dominant (V or V7) chords on the appropriate scale degrees.

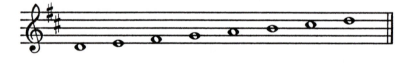

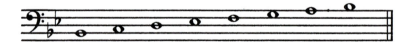

15. Describe the following musical terms.

a. Scale degrees

b. Syllable names

c. Key signature

d. Circle of Fifths

e. "Piano position" for I and V7 chords

f. Staccato touch

A Couple of Reading Tips

TIPS FOR SIGHT-READING

- Visually scan the piece to get a "picture" of what it is all about. Notice whether it breaks into easily recognizable parts. Look for tempo and dynamic markings, and observe how the pitches move in both the left- and right-hand parts.

- Next, check the meter signature, kinds of notes and rests, and any particular rhythmic patterns. Clap or tap the rhythm.

- Observe any similar patterns of notes and/or phrases; especially, determine if any of these are repeated.

- Put hands in correct position at the keyboard and locate your starting pitches.

- Play through the piece slowly hands together, looking ahead as you read and listening carefully. Remember that you are reading at sight, so you are bound to make mistakes.

TIPS FOR PRACTICING A PIECE *AFTER* SIGHT-READING

- After sight-reading a piece, repeat, but this time take note of where you are making mistakes and need work.

- Work on specific sections where you are playing wrong notes or rhythms. Practice these problems spots slowly—hands separately and hands together.

- Play the entire piece again, looking ahead as you read and observing tempo and dynamic markings.

- Continue practicing the piece until you can play it without pausing.

chapter seven

The Primary Chords and 12-Bar Blues

OBJECTIVES

After completing this chapter, you will be able to

- ✔ Construct and play primary chords in root position
- ✔ Improvise a blueslike piece using primary chords in the 12-bar blues progression
- ✔ Demonstrate understanding of syncopation through performance
- ✔ Perform musical pieces in the chapter with pitch and rhythmic accuracy and with expression, performing at least one from memory
- ✔ Compose a piano blues piece
- ✔ Demonstrate legato pedaling

THE SUBDOMINANT CHORD

The I (tonic) and the V (dominant) chords were presented in Chapter 6. By adding the IV (subdominant) chord, we complete the identification of the **primary chords.** These are the three most frequently used chords in tonal music.

The **subdominant** chord is built on the fourth degree of the scale and, like the I and the V chords, is a major triad in a major key. The IV chord includes pitches 4, 6, and 8 (1) of the major scale.

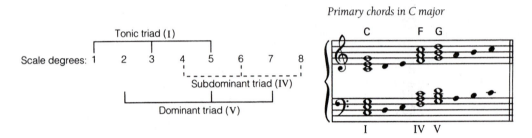

Primary chords in C major

K e y   T e r m   The tonic triad is always the last chord in a final cadence. When the tonic triad is preceded by a subdominant chord, the result is a **plagal cadence** (IV–I).

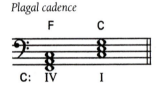

Plagal cadence

PERFORMING PRIMARY CHORDS

1. Practice the following exercise, which changes between these three chords. Play in the designated block-chord form and in arpeggio form. Transpose to other major keys.

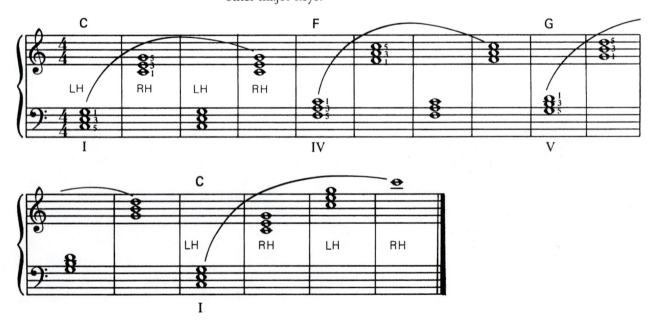

2. Practice Technique Exercise 2 at the end of this chapter. Try the technique described there with the preceding block-chord exercise. Hold the pedal down until a new chord is indicated.

3. Perform the chords in "Tar Paper Stomp" with your LH while your instructor performs the RH melody. Notice that the entire melody consists of pitches in each of the three chords. Also note the concluding plagal cadence of IV to I.

Tar Paper Stomp

Wingy Manone (United States, 1904–1982)

plagal cadence

JOSEPH ("WINGY") MANONE ● *(United States, 1904–1982), Swing-era jazz trumpeter, with one arm; also a singer and bandleader. His "Tar Paper Stomp" became the hit "In the Mood" for Glenn Miller's band.*

4. Try "When the Saints Go Marching In" with just the chord roots notated. Recall that you played this song in Chapter 2 and read from informal notation. Your instructor can add the *Piano 2* part (p. 24) or let CD track 4 accompany your performance. Also try playing all the chord tones in each chord, but be prepared to play the F and G7 chords down an octave in order not to collide with your RH part.

African American Spiritual

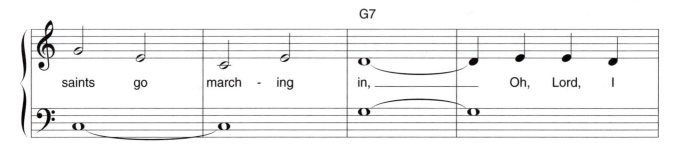

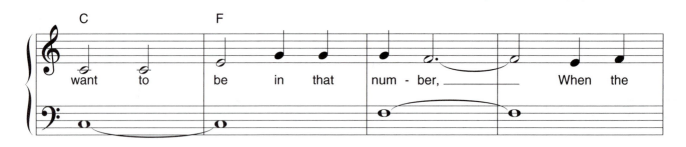

unit two • *The 12-Bar Blues Progression*

The blues, that special type of music that developed in the late 1800s, most often uses the three primary chords (I–IV–V) in a distinctive progression. One popular version of the traditional 12-bar **blues** (twelve measures) progression is:

Bar	1	2	3	4	5	6	7	8	9	10	11	12
Chord	I	I	I	I	IV	IV	I	I	V	IV	I	I

PERFORMING THE 12-BAR BLUES PROGRESSION

1. Practice this blues progression in C major. First play just the root of each chord; then gradually add all the pitches in the chords. Develop a feel for the distances of these chord jumps so that you do not have to look down at the keys.

12-bar blues progression—C major

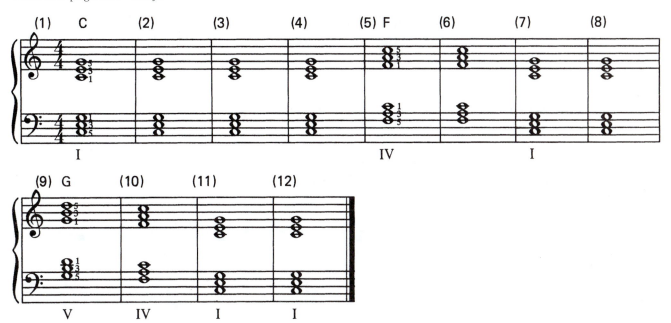

2. To create a RH melody based on the blues progression, play the tones in each chord one at a time as in "Chordal Blues." Practice "Chordal Blues" looking at the music, not at your hands. When you are comfortable with the chords, vary the rhythm and the order of chord tones to create a new version. Finally, transpose to primary chords in other major keys.

Chordal Blues

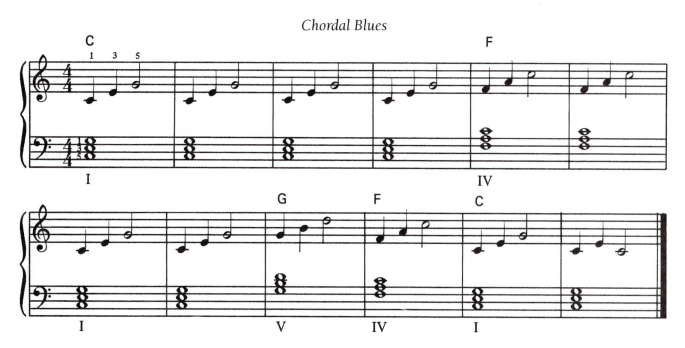

PERFORMING BLUES COMPOSITIONS

K e y   T e r m   **Blue notes** make blues pieces distinctive. They are part of the blues scale (introduced in Chapter 10). However, by lowering the middle note of a major chord a half step, you can incorporate a blue note—you will notice that this produces a mix of the major and minor chords.

1.   "Plain Blues" incorporates blue notes. Use the same fingering for each chord and keep the same hand position. Notice the accent marks (>) on beat 2 in each measure—emphasize this note and a more bluesy feel will result.

K e y   S i g n s   **Accent marks** (>) are musical signs indicating that the note should be stressed and played louder. A **fermata** (⌢) is a musical sign indicating that the designated note, chord, or rest is to be held beyond its normal duration.

Plain Blues

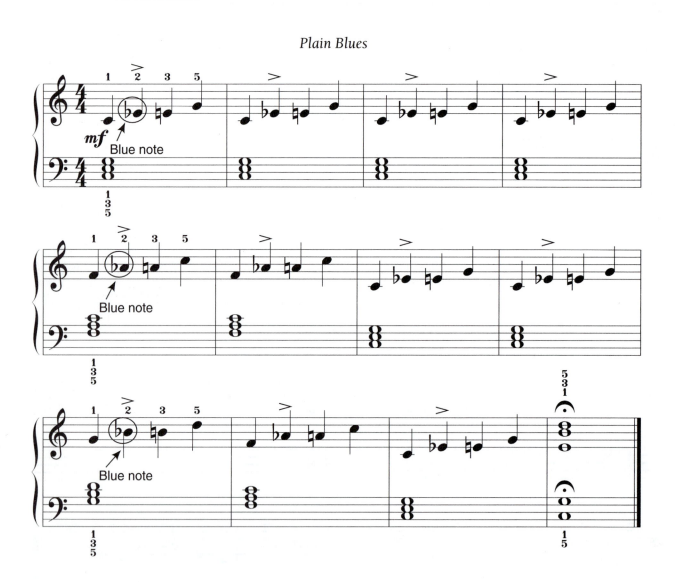

2. In "Leftie Blues," the LH plays the individual chord tones and blue notes (an octave lower than written) while the RH plays the block chords. Notice the accent mark on beat 2—again, observe the result.

Playing Tip   Remembering that the fingering is identical for each chord, keep the same hand shape.

Leftie Blues

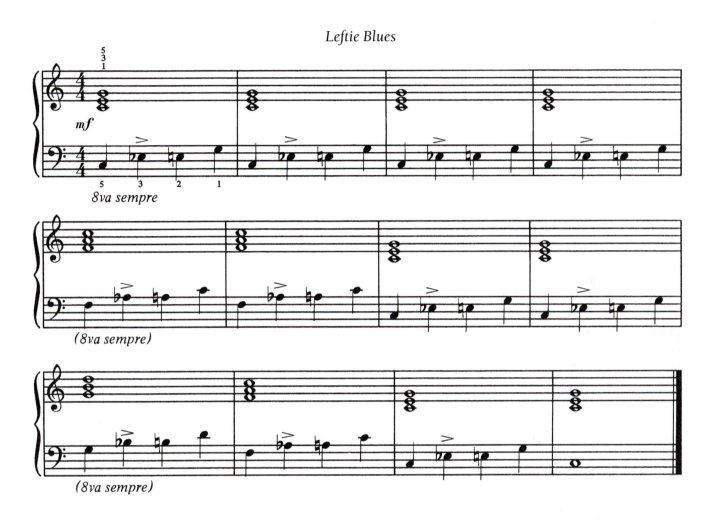

3. More blues pieces may be found on pp. 151, 164, 234, 281, and 286.
4. "Blue Jeans," a Lee Evans ensemble piece, features just the D major chord (I) in the student part. Note the bluesy flavor, though, created by the blue note. The addition of the *Piano 2* part (instructor or CD Track 34) results in a more interesting arrangement.

Blue Jeans

Student, Piano 1

Not too slowly (in 4) (Both hands an octave higher when played as a duet.)

Lee Evans (United States, b. 1933)

 TRACK 34

Instructor, Piano 2

Syncopation

Syncopation is a rhythmic device that gives variety and interest to all kinds of music. It is integral to **jazz** and occurs in the music of many cultures around the world.

K e y   T e r m   **Syncopation** is the placement of accents on weak beats or offbeats.

Nonsyncopated Major Scale Example

The following scale example is notated in 4/4, which indicates that the strong beats (beats 1 and 3) will be slightly accented and the weak beats (beats 2 and 4) will not be accented. Play the scale, making those accented notes slightly louder than those without accents.

C major scale with accents on 1 and 3

Syncopated Major Scale Example

The following scale example is noted in 4/4. However, in this example, the weak beats (2 and 4) are accented, which creates syncopation. Play the scale, accenting the weak beats.

C major scale with accents on 2 and 4

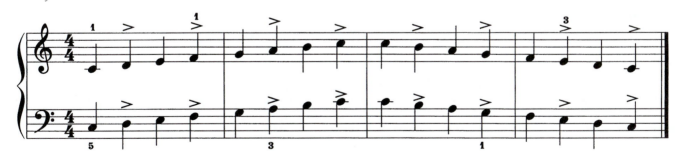

Rhythm Exercise. Syncopation—
accented offbeats, omitted accents (rests and ties)

Clap, chant, or play the following examples on any key(s) or any chord.

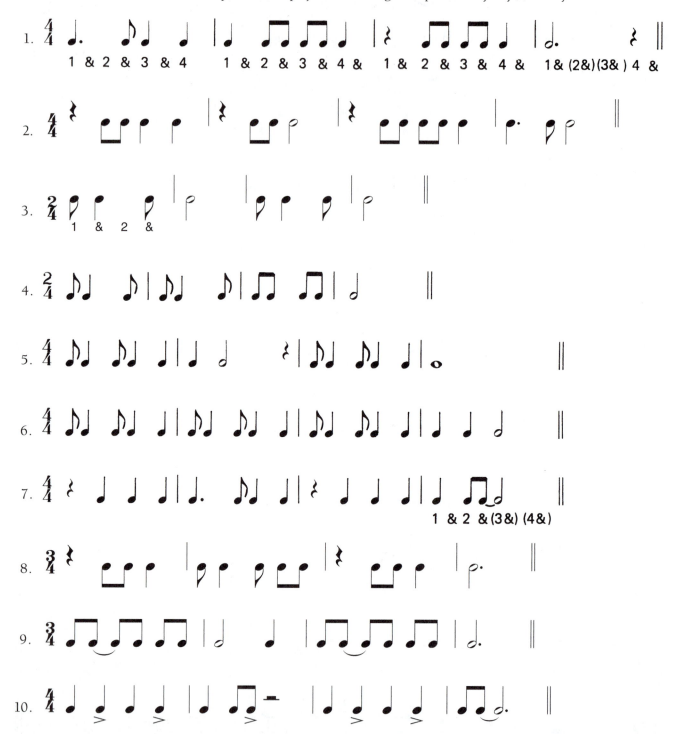

PERFORMING SYNCOPATED MUSIC

"Shabat, Shalom" includes accents on offbeats to create syncopation. Clap the rhythm of the melody before playing. The RH part falls within the D minor five-finger pattern (D E F G A).

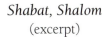

Shabat, Shalom
(excerpt)

Hebrew Song

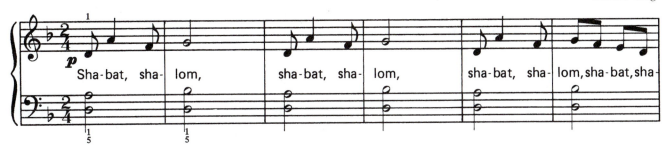

Sha-bat, sha- lom, sha-bat, sha- lom, sha-bat, sha- lom, sha-bat, sha-

lom, sha - lom!

"Syncopated Blues" creates syncopation by accents and by placing a rest on the first beat of each measure. Clap the rhythm of the RH part before playing.

Syncopated Blues

Check all dynamic and articulation markings in "jazz around the clock."
Notice the pedal markings in the last two measures. Is this piece based on the 12-bar blues progression? Does it include blue notes and syncopation?

K e y   S i g n   ♪♪♩ is a **triplet** (three notes of equal value within a beat that normally divides into two: ♪♩).

TRACK 35

jazz around the clock

Fast and upbeat

Catherine Rollin (United States, b. 1952)

LH sempre legato

CATHERINE ROLLIN ● *American composer, pianist, and educator. She combines a busy performing career with teaching prize-winning students and giving clinics and workshops throughout the United States and Canada.*

In this ensemble piece you'll find the syncopated pattern you performed in Rhythm Exercise No. 6 on page 150. An expanded position will be required for this popular ragtime song.

TRACK 36

Student, Piano 1

Hello! Ma' Baby

Joseph E. Howard (United States, 1878–1961)
Ida Emerson (United States, late 19th–20th c.)

TRACK 37

Instructor, Piano 2

COMPOSING PROJECT

Blues Piece

Create a piano blues piece based on the 12-bar progression.

Step 1. Choose a flat key, such as F major, for your blues piece. Determine the three primary chords for that key as well as the blue note for each chord.

Step 2. On staff paper, prepare a skeleton of your composition by blocking out the twelve measures (or bars) on the grand staff and notating the appropriate chords in each measure. Also indicate the blue note for each.

Step 3. Using your 12-bar chord progression, experiment with the pitches in the designated chords and the blue notes. A meter of $\frac{4}{4}$ is a good place to start with rhythm. Try to incorporate some syncopation, too.

Step 4. When your ideas become final, notate your blues piece, and then play, reading from staff notation. Exchange your blues piece with a classmate's. Play your pieces for each other, and assess your work for accuracy and creativity.

SOLO REPERTOIRE

Study the Bartók piece and identify the five-finger pattern used in both hands. Does the first phrase use parallel or contrary motion between hands? Notice the legato and staccato markings. Practice Technique Exercise 2 in this chapter before playing the piece.

 TRACK 38

What interval is exclusively used in "Chimes"? Review pedal techniques on page 159 before performing this piece.

Chimes

Lynn Freeman Olson (United States, 1938–1987)

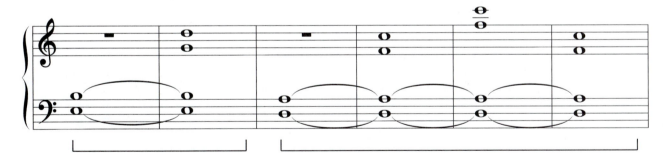
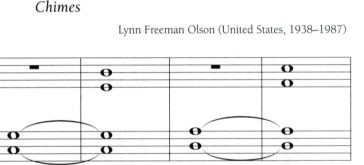
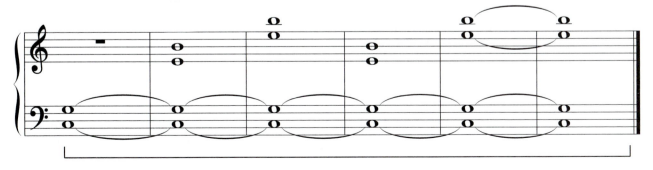

Morning Song
(No. 5 from *First Term at the Piano*)

Moderato

Béla Bartók (Hungary, 1881–1945)

What do you notice about phrases 1 and 2 in "Up or Out"? Note the change in dynamics and the register change of the RH in phrase 2.

Up or Out

Moderato

Nancy Van de Vate (United States, b. 1930)

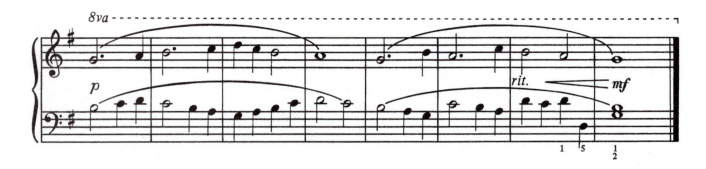

Konowitz encourages playing "Feelings" in an easygoing, relaxed manner. He suggests changing the mood by playing the piece in other ways as well—faster, slower, louder, softer, higher, or lower, and so on.

TRACK 41

Feelings

Easy, relaxed tempo

Bert Konowitz

BERT KONOWITZ ● *composer, arranger, and professor of music at Teachers College, Columbia University. Dr. Konowitz included "Feelings" in his* Jazz/Rock Course: A Complete Approach to Playing on both Acoustic and Electronic Keyboards.

What can you say about the four-measure phrases of this Beethoven piece? Are they parallel? contrasting? Practice one section at a time (section A = 2 phrases; section B = 2 phrases).

TRACK 42

Russian Folk Song, Op. 107, No. 3

Ludwig van Beethoven (Germany, 1770–1827)

TECHNIQUE EXERCISES

Technique Exercise 1. Independent Hands and Hand Coordination

Establish a good hand position. Practice this exercise with good finger action. Feel the weight of your arm shift from one finger to the next. Connect pitches as smoothly as possible. Transpose to other major keys.

Technique Exercise 2. Drop/Lift

Practice these two-note slurs with action mainly from the wrist. Elevate the wrist a bit, and as you play the first note, drop the wrist to key level with a slight bounce. On the second note, lift the wrist to the original position. Keep your fingers firm. Transpose to other major keys.

Pedal Technique

When the **damper pedal** (located to the far right) is pressed down, pitches can be sustained to produce a legato effect. This depressing of the pedal releases the felt dampers from the strings and permits the strings to vibrate freely.

To use the damper pedal, rest the ball of your right foot lightly on the pedal, keeping your heel on the floor. Practice depressing and releasing the pedal. Check that your heel does not leave the floor. Listen for any mechanical noises—you should pedal with as little noise as possible.

Special markings in music indicate when to use the damper pedal.

Pedal down		Pedal up
	Hold pedal	

Pedal down	Pedal up and down	Pedal up

Technique Exercise 3. Legato Pedaling

To legato-pedal, you must learn to connect several notes or chords with the pedal. To do this, you must play a note, depress the pedal, play another note releasing the pedal, and immediately depress again. The idea is to create a seamless effect. Try this exercise connecting one pitch to the next without a break. Listen carefully to make sure the pedal has sustained only one note.

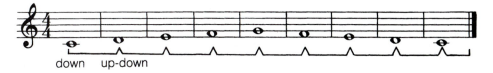

down   up-down

Perform the primary chords in C major adding the legato pedaling. Transpose the primary chords to other major keys.

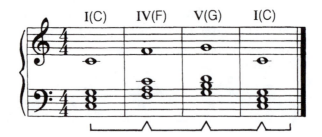

END-OF-CHAPTER EVALUATION

1. Play I, IV, and V chords (in root position) in the keys of C, G, D, F, and B♭.

2. At the keyboard, improvise a blueslike piece using primary chords in the 12-bar blues progression.

3. Demonstrate legato pedaling with the primary chords in Technique Exercise 3 in this chapter, or in the I–IV–V exercise earlier in the chapter.

4. Demonstrate understanding of syncopation by performing one of the lines in the rhythm exercise in this chapter.

5. Perform by memory one of the pieces in this chapter.

6. Write the I, IV, and V chords (in root position) for the following major keys:

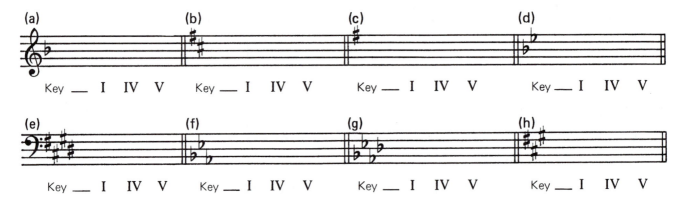

7. Identify the primary chords by letter name for the 12-bar blues progression in B♭ major.

I (_____)	I (_____)	I (_____)	I (_____)
IV (_____)	IV (_____)	I (_____)	I (_____)
V (_____)	IV (_____)	I (_____)	I (_____)

8. Notate possible pitches for a melody line as indicated by the LH chords in each measure.

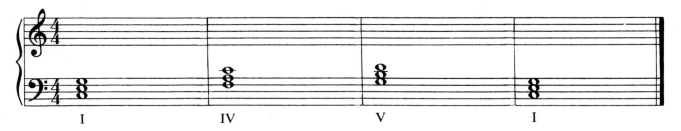

I   IV   V   I

9. Describe the following musical terms:

a. Subdominant chord

b. Syncopation

c. Blue note

d. Damper pedal

e. Primary chords

f. Plagal cadence

10. Identify and explain the following musical symbols:

a.

b. I

c. IV

d. V

e. *8va sempre*

f. 𝆄

chapter eight

Performing and Harmonizing with Primary Chords (Major Keys)

OBJECTIVES

After completing this chapter, you will be able to

✔ Construct and play primary chords in root position and in the I-IV$^6_4$-V$^6_5$ position

✔ Harmonize melodies with primary chords

✔ Demonstrate understanding of compound meter through performances

✔ Perform musical pieces in the chapter with pitch and rhythmic accuracy and with expression, performing at least one from memory

✔ Compose a two-phrase melody based on a tonic and dominant chord progression

✔ Demonstrate legato pedaling, extension fingering, and the Alberti bass accompaniment figure

Chords and Inversions

THE SEVENTH CHORD

The **seventh chord** includes four notes: a triad with an added third. There are several kinds of seventh chords, but the one frequently used is the *major-minor seventh chord.*

Key Term The major-minor seventh chord, also commonly referred to as the **dominant seventh chord**, includes a major triad with an added seventh above the root.

Performing Major-Minor Seventh Chords

"Seventh Chord Blues" includes open minor sevenths (m7) in the LH part. Decide what the other chord tones are in each of the seventh chords.

Seventh Chord Blues

In "Walkin' Boogie," the LH part walks through the tones in each seventh chord.

Walkin' Boogie

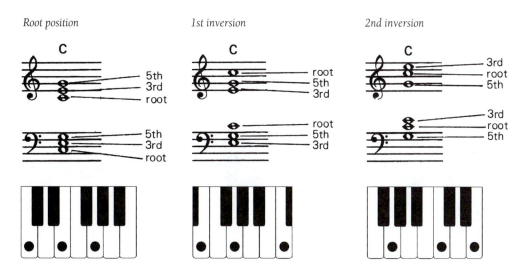

Key Term   **Boogie-woogie** is a jazz piano style (fast blues) in which the LH repeats a fast-moving bass (generally moving through I, IV, and V harmonies) while the RH often improvises a melody part.

CHORD INVERSIONS OF TRIADS AND SEVENTH CHORDS

Triads and seventh chords are not always written in root position (the root of the chord positioned as the lowest pitch). Chord tones may be rearranged, or *inverted*. The triad can be written in root position, first inversion, and second inversion.

Root position

C
— 5th
— 3rd
— root

— 5th
— 3rd
— root

1st inversion

C
— root
— 5th
— 3rd

— root
— 5th
— 3rd

2nd inversion

C
— 3rd
— root
— 5th

— 3rd
— root
— 5th

The seventh chord has three inversions and can be written in root position, first inversion, second inversion, and third inversion.

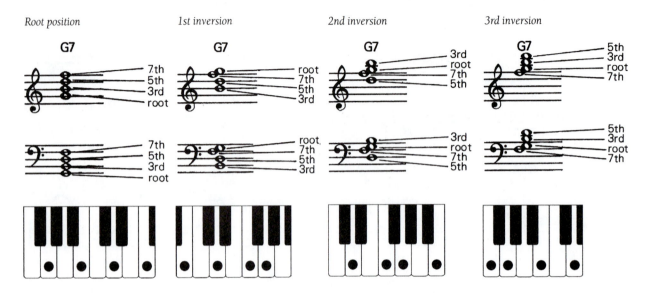

Chord Inversions with Figured Bass

Arabic numerals are sometimes added to roman numerals to indicate specific chord inversions, as in V7. The use of arabic numerals originated in the *figured bass* system of the **Baroque period** (c. 1600–1750), when keyboard players were skilled in improvising elaborate compositions from a given series of pitches and numerals (*figures*).

The arabic numerals added to the roman numerals to indicate the root position and various inversions of the triad and seventh chord are shown below.

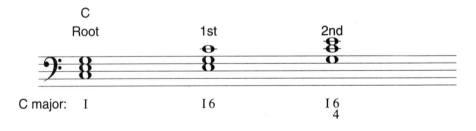

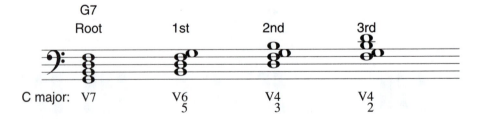

To understand what the arabic numerals stand for, see the Figures for triads and the Figures for seventh chords below. Notice that the arabic numerals show intervals within the chord and are measured from the lowest (bass) note to the other notes in the chord. For example, a 3 indicates an interval of a third up from the bass note, and a 5 specifies a fifth up from the bass note (the root position). In the following illustration, parentheses identify numbers not commonly shown but understood to be in the chord.

Figures for triads

Triad	Arabic numerals
Root	none
1st inversion	6
2nd inversion	$\begin{smallmatrix}6\\4\end{smallmatrix}$

Figures for seventh chords

Seventh chord	Arabic numerals
Root	7
1st inversion	$\begin{smallmatrix}6\\5\end{smallmatrix}$
2nd inversion	$\begin{smallmatrix}4\\3\end{smallmatrix}$
3rd inversion	$\begin{smallmatrix}4\\2\end{smallmatrix}$

I AND IV$\begin{smallmatrix}6\\4\end{smallmatrix}$ CHORDS

To make the hand and finger moves easier between two or three chords, some chords are performed in inversions. These inversions allow the hand to stay in one position and play two or three chords.

Of the two inversions of the IV triad, the second inversion (IV$\begin{smallmatrix}6\\4\end{smallmatrix}$) is the closer to the tonic (I) in root position. Notice that the bottom notes stay the same for the two chords but the middle note of the IV$\begin{smallmatrix}6\\4\end{smallmatrix}$ moves up a half step and the top note moves up a whole step.

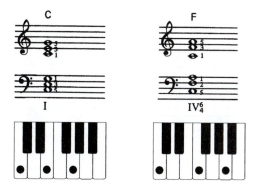

I–IV$_4^6$ Chords in Selected Major Keys

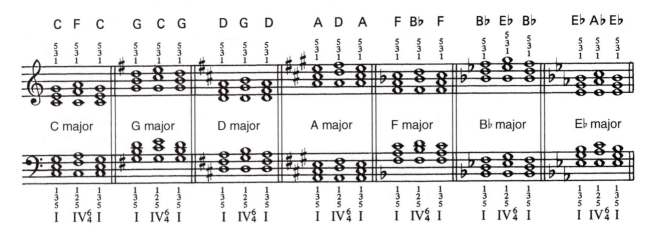

Performing I–IV$_4^6$ Chords

1. Perform Part A of the following exercise, which prepares the hands for the I–IV$_4^6$–I fingerings.

2. Perform Parts B and C of the following exercise to practice the necessary moves between the two chords. Transpose to other major keys.

Part A

Part B

Part C

3. Perform "Lovely Evening" using these chords for an accompaniment. First, practice playing a block chord on the first beat of each measure, holding the chord for the full three beats. Then try the broken-chord accompaniment shown here. Other broken-chord patterns are notated in Appendix I. (This piece may be performed as a round with two or three pianists or groups of pianists.)

Lovely Evening

Traditional Round

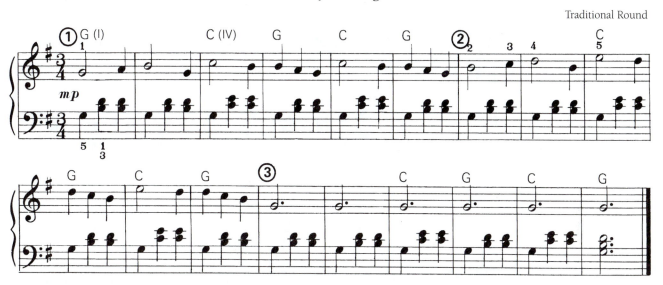

4. Practice Technique Exercise 1 at the end of this chapter. This exercise stresses contrary motion and the arpeggio style.

I AND V⁶₅ CHORDS

The first inversion (V^6_5) is commonly used when playing the I and the V7 because it is the closest to the tonic in root position. The top notes stay the same for the two chords, but the middle note of the V^6_5 moves up a half step and the bottom note moves down a half step.

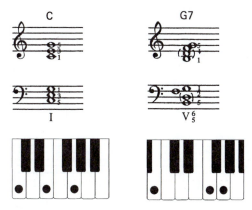

I and V$_5^6$ Chords in Selected Major Keys

Practice the I and the V$_5^6$ chords with the RH and the LH in the following frequently used major keys. (All chords are in Appendix H.)

Playing Tip   Try to develop a feel for this progression, and be ready to change chords. Feel the shape of the next chord, and actually touch the keys just before playing.

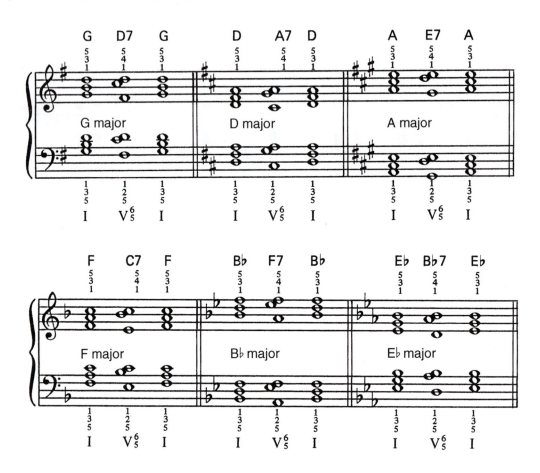

Performing I–V$_5^6$ Chords

1. Review the I–V7–I exercise on p. 129.

2. Perform the following pieces using the I–V$_5^6$ for an accompaniment. Transpose to other major keys.

Mary Ann

Calypso Song

Tom Dooley

American Folk Song

More Rhythm Reading—Compound Meters

All the meters studied so far are classified as simple, and in simple meter the beat is divided into two equal parts. When the beat divides into three equal parts, the meter is referred to as **compound**.

Simple　　　　　　*Compound*

Selected Time Signatures (Compound Meter)

In compound meter, the beat is represented by a dotted note, which divides into three equal parts. Since there is no number to designate a dotted note, the bottom number of a compound time signature shows divisions of the beat and the top number shows how many divisions in a measure. The top number is always a multiple of 3. To determine the meter—for example, duple—divide the top number by 3.

Compound duple meter

6 — 6 beat divisions per measure

8 — ♪ is the value of each division

Compound triple meter

9 — 9 beat divisions per measure

8 — ♪ is the value of each division

Compound quadruple meter

12 — 12 beat divisions per measure

8 — ♪ is the value of each division

Rhythm Exercise. Compound Meter

Compound meters may be counted several ways. One way is to count the division values of the beat stressing 1 and 4 (7 and 10). A second way is to say a sound such as "eh" and "ah" on the second and third division of each group of three. (See dotted rests in Appendix B.)

8. 1 (eh) (ah) 2 (eh) (ah) 3 eh ah
   1 (2) (3) 4 (5) (6) 7 8 9

9.

10.

11.

12.

Primary Chords in "Piano Position"

So that the fingers move smoothly between the I, IV, and V7 chords, the following inversions are used. These inversions allow the hand to stay in one position and play all three chords. This particular pattern is referred to as the "piano position" for primary chords in *PianoLab*. (The I, IV, and V7 chords for all major keys are notated in root position and in I—IV$^6_4$—V$^6_5$ form in Appendix H.)

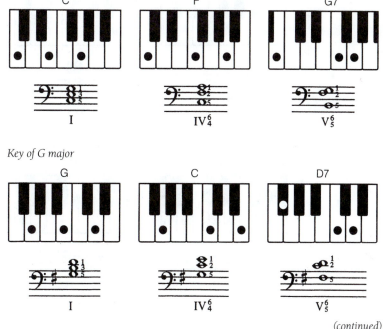

Key of C major

C   F   G7

I   IV$^6_4$ V$^6_5$

Key of G major

G   C   D7

I   IV$^6_4$ V$^6_5$

(continued)

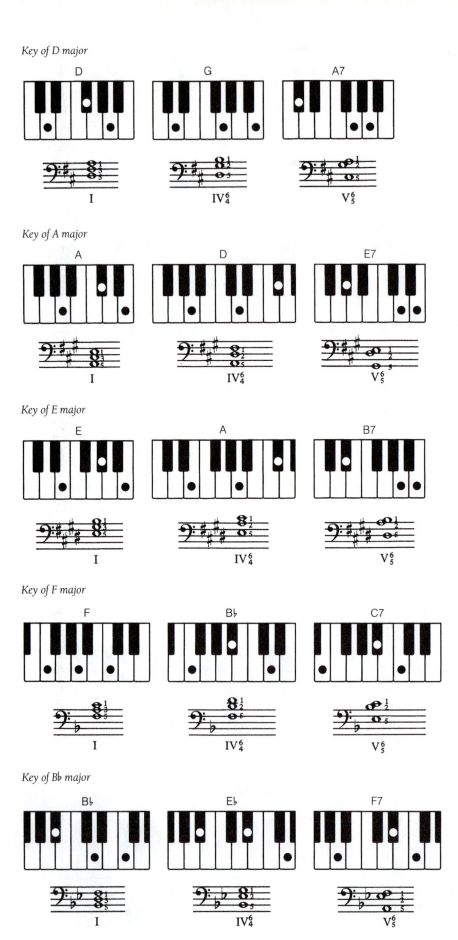

Key of E♭ major

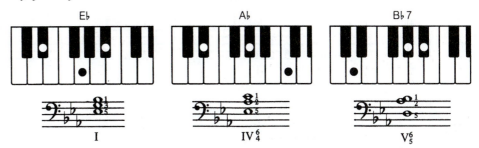

PERFORMING I–IV$_4^6$–V$_5^6$ CHORDS

1. Perform the following exercise to practice the moves between the three chords. The fingerings and the whole-step–half-step moves will be the same in any major key. Memorize this progression. Transpose this exercise to other major keys.

Playing Tip   Learn to shift quickly and smoothly from one chord to another. Feel the shape of the next chord, and actually touch the keys just before playing.

Part A

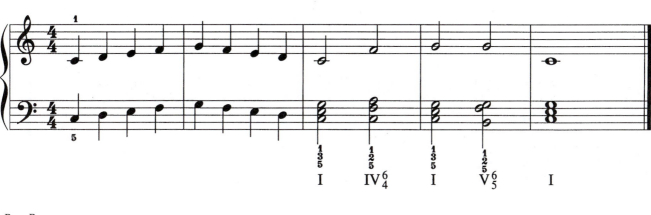

Part B

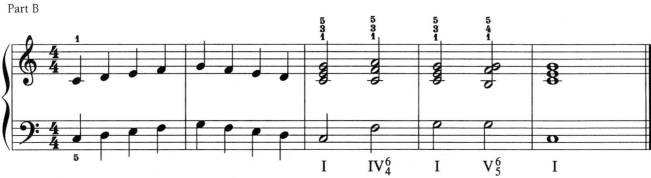

(continued)

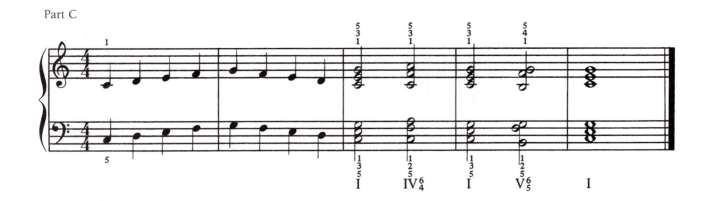

2. Use legato pedaling for the arpeggio exercise of the primary chords. Try not to blur chord tones or overlap sounds of single notes. Connect evenly when crossing hands. Transpose to other major keys.

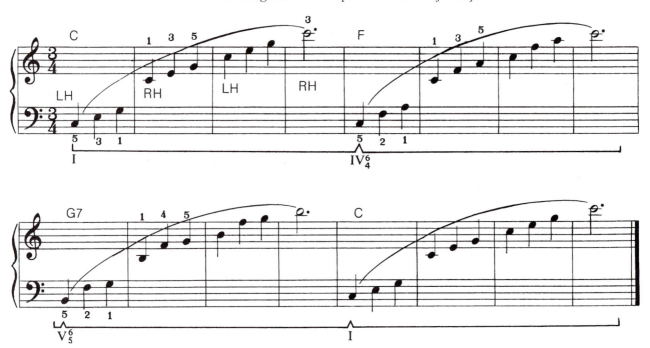

3. Perform the following pieces. Determine the major key and the primary chords first; then practice the chord progression and any special accompaniment pattern. Review the rhythm and the fingerings for each piece before performing. Transpose to other major keys.

I Never Will Marry

American Folk Song

tend to live sin - gle____ All the days of my life.____

Vive l'amour
(excerpt)

Traditional

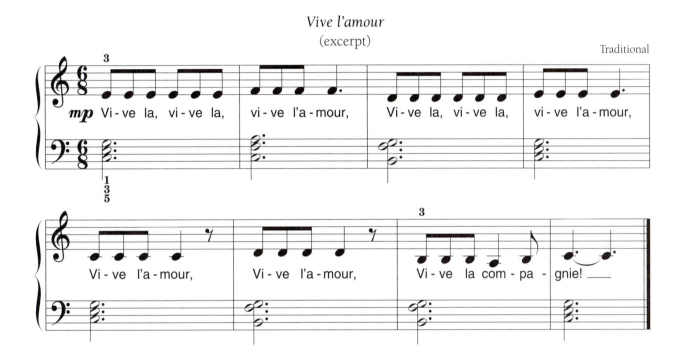

Vi - ve la, vi - ve la, vi - ve l'a - mour, Vi - ve la, vi - ve la, vi - ve l'a - mour,

Vi - ve l'a - mour, Vi - ve l'a - mour, Vi - ve la com - pa - gnie!____

Key Sign 1.   2.   are signs indicating first and second endings. Play through the first ending to the repeat sign, then go back to the beginning and repeat, but this time skip the first ending and perform the second.

The Victors

Louis Elbel (United States, 1877–1959)

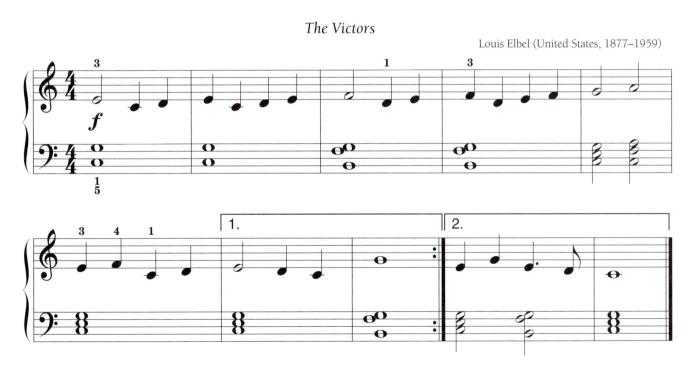

Key Sign   *D. C. al fine* (*Da capo al fine*) is a musical sign meaning to return to the beginning and conclude with the measure marked *fine*.

For He's a Jolly Good Fellow

Traditional

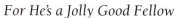

Bohemian Christmas Carol

Simple Gifts

American Shaker Hymn
Joseph Brackett (United States, 1797–1882)

4. For other songs that can be accompanied with the primary chords, see

"The First Noel"   p. 118

"Joy to the World"   p. 296

"De colores"   p. 300

"John B"   p. 299

"Silent Night"   p. 290

unit three ●   # Harmonizing

Harmony (chords) and melody are related. Selecting appropriate chords for a melody is referred to as harmonizing or harmonization. To select appropriate chords, one must determine what chord(s) matches pitches in the melody. For example, in Chapter 7, the melody of "Tar Paper Stomp," page 143, is made up entirely of pitches in the primary chords, and the blues pieces are based primarily on chord tones.

Although the framework of a melody is mostly chord tones, other pitches are added between them. These tones are called *nonchord tones*.

NONCHORD TONES

Passing tones and **neighboring tones** are two kinds of nonchord tones. They often fall on unaccented beats (2 and 4 in quadruple meter; 2 in duple; and 2 and 3 in triple) or on unaccented parts of beats.

Passing tones (p.t.) come between pitches that are a third apart.

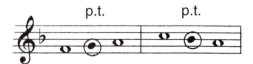

Neighboring tones come stepwise between repeated pitches and can be either upper neighbors (u.n.) or lower neighbors (l.n.).

Practice with Nonchord Tones

In the following melody, the I (F) and the V7 (C7) chords serve as the chord framework. The circled pitches are nonchord tones. Label the nonchord tones as p.t. and u.n. or l.n. and perform.

Melody 1
(with nonchord tones circled)

HARMONIZING MELODIES WITH PRIMARY CHORDS

There are some general guidelines to follow in learning how to harmonize melodies. Follow the three steps outlined in the box on the following page.

GUIDELINES FOR HARMONIZING MELODIES WITH PRIMARY CHORDS

Step 1. Determine the key of the melody and the pitches in the I, IV, and V7 chords for that key.

Step 2. For each measure, compare the pitches in the melody with those in the three chords. Decide which chord (or chords) includes *most* of the pitches in that measure. (The first pitch in the measure and pitches on the other strong beats are especially important in making this choice.) Many melodies can be harmonized with one chord per measure; others may need two or more. (There may be a few pitches in the melody that are nonchord tones.) If the melody begins on an upbeat, the upbeat is usually not chorded. Also remember that a melody normally ends on the tonic pitch and the tonic chord.

Step 3. Try the chosen chords with the melody. It is important to *always check each musical decision by playing at the keyboard.* Write the roman numerals or the letter names for the selected chords above or below each measure of the melody. (Or notate the correct chords in root position or in the I—IV$^6_4$—V$^6_5$ position below the melody. See the "Tante Minna" example.)

Tante Minna
(harmonized)

Example: C major (I = C E G, V7 = G B D F)

German Folk Melody

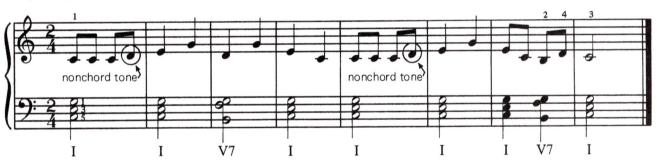

I   I   V7   I   I   I   I   V7   I

Practice in Harmonizing Melodies

Harmonize the following melodies. Play the harmonizations, and notate the melodies and the chords on a staff.

German Folk Melody 2

The Cradle

Austrian Carol

English Folk Melody 3

English Folk Melody 4

French Canadian Round

On Top of Old Smoky

American Folk Melody

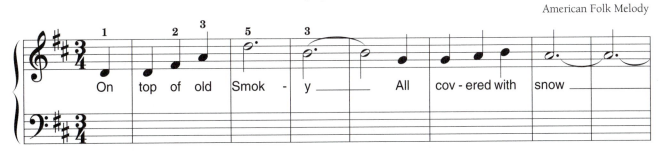

On top of old Smok - y ___ All cov - ered with snow ___

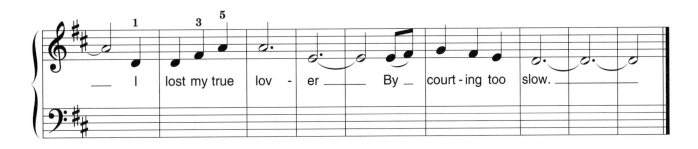

___ I lost my true lov - er ___ By _ court - ing too slow. ___

Lullaby

Johannes Brahms (Germany, 1833–1897)

JOHANNES BRAHMS ● *(Germany, 1833–1897), Late Romantic period composer and pianist. He was a master of the "variation" compositional device. Brahms wrote concertos, chamber music, choral works, songs, keyboard pieces, and four symphonies.*

Kum Ba Yah

African American Song

Kum - ba - yah, my Lord, Kum - ba - yah, Kum - ba - yah, my Lord, Kum - ba -

yah, Kum - ba - yah, my Lord, Kum - ba - yah, oh, Lord ____ Kum - ba - yah.

COMPOSING PROJECT

Two-Phrase Melody

Create a two-phrase melody based on the following major chord progression.

Phrase 1: | I | I | V7 | V7 |
Phrase 2: | I | I | V7 | I ||

Step 1. Decide which major key you wish to use for your melody, and determine the I and the V7 chords in that key.

Step 2. On staff paper, prepare a skeleton of your melody by blocking out the eight measures and notating the appropriate chords in both treble and bass clefs.

Step 3. Decide on a meter signature and then experiment with the pitches in the designated chords. You might want to limit yourself to quarter and half notes and use only chord tones for the melody part. Your accompaniment could include block chords in the I and the V_5^6 positions, or it could be varied to suit the melody.

Step 4. Notate your melody and accompaniment on the staff, and then play, reading from staff notation. Exchange your melody with a classmate's. Play your pieces for each other, and assess your work for accuracy and creativity. Are the phrases of your melody parallel or contrasting?

SOLO REPERTOIRE

Diabelli's piece divides into two sections (A and B). Are there any similar phrases within each section?

TRACK 43

Melody

Anton Diabelli (Austria, 1781–1858)

Moderato

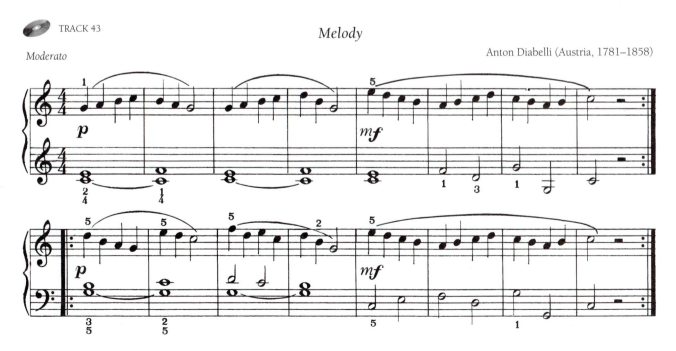

Analyze Bielawa's "Promenade" for rhythmic features and new sounds and combinations of sounds.

TRACK 44

Promenade

Herbert Bielawa (United States, b. 1930)

HERBERT BIELAWA ● *(United States, b. 1930), composer and professor emeritus of theory and composition at San Francisco State University. His compositions include **electronic music**, chamber music, keyboard works (solo and ensemble), and a variety of vocal and instrumental pieces.*

Kabalevsky uses the F major, G minor, and G major triads in "A Little Dance." Practice the RH triads in block form and with tones one at a time. Practice LH block chords; notice the added F in the G minor and G major triads.

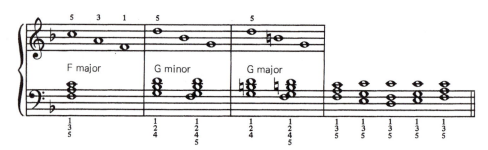

TRACK 45

A Little Dance, Op. 39, No. 9

Allegro molto

Dmitri Kabalevsky (Russia, 1904–1987)

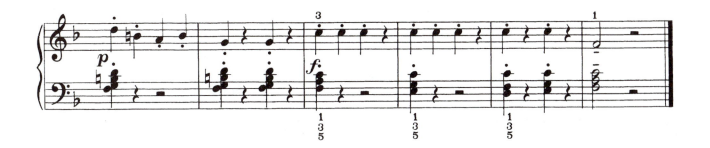

TECHNIQUE EXERCISES

Technique Exercise 1. Contrary Motion and Arpeggio

Practice the following exercise using arpeggios. Keep the wrists flexible and the arms moving in a gentle outward and upward movement. Transpose to other major keys.

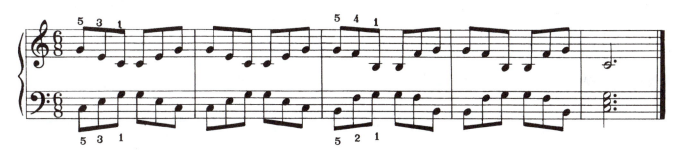

Technique Exercise 2. Extension Fingering

This Hanon exercise requires the fingers to expand to the six-finger position (fingers 1 and 2 skip a note between them) and focuses on the stretch between the fifth and the fourth fingers of the LH ascending and the fifth and the fourth fingers of the RH descending. Begin practicing slowly, lifting the fingers high and playing each note with precision. Gradually increase the speed.

CHARLES-LOUIS HANON ● *(France, 1819–1900). Hanon prepared a collection of sixty technique exercises* (The Virtuoso Pianist) *that has become one of the standard technical keyboard works.*

The Virtuoso Pianist, No. 1
(simplified version)

Charles-Louis Hanon (France, 1819–1900)

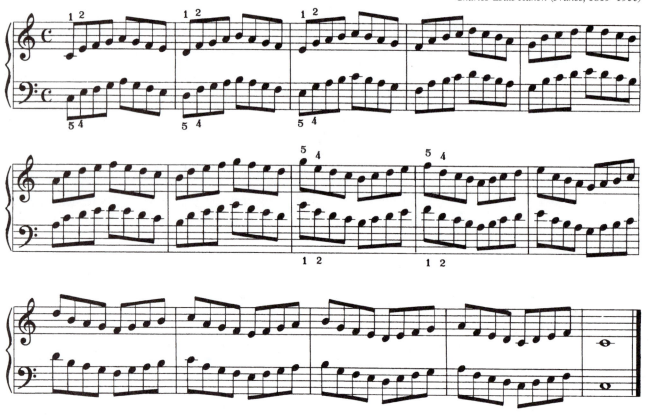

Technique Exercise 3. Broken Chord (Alberti Bass)

Practice the following two studies for facility in using the broken-chord figure. This figure when performed in the bass is often called the **Alberti bass**. (Eighteenth-century composer Domenico Alberti used these figures in his sonatas.)

Part A

Part B

END-OF-CHAPTER EVALUATION

1. Play the primary chords in the I–IV$_4^6$–V$_5^6$ position in the following major keys with correct fingering: C, G, D, A, E, F, B♭, E♭, A♭.

2. Demonstrate legato pedaling by performing the exercise on p. 176.

3. Harmonize one of the melodies on pp. 181–184 with primary chords.

4. Play with rhythmic accuracy a piece in this chapter that has a compound meter.

5. Construct major-minor seventh chords (dominant seventh chords) on the given roots. Label each chord as C7, F7, and so on.

6. Label these major triads and major-minor seventh chords as follows: root position (R), first inversion (1st), second inversion (2nd), or third inversion (3rd).

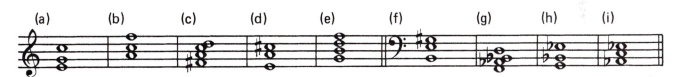

7. Write the primary chords for the stated key in root position and then in the I–IV$_4^6$–V$_5^6$ position.

$$I \qquad IV \qquad V7 \qquad I \qquad\qquad\qquad I \qquad IV_4^6 \qquad V_5^6 \qquad I$$

8. Harmonize Melody 2 and Melody 3 with the appropriate chords. Notate the chords on the staff below the melody. Write the chords in the I–IV$_4^6$–V$_5^6$ position.

Melody 2

Key: _____

(continued)

Key: _____

Melody 3

9. Create and notate a rhythmic phrase in the specified time signature and length. Use a variety of note and rest possibilities.

$\frac{6}{8}$ | | | ‖

10. Describe the following musical terms and symbols:

a. Dominant seventh chord

b. Root-position chord

c. Chord inversions

d. Harmonizing

e. Compound meters

g. IV$^{6}_{4}$

h. V$^{6}_{5}$

i. $\frac{9}{8}$

Lindeman's Top Ten Practice Tips

10. Just Do It!

Developing a skill takes practice whether it's a sport or playing the piano. Allocate time daily for practice—a little time each day is better than a longer practice session a couple of days a week. Keep a practice journal (p. 46)—write down what you have accomplished and what you want to accomplish the next time you practice. Make the commitment and have some fun!

9. Plan Your Attack!

Decide what needs to be tackled at each practice session and carry out the plan. (Use your practice worksheet, p. 45.) Always begin with a warm-up, but the rest of the practice time is up to you. Some students like to review older pieces first; others like to begin by working on newer ones. Some like to mix improvising and other creative projects in between older and newer pieces. Setting goals for each practice session works!

8. Warm Up!

Begin each practice session with one or two warm-up exercises so that you can concentrate on seeing and feeling correct hand and finger positions and listening for good tone production. There are many technique exercises in *PianoLab*. Quickly memorize the patterns of the exercise so that you can give full attention to your technique development instead of reading notes.

7. Hands Together/Hands Separate.

Practice your pieces both hands together and hands separately. Practicing hands separately allows you to isolate problems and devote twice as much mental energy to the right or left hand. However, coordinating the two hands, not to mention reading two different lines, is critical too!

6. Divide and Conquer!

Work or focus on specific spots that are causing you trouble instead of repeating the entire piece all the way through. Practice problems spots slowly and correctly—hands separately and hands together. If you learn something incorrectly, it takes about twenty times of doing it right to unlearn your mistakes!

5. Sloooooooooow Down!

If you're having difficulty playing a piece at the correct tempo, slow down and play at a speed that you can handle. Once your fingers learn the moves, you can gradually increase the tempo.

4. Relax!

No tension in arms or hands should be your motto. Check and recheck your playing position throughout your practice session. Stop from time to time and dangle arms at your sides to relax the arms and hands.

3. Read/Preread/Reread.

To be a good reader, you must keep your eyes on the music—not on the keys. That means that you must see groups of notes, not just one note at a time. Visually analyze each piece before playing—check fingerings, hand positions, sharps and flats, intervals, dynamic and tempo markings, and so on. Do a little sight-reading at each practice session to hone your reading skills.

2. Improvise!

Always, always, always experiment and play with sounds at the keyboard. Explore and create your own music. Remember that playing only on the black keys is an excellent place to begin improvisations. The main thing is to get your creative juices flowing.

1. Enjoy!

As you take on this new task, enjoy the excitement of learning to play the piano. Try not to become frustrated by the challenges. Allow yourself the opportunity to soak up as much as you can about the language of music too— how music "works" and how it is put together. Most important, enjoy the piano experience. Research suggests that being involved in music, and especially playing the piano, works wonders for our well-being. Music and piano playing are good for you!!!

chapter nine

An Introduction to the Minor Scales and Primary Chords in Minor

Unit 1.   The Minor Scales
          The Natural Minor Scale
          Minor Key Signatures
          The Harmonic Minor Scale
          The Melodic Minor Scale
          Identification of Scale Tones
          Performing Pieces in Minor Keys
Unit 2.   Primary Chords in Minor
          Performing i, iv$^6_4$, V$^6_5$ Chords
          Harmonizing Melodies with Primary Chords
More Rhythm Reading
Unit 3.   Relative and Parallel Majors and Minors
          Relative Majors and Minors
          Parallel Majors and Minors
Composing Project
Solo Repertoire
Technique Exercises
End-of-Chapter Evaluation

OBJECTIVES

After completing this chapter, you will be able to

✔ Construct and perform the three forms of the minor scale

✔ Transpose and harmonize minor melodies at the keyboard and in writing

✔ Demonstrate understanding of parallel and relative majors and minors

✔ Play and construct the primary chords in minor in root position and in the i–iv$^6_4$–V$^6_5$ position

✔ Perform musical pieces in the chapter with pitch and rhythmic accuracy and with expression, performing at least one from memory

✔ Create a theme-and-variations composition

✔ Demonstrate contraction and extension fingering

The Minor Scales

The major and minor scales are the scale patterns that serve as the basis for most tonal music. Major scales have one pattern, whereas minor scales come in three forms: *natural minor, harmonic minor,* and *melodic minor.* Each has a particular whole-step–half-step pattern.

Key Fact   All three forms of the **minor scale** have in common a half step between the second and the third scale degrees.

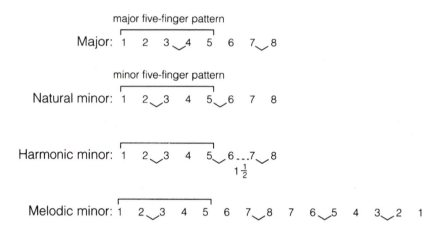

THE NATURAL MINOR SCALE

The **natural minor scale** (probably the oldest form of the minor scale) includes five whole steps and two half steps. The half steps occur between scale degrees 2 and 3 and between scale degrees 5 and 6. The natural minor scale pattern is illustrated by the white keys from A to A.

The A natural minor scale

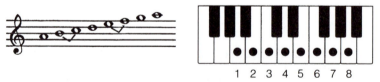

Performing the Natural Minor Scale

1. Play the A natural minor scale with the tetrachord fingering. Then, sight-read "Hatikvah."

Hatikvah
(excerpt)

Israeli National Anthem

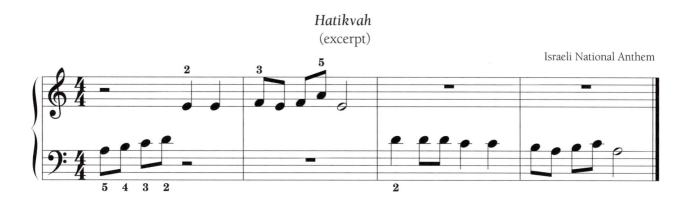

2. Perform the following piece, which uses pitches in the D natural minor scale. The RH stays within the minor five-finger pattern.

Melody, Op. 39, No. 3
(from *24 Little Pieces*)

Dmitri Kabalevsky (Russia, 1904–1987)

3. Try playing "Zum Gali Gali" in E minor.

Zum Gali Gali

Israeli Folk Melody

Zum ga - li, ga - li, ga - li, Zum ga - li, ga - li, Zum ga - li, ga - li, ga - li, Zum ga - li, ga - li,

He - cha lutz le 'man a - vo - dah, A - vo - dah le 'man - he - cha - lutz.

Natural Minor Scale Fingering

Cross-over and cross-under fingering is needed to play the natural minor scale with one hand. One-hand fingerings for selected natural minor scales are in Appendix F.

One-Hand Fingering in Two Octaves

The fingering for the A natural minor scale in two octaves (also the same for E, D, G, and C minor scales) is as follows:

RH: 1 2 ③ 1 2 ③ 4 ① 2 ③ 1 2 ③ 4 5
LH: 5 4 ③ 2 1 ③ 2 ① 4 ③ 2 1 ③ 2 1

A natural minor scale

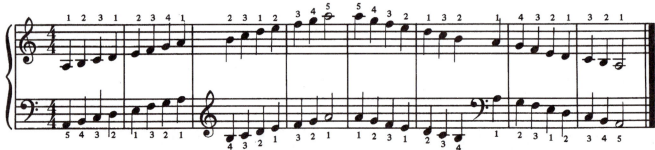

Performing the Natural Minor Scale

1. Practice the following thumb-under exercise in preparation for one-hand minor scale playing. Keep the hand in position and let the thumb do all the work.

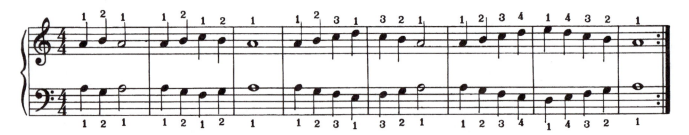

2. Perform the preceding A natural minor scale with one-hand fingering in two octaves—in contrary motion and in parallel motion.

MINOR KEY SIGNATURES

Relative Major and Minor Key Signatures

Each major key shares a key signature with a minor key. Major and minor scales with the same key signature are referred to as **relative.**

Relative major and minor key signatures

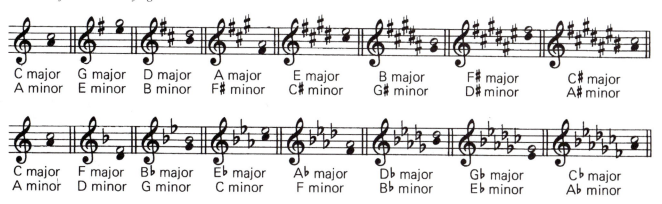

C major	G major	D major	A major	E major	B major	F♯ major	C♯ major
A minor	E minor	B minor	F♯ minor	C♯ minor	G♯ minor	D♯ minor	A♯ minor

C major	F major	B♭ major	E♭ major	A♭ major	D♭ major	G♭ major	C♭ major
A minor	D minor	G minor	C minor	F minor	B♭ minor	E♭ minor	A♭ minor

GUIDELINES FOR USING THE KEY SIGNATURE TO DETERMINE THE TONIC OR MINOR KEY

Step 1. To identify the tonic or minor key, it is easiest to first check the key signature and determine the major tonic or key.

Step 2. Count down three half steps (or a minor third) from the major tonic to determine the minor tonic or key. When a major tonic is in a space, the minor one is in the next lower space. When a major tonic is on a line, the minor one is on the next lower line.

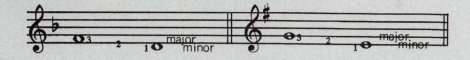

Key Fact The key signatures and tonics are the same for the natural, harmonic, and melodic minor scales. The natural minor is the only one that uses exclusively the pitches indicated by the key signature.

The Circle of Fifths (Minor Keys)

The fifteen minor key signatures progress in a sequence of perfect fifths and can be arranged in a circle (page 198), as the major keys are. By moving clockwise *up* the interval of a perfect fifth to the tonic, each new key adds one more sharp. By moving counterclockwise *down* a perfect fifth, each new key adds one more flat. The three enharmonic keys appear at the bottom.

Circle of Fifths
(minor keys)

Enharmonic Keys

THE HARMONIC MINOR SCALE

The **harmonic minor scale** is the most frequently used. It is the form upon which chords (harmonies) are usually built.

The harmonic minor scale has the same half steps between 2 and 3 and between 5 and 6 as the natural minor but raises the seventh degree one half step, creating a step and a half between 6 and 7. (The raised seventh also establishes a half step between 7 and 8, as in the major scale.) The raising of the seventh tone is accomplished by an **accidental** rather than by a change in the key signature. The key signature is the same for natural minor and harmonic minor.

The A harmonic minor scale

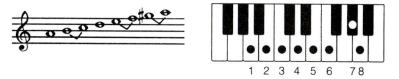

Performing the A Harmonic Minor Scale

Perform Israeli Folk Melody 3 and Witthauer's "Gavotte." Both use the A harmonic minor scale. Notice that the G♯ (seventh step) is added in the music.

Israeli Folk Melody 3

K e y   T e r m   A **gavotte** is a French dance in moderately quick duple meter, often with an upbeat of two quarter notes.

Gavotte

Andante

Johann Georg Witthauer (1750–1802)

Harmonic Minor Scale Fingering

The harmonic minor scales have different one-hand fingerings. (One-hand fingerings for selected minor scales are in Appendix F.)

One-Hand Fingering in Two Octaves

The fingering for the A harmonic minor scale in two octaves (also the same for the E, D, G, and C minor scales) is as follows:

RH: 1 2 ③ 1 2 ③ 4 ① 2 ③ 1 2 ③ 4 5
LH: 5 4 ③ 2 1 ③ 2 ① 4 3 2 1 ③ 2 1

A harmonic minor scale

Performing the Harmonic Minor Scale

1. Practice the preceding A harmonic minor scale with one-hand fingering in two octaves—first in contrary motion and then in parallel motion.

2. Once the fingering is secure for the A minor scale, try the E, D, G, and C minor scales.

THE MELODIC MINOR SCALE

Of the three forms of minor, the **melodic minor** is used the least. This scale has the same half steps between 2 and 3 as natural and harmonic but raises both the sixth and the seventh pitches one half step. The melodic minor usually descends in the natural minor form. (As with the harmonic form, if the raising of the sixth and seventh steps requires an accidental, this is added in the melody, not in the key signature.)

A melodic minor scale

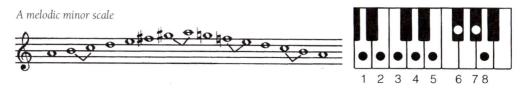

Melodic Minor Scale Fingering

One-Hand Fingering in Two Octaves

The one-hand fingering for the A melodic minor scale in two octaves (also the same for the E, D, G, and C melodic minor scales) follows. Try playing the scale listening for the raised sixth and seventh ascending and the return to natural minor in the descending portion.

RH: 1 2 (3) 1 2 (3) 4 (1) 2 (3) 1 2 (3) 4 5
LH: 5 4 (3) 2 1 (3) 2 (1) 4 (3) 2 1 (3) 2 1

A melodic minor scale

IDENTIFICATION OF SCALE TONES

Scale Degrees

The degrees of the minor scales are identified by the same names as those of the major scale—with the exception of the seventh in the natural minor form. Since the natural minor scale does not have a half step between the seventh and the eighth degrees, the seventh degree is often referred to as the **subtonic**.

Minor scale degrees

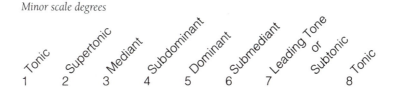

Syllable Names

Pitches in the minor scales may be referred to with syllable names, just as in major. Two approaches are used for associating syllables with pitches in minor keys.

1. Scales begin with *do* as in major, and the remaining syllables are altered when necessary. This approach stresses the relationship of the sound of the tonic with the syllable *do*.

2. Scales begin with *la* and end on *la* (the tonic or keynote is *la*). This approach stresses the relationship between the major and minor scales.

A natural minor scale

do	re	me	fa	sol	le	te	do
la	ti	do	re	mi	fa	sol	la

A harmonic minor scale

do	re	me	fa	sol	le	ti	do
la	ti	do	re	mi	fa	si	la

A melodic minor scale

do	re	me	fa	sol	la	ti	do	te	le	sol	fa	me	re	do
la	ti	do	re	mi	fi	si	la	sol	fa	mi	re	do	ti	la

PERFORMING PIECES IN MINOR KEYS

Determine the minor key for the following pieces, then perform each. To identify the minor key

1. Examine the key signature to determine the major key possibility and the minor key possibility.

2. Check the final pitch of the piece to eliminate one possibility (from step 1). Most often, that final pitch will be the tonic.

3. Check the melody to see if accidentals are used if you think a minor tonic is indicated. (Remember that the harmonic and melodic minor scales will have accidentals added to the melody.)

The results of steps 1 and 2 will identify the minor key.

Adagio

Daniel Gottlob Türk (Germany, 1756–1813)

English Carol

Canon

Konrad Max Künz (Germany, 1812–1875)

Student, Piano 1

Shalom, Chaverim

Israeli Round

Sha - lom, cha-ve-rim! Sha - lom, cha-ve-rim! Sha - lom, sha - lom! Le -

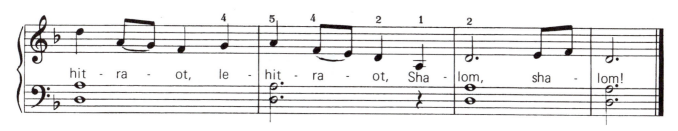

hit - ra - ot, le - hit - ra - ot, Sha - lom, sha - lom!

Instructor, Piano 2

Primary Chords in Minor

The harmonic minor scale usually serves as the framework for constructing the primary chords in minor. The i and the iv chords are always minor, and the V and the V7 chords are always major and major-minor sevenths (as in a major key).

Primary chords in A minor

The i, iv, and V7 chords for selected minor keys are shown in Appendix H. RH and LH fingerings are also provided.

The i, iv$_4^6$, and V$_5^6$ Chords in Selected Minor Keys

As in major, the primary chords in minor can be rearranged or inverted for ease in moving from one chord to the next. The same inversions for the iv (second inversion) and the V7 (first inversion) are used in harmonic minor.

Key of A minor

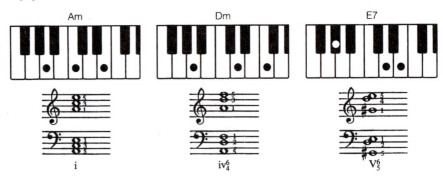

Key of E minor

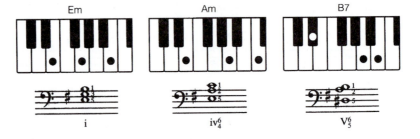

Key of B minor

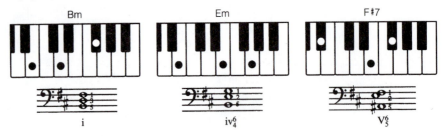

Key of D minor

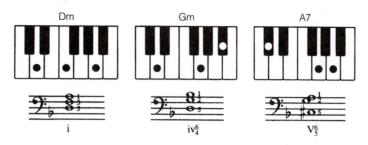

Key of G minor

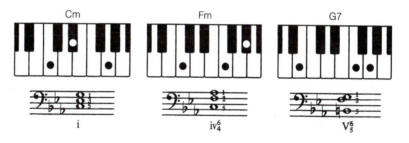

Key of C minor

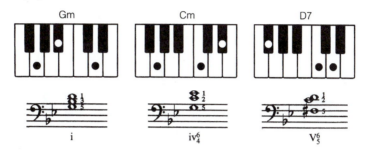

Key of F minor

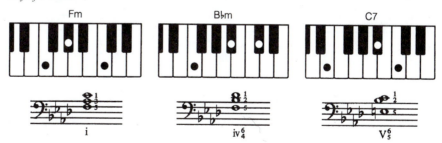

Performing i–iv$_4^6$–V$_5^6$ Chords

1. Perform the following exercise to practice the chord moves. The fingerings and the whole-step–half-step moves will be the same in any minor key. Transpose this exercise to other minor keys.

Playing Tip   Memorize this progression. Learn to shift quickly and smoothly from one chord to another. Feel the shape of the next chord, and actually touch the keys just before playing.

i–iv$_4^6$–V$_5^6$ Exercise

Part A

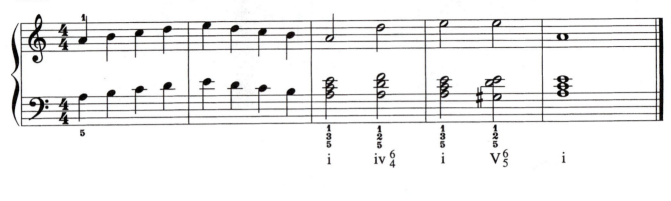

i   iv $_4^6$ i   V $_5^6$ i

Part B

i   iv $_4^6$ i   V $_5^6$ i

Part C

i   iv $_4^6$ i   V $_5^6$ i

2. Use legato pedaling for the following arpeggio exercise. Try not to blur chord tones or overlap sounds of single notes. Connect evenly when crossing hands. Transpose to other minor keys.

Arpeggio Exercise: i–iv$_4^6$–V$_5^6$

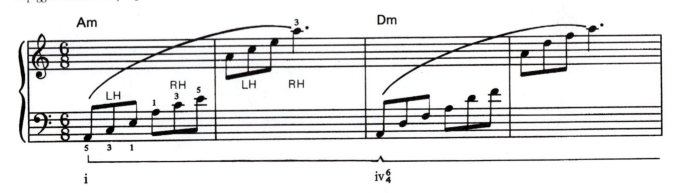

i   iv $_4^6$

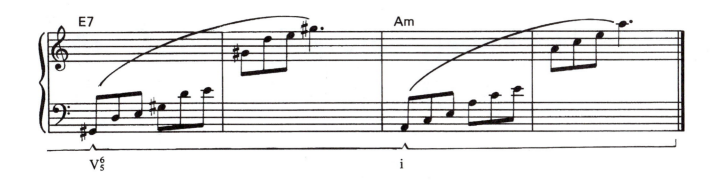

V_5^6 i

3. Perform the following pieces with the i and V_5^6 chords. Determine the minor key and the i and V_5^6 chords first; then practice the chord progression. Be sure to review the rhythm, form, and fingering for each piece before performing. Transpose to other minor keys.

Folk Melody 5

Folk Melody 6

4. Perform the following pieces with the i–iv$_4^6$–V$_5^6$ chords.

This Old Hammer

American Folk Melody

This old ham-mer___   killed John Hen-ry,___   This old ham-mer___

(continued)

Joshua Fought the Battle of Jericho

African American Spiritual

Key Sign *D.C. al fine* is the Italian sign indicating that a piece is to be repeated from the beginning to the measure marked fine (the end). Symbols such as these are used to reduce the amount of music needed to notate a piece.

Czech Folk Melody 2

Harmonizing Melodies with Primary Chords

1. Accompany the following melodies with the i and V$\frac{6}{5}$ chords. (Refer to Guidelines on p. 181). Try different accompaniment patterns (broken-chord and arpeggio), too.

Folk Melody 7

Hungarian Folk Melody 2

German Dance No. 1
(excerpt)

Franz Schubert (Austria, 1797–1828)

FRANZ SCHUBERT ● *(Austria, 1797–1828), one of the leading composers of the early* **Romantic period**. *His works include over six hundred songs, eight symphonies, piano works, chamber music, and music for the stage.*

2. Accompany the following melodies with i–iv$^6_4$–V$^6_5$ chords. Try different accompaniment patterns.

Canterbury

English Folk Melody

Folk Melody 8

More Rhythm Reading

Rhythm Exercise — $\frac{2}{4}$ $\frac{3}{4}$ $\frac{4}{4}$ $\frac{3}{8}$ ♫♪♪♪♪ ♪ ♫♪♪

Clap, chant, or play the following examples on any key(s) or any chord. Check the number of beats per measure and the number of beats or fractions of beats each note and rest receive.

1. 4/4 — counting: 1  & 2 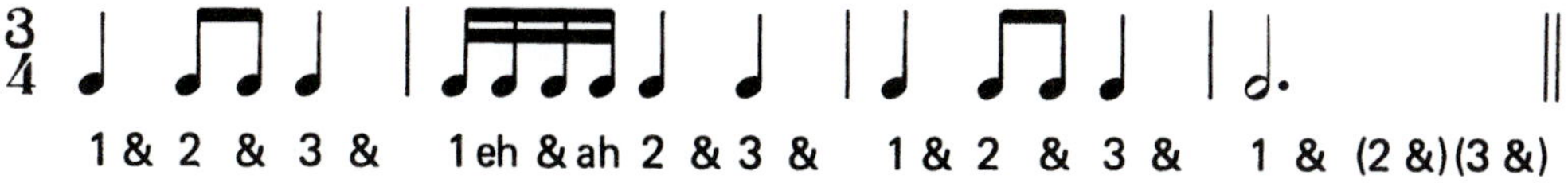 & 3  & 4  &   1 & 2 & 3 & 4 &   1 eh & ah 2 & 3 & 4 &   1 & 2 & 3 & (4 &)

2. 3/4 — counting: 1 & 2 & 3 &   1 eh & ah 2 & 3 &   1 & 2 & 3 &   1 & (2 &)(3 &)

3. 2/4 — counting: 1 & 2 &   1 eh & ah 2 &   1 & 2 &   1 & 2 &

4. 4/4

5. 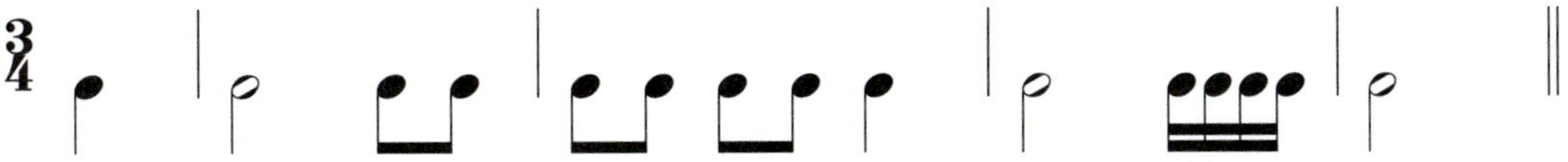 3/4

6. 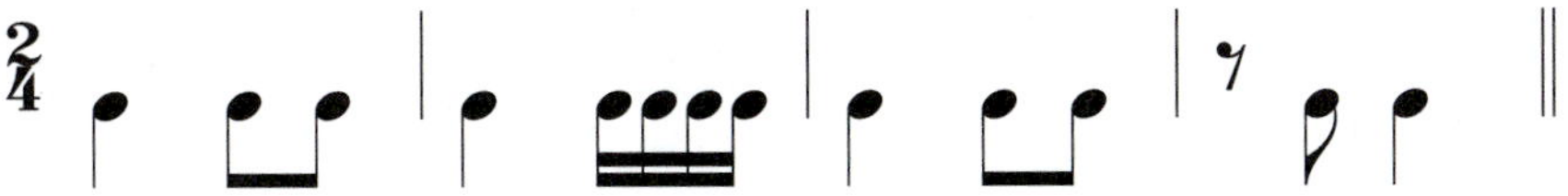 2/4

7.  3/8 — counting: 1 2 3

8. 3/8 — counting: 1 & 2 & 3 &

9.  4/4

10. 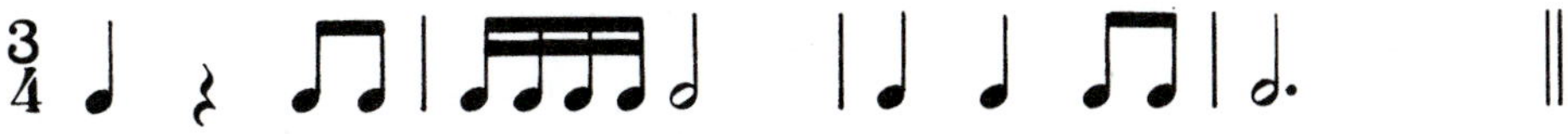 3/4

unit three • *Relative and Parallel Majors and Minors*

RELATIVE MAJORS AND MINORS

Major and minor scales sharing the same key signatures are *related* (see "Minor Key Signatures" earlier in this chapter). Often in compositions, especially long pieces, both the major and the relative minor (or vice versa) are used.

"We Three Kings" is in E minor in the A section and in G relative major in the B section. Practice one section at a time. Notice the $\frac{3}{8}$ time signature.

We Three Kings

John H. Hopkins, Jr. (United States, 1820–1891)

PARALLEL MAJORS AND MINORS

Just as major and minor scales and keys can have the same key signature but different tonics, so major and minor scales and keys can have the same tonic but different key signatures. When a major and a minor scale begin on the same tonic, they are said to be *parallel majors and minors*. For example, C major and C minor are **parallel keys.**

"Ah, vous dirai-je, Maman" ("Twinkle, Twinkle, Little Star") is presented here in its original scale (C major) and in the parallel minor. Play both versions.

Ah, vous dirai-je, Maman (C major)

French Folk Melody

Ah, vous dirai-je, Maman (C minor)

Key Fact   A **theme and variations** is a series of variations on a given melody. Although some theme and variations are improvised at the keyboard, many composers over the years have written a set of variations on a popular song or dance, a chorale tune, or a theme they or someone else composed. Variations are created by altering the rhythm, the melody, or the harmony (or all three) of the **theme.**

In 1778 Wolfgang Amadeus Mozart composed a set of twelve variations on the theme "Ah, vous dirai-je, Maman." (The "K" that appears with the titles of Mozart's works is an abbreviation for Köchel. Ludwig von Köchel chronologically catalogued Mozart's more than six hundred compositions.) The theme appears in its entirety below, followed by excerpts of ten of the twelve variations.

Study this example and determine the melodic, rhythmic, and harmonic changes made for each variation. A live or recorded performance of Mozart's entire composition will help you to *hear* what you *see* and *see* what you *hear*.

12 Variations on "Ah, vous dirai-je, Maman," K. 265

Theme

Wolfgang Amadeus Mozart (Austria, 1756–1791)

Variation I (excerpt)

Variation II (excerpt)

Variation III (excerpt)

Variation IV (excerpt)

Variation V (excerpt)

Variation VI (excerpt)

Variation VIII (excerpt)

Variation IX (excerpt)

Variation XI (excerpt)
Adagio

Variation XII (excerpt)
Allegro

This ensemble piece, Diabelli's "Scherzo," is in C major, but notice the momentary shift to C minor in the third staff. This adds interest and color.

Scherzo from Melodious Pieces, Op. 149, No. 6

Student, Piano 1

Allegro

Anton Diabelli (Austria, 1781–1858)

(continued)

TRACK 50

Instructor, Piano 2

Allegro

ANTON DIABELLI ● (*Austria, 1781–1858*), *Viennese publisher and composer. He composed and then cleverly distributed a waltz theme to prominent Austrian composers, asking them to create a set of variations on his theme. Beethoven responded and the* Diabelli Variations *were the result.*

COMPOSING PROJECT

Theme and Variations

Since the 1600s, keyboard players have performed compositions based on the theme-and-variations form. Variations are created by altering the rhythm, the melody, or the harmony (or all three) of the theme. For example, the rhythm could be altered by changing the meter, or the melody could be varied by changing from major to minor or vice versa. If "Ah, vous dirai-je, Maman" were used as the theme for such a composition, one variation could include the change of mode from major to minor (as in the parallel minor example). Another variation could feature a change of meter from $\frac{4}{4}$ to $\frac{3}{4}$.

Create a theme-and-variations composition based on a familiar melody.

Step 1. Choose a familiar melody that you can play well. Some possibilities are "When the Saints Go Marching In," p. 144; "Love Somebody," p. 58; "I Never Will Marry," p. 176; and "Kum Ba Yah," p. 184.

Step 2. Using the selected melody, create one variation that illustrates a change of mode. (If your melody is in major, use the parallel minor, and if your melody is in minor, use the parallel major.) Experiment, and when you have finalized your variation, notate it on the staff.

Step 3. Create a second variation on the original melody, illustrating a change of rhythm. You can either vary the rhythm of the melody or change the meter. Notate your variation.

Step 4. Play your Theme and Two Variations, reading from staff notation. Exchange your melody with a classmate's. Play your pieces for each other, and assess your work for accuracy and creativity.

SOLO REPERTOIRE

In this Kabalevsky piece, which interval is used almost exclusively? Notice the jump from the ascending interval to the descending one. First practice measures 1–3 separately very slowly, using the drop/lift technique (see Chapter 7). Then work on the entire piece.

TRACK 51

Op. 39, No. 4
(from 24 *Little Pieces*)

Dmitri Kabalevsky (Russia, 1904–1987)

Notice the minor five-finger range for Bartók's "Round Dance." What can you say about the pitches in the final measure?

TRACK 52

Round Dance
(from *First Term at the Piano*)

Andante moderato

Béla Bartók (Hungary, 1881–1945)

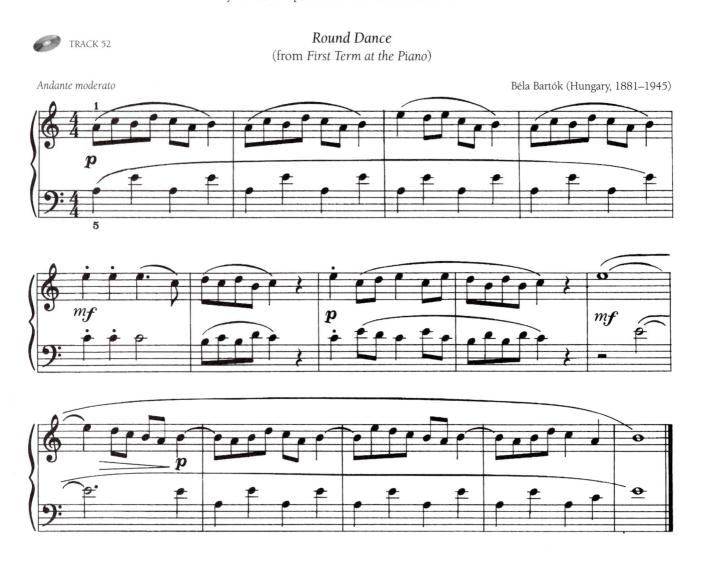

Notice that the first section (A) of this Leopold Mozart minuet is in minor. (Which form?) The second section (B) begins in relative major F but quickly moves back to D minor.

TRACK 53

Minuet

Leopold Mozart (Austria, 1719–1787)

LEOPOLD MOZART ● *(Austria, 1719–1787), composer, pianist, and father of Wolfgang Amadeus Mozart. His works include operas, oratorios, cantatas, symphonies, concertos, and chamber music.*

TECHNIQUE EXERCISES

Technique Exercise 1. Extension Fingering and Interval Study

This exercise focuses on the intervals within the three minor scales. Notice the new intervals: the minor sixth (m6) and the minor seventh (m7). (Remember, minor intervals are always a half step smaller than major ones.) Practice hands separately and hands together. Transpose to other minor keys.

Playing Tip   *Feel* the distance of each interval as you play, and listen to the sound of each.

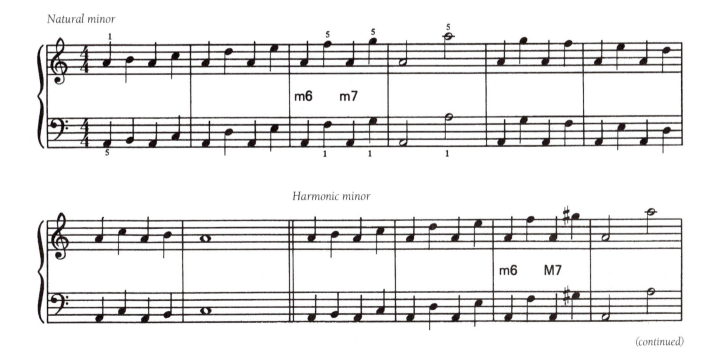

(continued)

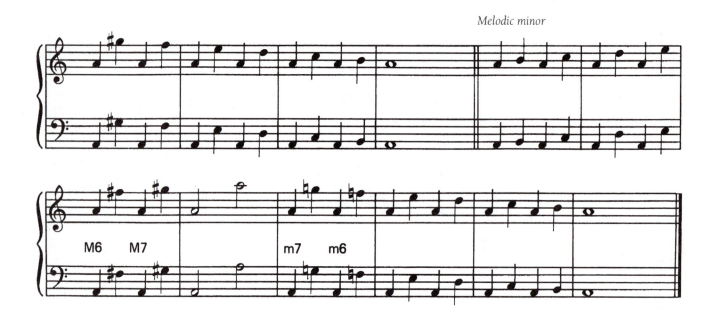

Technique Exercise 2. Contraction Fingering

This exercise stresses contraction within the five-finger pattern. Fingers are actually brought closer together. Practice hands separately and hands together. Play without accidentals (in parentheses) for the major pattern and with accidentals for the minor pattern. Transpose to the parallel major and minors of G, F, D, A, E, and B.

Technique Exercise 3. Technical Study

After this study is secure as notated, change to the C parallel minor (harmonic).

Study from Op. 823

Carl Czerny (Austria, 1791–1851)

CARL CZERNY ● *(Austria, 1791–1857), pianist and pedagogue who composed symphonies, overtures, chamber music, and Masses and other sacred music. He is known for his numerous collections of piano studies and exercises.*

END-OF-CHAPTER EVALUATION

1. Play the pitches in the natural, harmonic, and melodic minor scales (one octave) on the following tonics: D, G, E, and C.

2. Perform the G harmonic minor scale in two octaves ascending and descending.

3. Play the i, iv$^6_4$, V$^6_5$ chords in the following minor keys (harmonic form): A, E, B, D, and G.

4. Demonstrate parallel majors and minors by choosing a major melody to play. Perform the melody in major and in the parallel minor.

5. Perform the following melody accurately and musically. Be able to describe its melodic and rhythmic characteristics. Transpose the melody to the key of D minor. Harmonize with i, iv, and V7 chords.

Bim Bom

Israeli Folk Melody

6. Write the specified minor scales. Use key signatures.

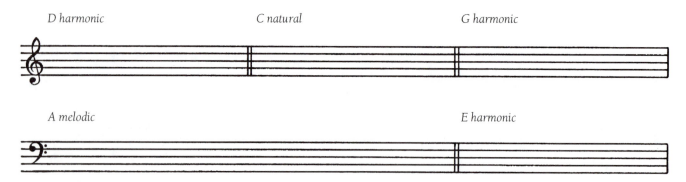

D harmonic   *C natural*   *G harmonic*

A melodic   *E harmonic*

7. Notate the minor tonics for the following key signatures on the staff. Write the letter name of the tonics below the staff.

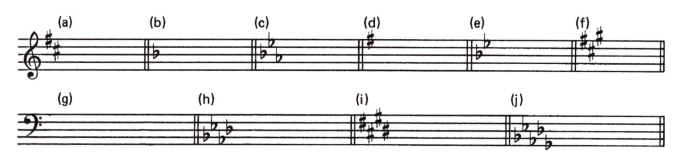

(a)   (b)   (c)   (d)   (e)   (f)

(g)   (h)   (i)   (j)

8. Write the primary chords for the stated key in root position and then in the i–iv$^6_4$–V$^6_5$ position. Use key signatures.

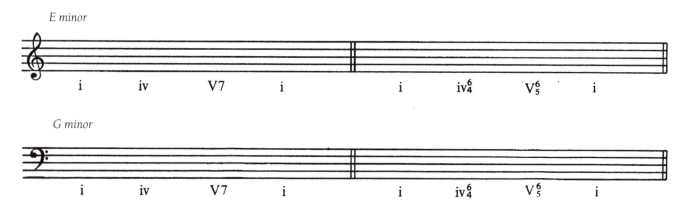

E minor

  i   iv   V7   i   i   iv$^6_4$ V$^6_5$ i

G minor

  i   iv   V7   i   i   iv$^6_4$ V$^6_5$ i

9. Describe the following musical terms:

    a. Relative majors and minors

    b. Parallel majors and minors

c. Theme and variations

d. Gavotte

10. Explain the meaning of the following musical symbols:
   a. $\frac{3}{8}$

   b. Bm

   c. E7

   d. *D.C. al fine*

chapter ten

Other Scales, Modes, and Tonalities

OBJECTIVES

After completing this chapter, you will be able to

✔ Demonstrate understanding of and play the pentatonic, whole-tone, and blues scales; modes; and twelve-tone row

✔ Perform a bitonal piece

✔ Demonstrate and perform rhythmic examples of shifting and asymmetric meters

✔ Perform musical pieces in the chapter with pitch and rhythmic accuracy and with expression, performing at least one from memory

✔ Compose a twelve-tone row composition

✔ Demonstrate changing fingers on the same key

unit one • # Other Scales and Modes

Although major and minor scales have been widely used in the music of Western civilization and are certainly the most familiar to us, other scales and modes have been used and are still being used today. It is not uncommon to find music based on the pentatonic, whole-tone, and blues scales. Modes, seven-tone scales that served as the basis of most Western music through the seventeenth century, were rediscovered by nineteenth- and twentieth-century composers. Often, contemporary composers mix modes and scales—even within a piece.

PENTATONIC SCALES

The **pentatonic scale** (*penta* means five) may be the oldest. This five-tone scale serves as the basis for much of world music, particularly music of Northeast Asia, Native America, Africa, and Europe, and it often forms the basis of **ostinati** in rock music. Pentatonic melodies are also found in the works of **Western art music** composers—for example, Debussy's *Voiles*. The pentatonic scale most frequently used includes no half steps and one interval of a whole step plus a half step. This familiar pentatonic scale can be illustrated on the five black keys and transposed to the white keys.

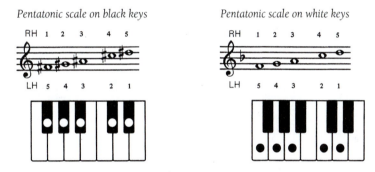

Pentatonic scale on black keys   Pentatonic scale on white keys

Key Fact   Major and minor key signatures are adapted for pentatonic music by choosing the signature that results in the five necessary pitches. The key signature will not always identify the tonic as it does for major and minor scales. Because there is no leading tone in the pentatonic scale, some pentatonic music does not have an obvious tonic.

Performing Pentatonic Melodies

1. Play the preceding pentatonic scale on the black keys, and then on the white keys.

2. Perform "Taiwan School Song" on the following page as written, then on the black keys by thinking of each note as being sharped.

Taiwan School Song

Yang wa__ wa Syan syi__ syi Yu le yi ge yang wa__ wa.

Ni tsung na li lai, Ni wang na li chu. Yu le yi ge yang wa__ wa.

3. Perform "Sakura," which uses a pentatonic scale that includes half steps (E F A B C). Notice the drone accompaniment.

Sakura

Japanese Folk Melody

p Sa - ku - ra, Sa - ku - ra, Yo - yo i - no so ra - wa,

Mi - wa ta su ka gi - ri. Ka su mi - ka ku - mo - ka, Ni - o - i - zo

i zu - ru I - za - ya, i - za - ya, Mi ni yu - ka - n.

4. Perform "Auld Lang Syne." Its melody is based on the pentatonic scale G A B D E, but its accompaniment uses broken chords.

Auld Lang Syne

Scottish Folk Melody

5. Perform other pentatonic melodies, such as "Tom Dooley" (p. 171) and "Kang Ding Ching Ge" (p. 287).

6. Improvise with the pentatonic scale by playing only on black keys. Review "Improvisation—Black Keys," in Chapter 1.

MODES

The **modes,** also referred to as *church modes,* are seven-tone scales that include five whole steps and two half steps. They are used today in **classical music,** jazz, and popular music. The Dorian and Mixolydian modes are especially popular with composers of jazz and commercial music. (Much of the Beatles' music is modal, frequently mixing modes and major and minor within a piece.)

Together with major and minor scales, modes can be illustrated on the white keys of the piano, as shown in "Modes and Scales" below. As with minor scales, two approaches are used for associating syllables with modes.

1. The mode begins with *do*. The remaining syllables are altered when necessary.

2. The keynote is *do*. Each mode begins with the syllable name that pitch would have in the major scale of that key. This approach stresses the relationship of the modes to the tonic of the major scale. (Dorian is up a major second, Phrygian is up a major third, and so on.)

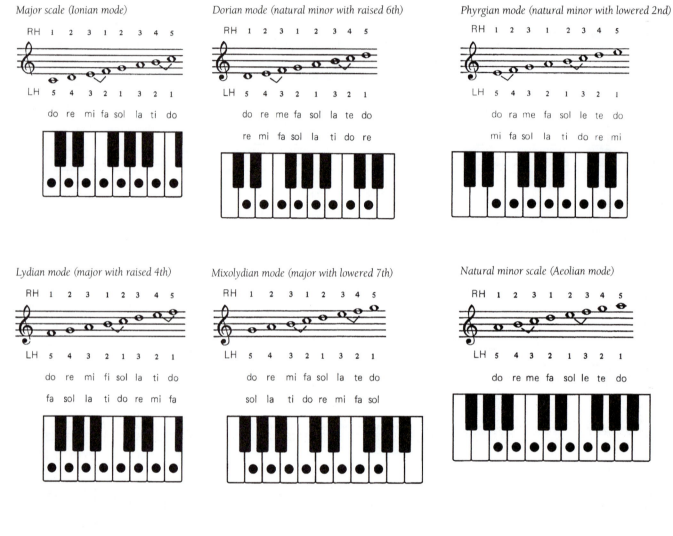

Major scale (Ionian mode)

do re mi fa sol la ti do

Dorian mode (natural minor with raised 6th)

do re me fa sol la te do

re mi fa sol la ti do re

Phyrgian mode (natural minor with lowered 2nd)

do ra me fa sol le te do

mi fa sol la ti do re mi

Lydian mode (major with raised 4th)

do re mi fi sol la ti do

fa sol la ti do re mi fa

Mixolydian mode (major with lowered 7th)

do re mi fa sol la te do

sol la ti do re mi fa sol

Natural minor scale (Aeolian mode)

do re me fa sol le te do

Locrian mode (seldom used)

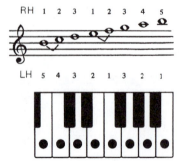

Key Fact The modes may be transposed to any pitch, but because of the variety of whole-step–half-step formulas, they may be more difficult to recognize in transposed form. Often, major and minor key signatures are adapted for transposed modal music.

Performing the Modes

1. Practice each of the preceding modes, listening for the special qualities of each. The fingering is indicated above and below the notes.

2. Choose a mode and improvise a bit at the keyboard with the pitches in that mode. Move freely between left and right hands. Experiment until you come up with something that pleases you.

3. Perform the following pieces. Determine which mode each is based on. (The first two are in original form, and the third is transposed.)

Scarborough Fair

English Folk Song

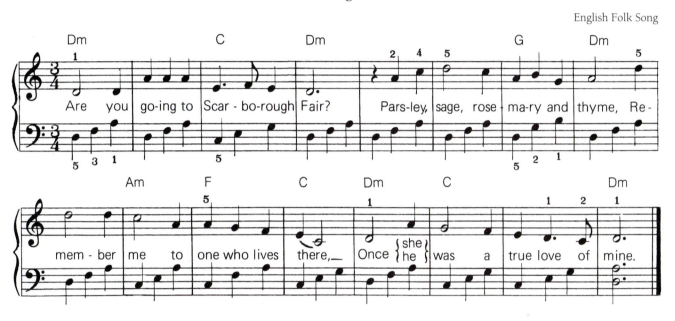

The Great Silke

Scottish Folk Melody

Every Night When the Sun Goes Down

Student, Piano 1

American Folk Song

TRACK 55

Instructor, Piano 2

THE WHOLE-TONE SCALE

Scales using equidistant tones are common in Southeast Asia and enjoyed a brief vogue in early twentieth-century Europe, especially in the music of the French Impressionist composers Debussy and Ravel. As used by the Impressionist composers, this scale lacks a feeling of tonic and conveys ambiguity, a sense of vagueness, and a musically indefinite quality (an impression, hence **impressionism**).

The **whole-tone scale,** a six-tone scale, consists solely of whole steps. The two forms of the whole-tone scale are shown here.

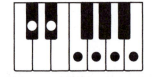   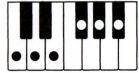

Performing Whole-Tone Scales

1. Improvise on the whole-tone scale with the damper pedal depressed. Freely move between the low, middle, and high registers of the piano. Use arpeggio figures. Be flexible with the beat, rhythm, and tempo, taking slight ritards for musical expression (*rubato*).

2. Identify the whole-tone scale in Vladimir Rebikov's "The Bear." What accompaniment figure is used in the LH?

TRACK 56

The Bear

Andante

Vladimir Rebikov (Russia, 1886–1920)

VLADIMIR REBIKOV ● *(Russia, 1866–1920), composer. His early works were in the Romantic style, but about 1900 he began writing expressionist dramatic and vocal pieces using whole-tone harmony and other contemporary idioms.*

THE BLUES SCALE

The special form of jazz called the blues uses a **blues scale.** This scale can only be approximated in traditional notation or on the keyboard because the "blue notes" fall somewhere between the pitches and keys we know. A blues scale, derived from a major scale, features the third, the fifth, and the seventh pitches lowered a half step.

Blues scale in C major

Performing the Blues Scale

1. Play the blues scale in C (as in the preceding example) hands separately. Experiment with rhythmic variations as you get familiar with the sound of the scale. Transpose the blues scale to F major and to G major.

2. Perform "Emily's Blues," noting the familiar 12-bar blues chord progression (see Chapter 7). Notice that the notes in the C blues scale are included when the C7 chord is featured, the F blues scale for the F7, and G blues scale for the G7. A new rhythmic combination (♪♫) is introduced, too, in "Emily's Blues."

TRACK 57

Emily's Blues

Diana Somers

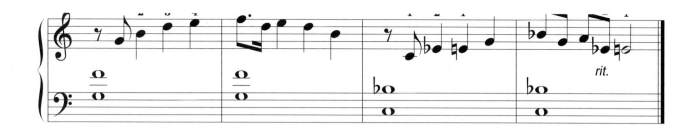

DIANA SOMERS ● *composed "Emily's Blues" while a student in a beginning piano and music fundamentals class at San Francisco State University.*

3. "Calico Rag" features elements of the blues scale and adds some of its own special jazzy features.

TRACK 58

Student, Piano 1

Calico Rag

Dennis Alexander (United States, b. 1947)

Allegro moderato

Instructor, Piano 2

DENNIS ALEXANDER ● *(United States, b. 1947), a prolific and popular composer of educational piano music who maintains an active composing and touring schedule for Alfred Publishing Company.*

unit two • *Bitonality and Atonality*

BITONALITY

Twentieth-century composers explored the use of two or more tonalities (or keys) occurring simultaneously. When two tonalities are performed at the same time, the result is **bitonality.**

Performing Bitonal Music

1. Perform Bartók's "Dialogue," which may be considered bitonal. The RH part is within the A minor five-finger pattern, and the LH part is within the E major pattern. Practice the parts separately and together.

TRACK 60

Dialogue
(from First *Term at the Piano*)

Moderato

Béla Bartók (Hungary, 1881–1945)

2. Improvise with bitonality. Use a different major or minor five-finger pattern in each hand. Be flexible with rhythm. Explore various registers of the piano and the use of pedal.

ATONALITY

Twentieth-century composers also experimented with pitch organizations that suggest no tonality or key. Music in which all pitches have an equal function and no one tone serves as the tonic is referred to as **atonal.**

Tone Rows

One atonal pitch organization involves arranging the twelve pitches of the **chromatic scale** (a twelve-tone scale consisting entirely of half steps) into a series (**serial music**), or a **twelve-tone row.** Thousands of rows can be formed from the chromatic scale. The series is then used without alteration according to the following rules.

1. O—Original: Row is played exactly in the planned order, one note after the other.

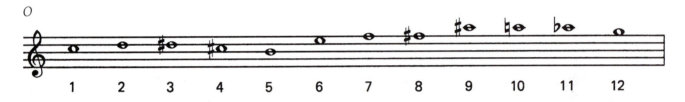

2. R—Retrograde: Row is played backwards, one note after the other.

3. I—Inversion: Row is played with the intervals of the original but with each interval inverted (upside down or in "mirror" version).

4. RI—Retrograde Inversion: Row is played in inverted form in retrograde (backwards and upside down).

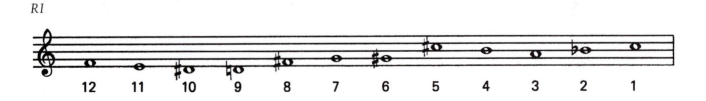

Performing Tone Rows

1. Perform the original form of the tone row in any rhythm you choose or without any rhythm at all. Use both hands to play each note in any register you wish. Follow this rule: Once you have used a tone in the row, do not reuse it until you have used the other eleven tones.

2. Perform all four forms of the tone row.

3. Discover which forms of the preceding tone row are used in "Two-Handed Duet." Remember that any octave position and enharmonic spelling of the pitches are possible, and any clef, range, simultaneous playing of tones, and repetition of tones may be used. Notice how the rhythm ties the composition together.

TRACK 61

Two-Handed Duet
(X from *32 Piano Games*)

♩ = 160

Ross Lee Finney (United States, 1906–1997)

ROSS LEE FINNEY ● *(United States, 1906–1997), composer. He wrote songs, piano and organ pieces, chamber music, choral works with orchestra, concertos, four symphonies, and other orchestral works.*

unit three ● *Shifting and Asymmetric Meters*

SHIFTING METER

A rhythmic effect of irregularity can be achieved by shifting meters. **Shifting meter** occurs when there are meter changes throughout a composition—for example, $\frac{3}{4}$ to $\frac{4}{4}$ to $\frac{3}{4}$. To indicate shifting meters, a new time signature is written within each measure where the meter changes.

Rhythm Exercise 1. Shifting Meter

Clap, count, or play on any key(s) the following examples of shifting meters.

Performing Shifting Meter

Stravinsky's "Andantino" shifts from $\frac{2}{4}$ to $\frac{3}{4}$ to $\frac{2}{4}$ at the end of the first section. Clap and count the rhythm before playing. Notice that both hands stay within the five-finger position; note that the piece divides into three sections—**A B A** or **ternary form.**

Andantino
(No. 1 from *The Five Fingers*)

Igor Stravinsky (Russia, 1882–1971)

IGOR STRAVINSKY ● (*Russia, 1882–1971*), *an original and sometimes revolutionary composer of the twentieth century. Stravinsky wrote influential scores for ballets, orchestral works, and operas and explored a wide variety of styles, including jazz and ragtime.*

ASYMMETRIC METER

Asymmetric meter occurs when the accents within a measure are spaced irregularly. This gives an effect of constant shifting of accents throughout an entire piece and is often heard in Eastern European and Greek music and in twentieth-century music. Frequently used asymmetric time signatures are $\frac{7}{8}$ and $\frac{5}{4}$.

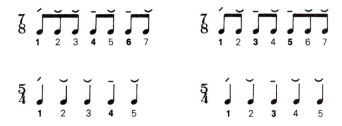

Rhythm Exercise 2. Asymmetric Meter

Clap, count, or play on any key(s) the following examples of asymmetric meters.

1.

1 2 3 4 5 6 7

2.

3.

1 2 3 4 5

4.

5.

6.

7.

8.

Performing Asymmetric Meters

1. Clap the rhythm of the RH part before playing. Perform "Yugoslavian Folk Melody" in $\frac{7}{8}$, observing that the accents occur on beats 1 and 5.

Yugoslavian Folk Melody

2. "Clusterphobia" includes shifting meter ($\frac{5}{4}$ to $\frac{3}{4}$), asymmetric meter ($\frac{5}{4}$), and no meter (0). The five-note clusters are to be performed entirely on white keys with fingers 1-2-3-4-5 in both hands. Both damper and soft pedals remain down throughout.

TRACK 63

Clusterphobia

Nancy Van de Vate (United States, b. 1930)

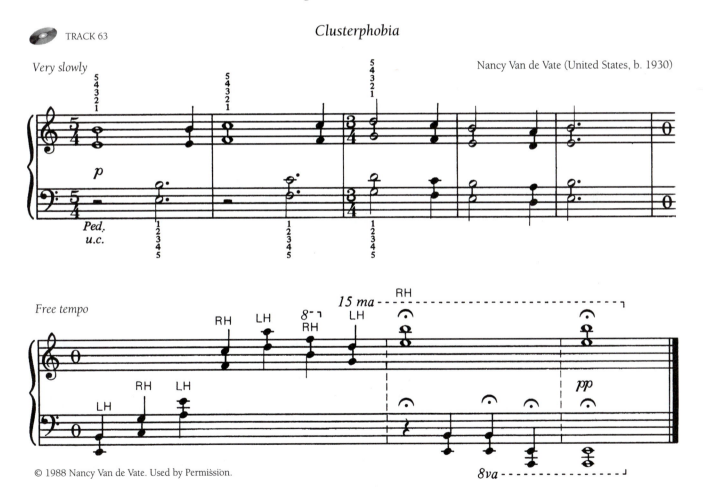

© 1988 Nancy Van de Vate. Used by Permission.

COMPOSING PROJECT

Twelve-Tone Row Composition

Create a composition based on a twelve-tone row.

Step 1. Decide on your tone row by arranging the twelve pitches of the chromatic scale in a specific order. (See the example on p. 238.) This arrangement will serve as your original form.

Step 2. Experiment with this original form, using any rhythm you choose. Distribute the row between the LH and the RH. When you have finalized your rhythm and your keyboard position, notate.

Step 3. Continue your composition by manipulating the row in original and retrograde forms (see the example on p. 238) as many times as you wish to complete the piece. Also, consider incorporating varying dynamics, tempo, and shifting meters. Notate your composition.

Step 4. Play your twelve-tone row composition, reading from staff notation. Exchange your melody with a classmate's. Play your pieces for each other, and assess your work for accuracy and creativity.

SOLO REPERTOIRE

Gurlitt's "Joy" stays within the D-to-A range in both hands. Notice the two measures that include chromatic tones in the RH. As you practice hands together, observe the imitation between lines.

TRACK 64

Joy

Allegretto

Cornelius Gurlitt (Germany, 1820–1901)

In Finney's "3 White-Note Clusters," the white and back rectangles are **tone clusters** of three notes. Play the blocked clusters (bunched seconds played simultaneously) with fingers 2, 3, and 4.

3 White-Note Clusters
(IV from *32 Piano Games*)

Ross Lee Finney (United States, 1906–1997)

♩ = 80

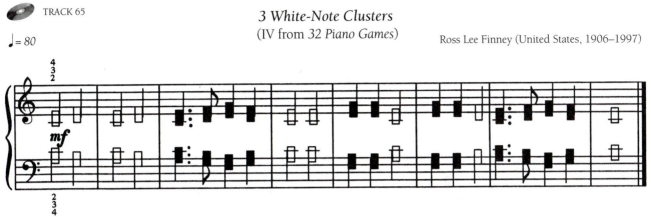

Visually analyze Kabalevsky's Op. 39, No. 8, for key or mode identification, phrase structure, interval movement, fingerings, and rhythm. Play legato, paying careful attention to slurs.

Op. 39, No. 8
(from *24 Little Pieces*)

Dmitri Kabalevsky (Russia, 1904–1987)

Andante

Leopold Mozart's Minuet (following page) is an example of **A B,** or **binary, form.** Notice that each section is repeated, and discover what part of A is repeated in B. Practice one section at a time.

Minuet

(from *Nannerl Notenbuch,* 1759)

Leopold Mozart (Austria, 1719–1787)

The interval of a major sixth (nine half steps) is featured in the following **etude** by John Biggs. Only fingers 1 and 5 are used. Practice the major sixths alone first, then the entire piece.

 TRACK 67

Etude No. 9

Very fast (♩ = 112)

John Biggs (United States, b. 1932)

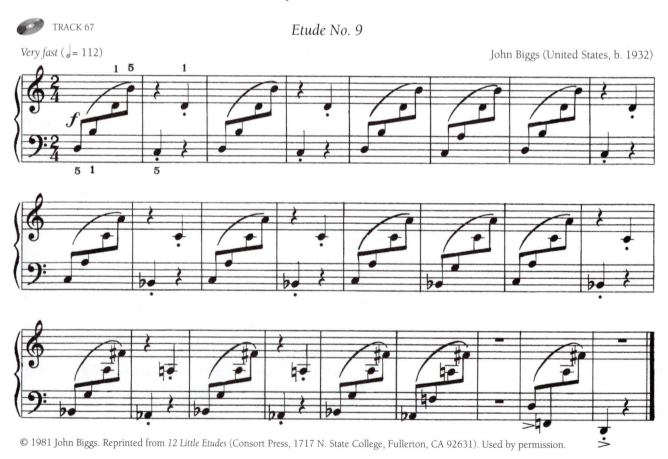

TECHNIQUE EXERCISES

Technique Exercise 1. Extension Fingering

This exercise extends beyond the five-finger range and works on the third, fourth, and fifth fingers of the LH ascending, and the third, fourth, and fifth fingers of the RH descending. At first, practice very slowly, playing each note distinctly and evenly (hands together and then hands separately). Gradually increase the speed. Play legato.

The Virtuoso Pianist, No. 4
(simplified version)

Charles-Louis Hanon (France, 1819–1900)

Technique Exercise 2. Changing Fingers

Practice this exercise with each hand separately. Change fingers while holding down the half notes. Also play the exercise changing between the following fingers:

RH: 3–2, 4–3, 5–4

LH: 2–3, 3–4, 4–5

Part A

Part B

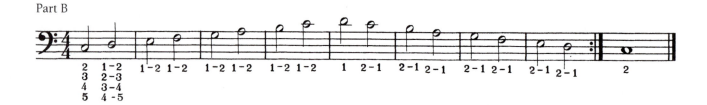

Technique Exercise 3. Legato Pedaling

Practice this Schumann piece slowly, using the legato or syncopated pedaling. Practice hands separately and then hands together.

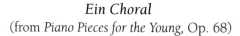

Ein Choral
(from *Piano Pieces for the Young,* Op. 68)

Robert Schumann (Germany, 1810–1856)

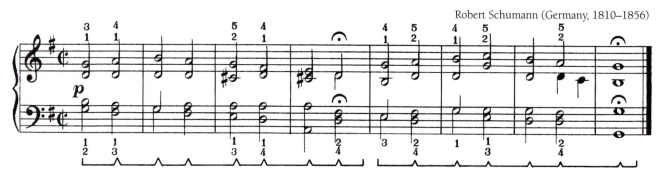

END-OF-CHAPTER EVALUATION

1. At the keyboard, demonstrate a pentatonic scale, the Dorian mode, the Mixolydian mode, and a whole-tone scale.

2. Demonstrate changing fingers on the same key by playing Technique Exercise 2 in this chapter.

3. Play the bitonal piece "Dialogue" (Bartók), p. 237, with pitch and rhythmic accuracy and with expression. Be able to identify the two scales used.

4. Perform the twelve-tone row composition "Two-Handed Duet," p. 239, with pitch and rhythmic accuracy and with expression. Be prepared to discuss the tone row and its manipulation in this piece.

5. Clap several examples of shifting meter in the rhythm exercise in this chapter.

6. Demonstrate legato pedaling by performing Schumann's "Ein Choral" (Technique Exercise 3).

7. Write the pitches in the pentatonic scale based on the following whole-step–half-step arrangement:

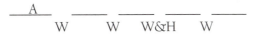

8. Notate the pitches in the designated modes on the staff and on the keyboard chart.

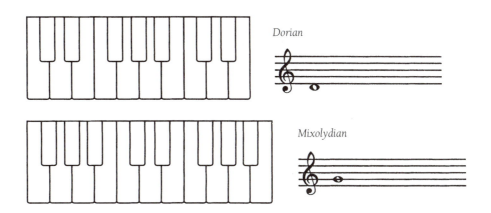

9. The following excerpt from a Chopin **mazurka** uses the pitches B♭ C D E F G A B♭. Determine on which mode this excerpt is based.

_____
(mode)

Mazurka in F Major, Op 68, No. 3
(excerpt)

Poco più vivo

Frédéric Chopin (Poland, 1810–1849)

10. Write whole-tone scales on the given pitches.

 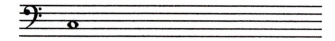

11. Create a twelve-tone row, and notate the row on the following staff. Number each note in the row.

12. One way to manipulate a tone row is to play it backwards or in _____ form.

13. Notate four measures of a rhythm in any asymmetric meter of your choice.

             | | | ||

14. Describe the following musical terms:

    a. Pentatonic scale

    b. Modes

    c. Whole-tone scale

    d. Blues scale

    e. Bitonality

    f. Atonality

    g. Shifting meter

Supplementary Music

Solo Repertoire

Folk Song
(No. 7 from *First Term at the Piano*)

Moderato

Béla Bartók (Hungary, 1881–1945)

One of Hungary's most outstanding composers, Béla Bartók wrote string quartets, orchestral works, operas, and a collection of piano pieces. *PianoLab* includes seven pieces from Bartók's *First Term at the Piano*. Like "Folk Song" above, Bartók based these pieces on folk melodies that he spent years collecting in Hungary and Romania.

Sunrise

Delicate (♩ = 120)

Jeanine Yeager

*Hold damper pedal down through the entire piece.

Slightly faster (♩ = 138)

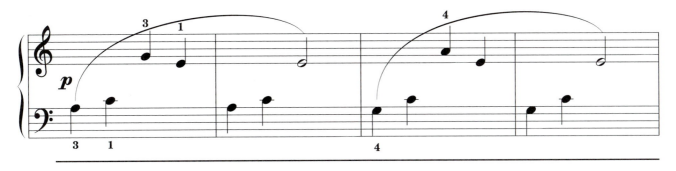

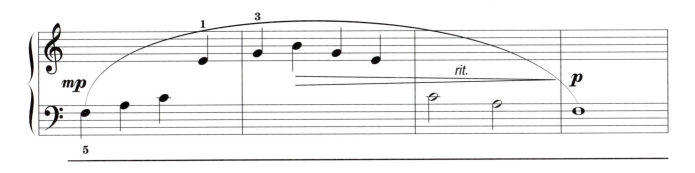

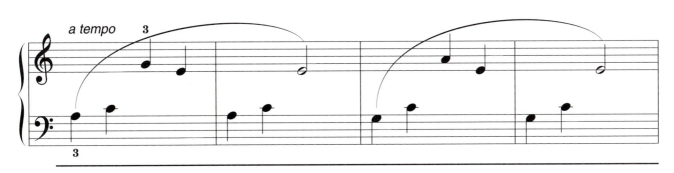

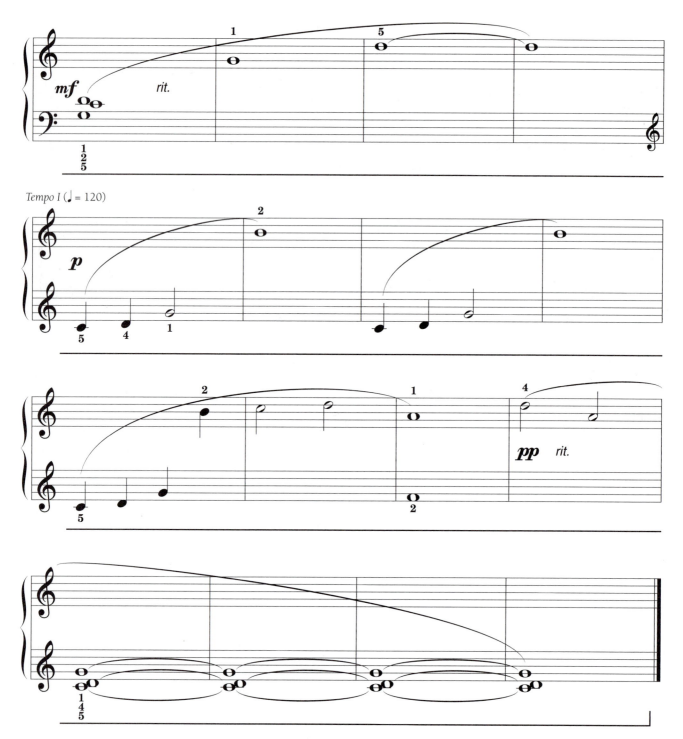

Tempo I (♩ = 120)

Jeanine Yeager is a contemporary American composer who enjoys creating compositions that are fresh and appealing to students. This piece is from a collection of her New Age music, which, as she describes it, "is flowing and resonant and evokes a feeling or mood, frequently one of introspection, peace, and calm."

Little Rondo

Daniel Gottlob Türk (Germany, 1756–1813)

Rondos have been popular since the time of Mozart and Haydn (and Türk). A **rondo** includes an initial section (A) that is repeated, usually in alternation with contrasting sections: A–B–A–C–A, A–B–A–C–A–D–A, and so on.

Bagatelle

Moderato

Anton Diabelli (Austria, 1781–1858)

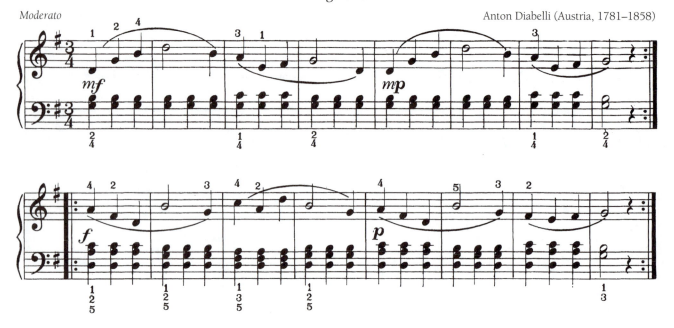

A **bagatelle** is a short, light piece. Bagatelles, minuets, and other short pieces written in the eighteenth century are often in two-part form (A B). Both Diabelli's Bagatelle and Mozart's Minuet in G are examples.

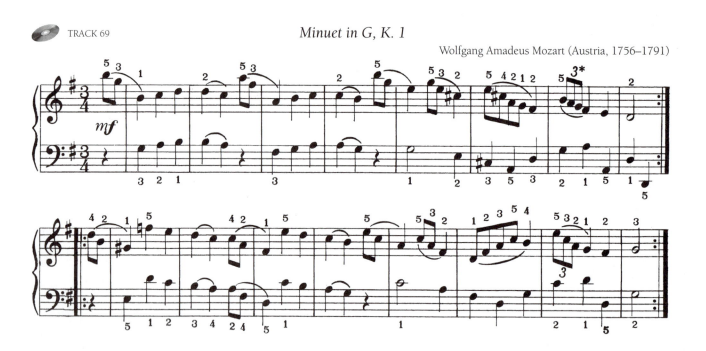

TRACK 69

Minuet in G, K. 1

Wolfgang Amadeus Mozart (Austria, 1756–1791)

Wolfgang Amadeus Mozart was one of the most outstanding composers the world has ever known. A child prodigy, Mozart dazzled audiences with his keyboard prowess and created more than six hundred compositions. This minuet is numbered as his first piece (K. 1), and the other minuet in this supplementary section is numbered K. 2. Both are believed to have been composed when he was just five or six years old.

* ♪♫ is a triplet (three notes of equal value within a beat that normally divides into twos: ♫).

Écossaise

Allegretto

Franz Schubert (Austria, 1797–1828)

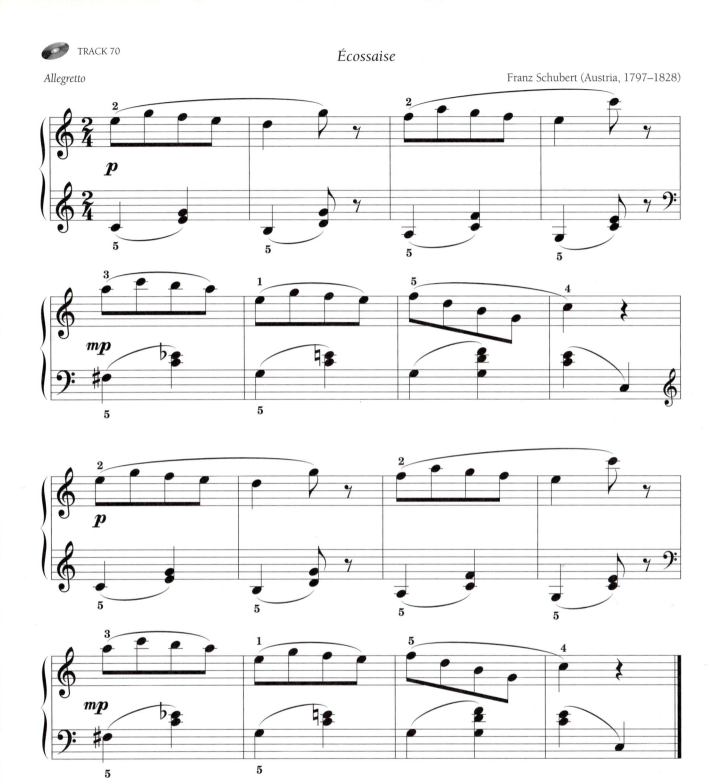

The **écossaise**, a lively English country dance in $\frac{2}{4}$ time, was popular in the eighteenth and nineteenth centuries. Schubert composed stylized écossaises for piano.

Minuet
(from *Notenbuch für Wolfgang*, 1762)

Carl Philipp Emanuel Bach (Germany, 1714–1788)

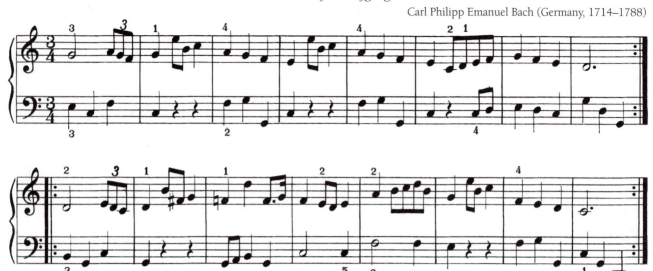

Sons of the great J. S. Bach, Carl Philipp Emanuel Bach and Johann Christoph Friedrich Bach composed keyboard works. C. P. E. Bach, a brilliant keyboard performer, was the author of the important treatise *Essay on the True Art of Playing Keyboard Instruments* (1753). J. C. F. Bach, the second youngest son of Bach's twenty children, was a court chamber musician at Bückeburg, Germany, and is known as the "Bückeburg Bach."

Schwaebisch

Johann Christoph Friedrich Bach (Germany, 1732–1795)

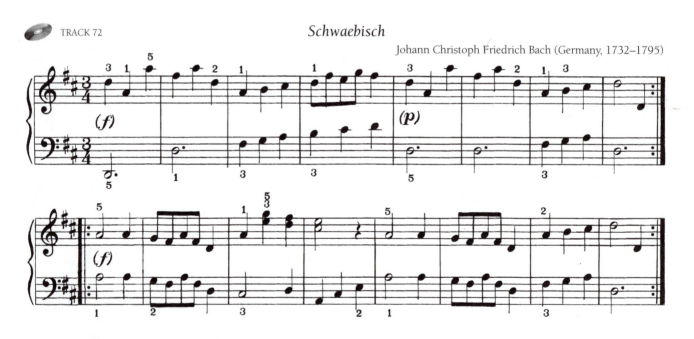

A **schwaebisch** is a rustic dance.

Growing

Emma Lou Diemer (United States, b. 1927)

Moderately slow

Emma Lou Diemer is professor emerita of theory and composition at the University of California, Santa Barbara. Her several hundred compositions include works for orchestra and band, chamber ensemble, organ, piano, and chorus as well as solo songs and song cycles.

Minuet

Allegretto

Jean-Philippe Rameau (France, 1683–1764)

Jean-Philippe Rameau, one of the most influential composers of eighteenth-century France, wrote numerous operas, ballets, and chamber and keyboard pieces; he was also an organist and theorist.

March
(from *Six Children's Pieces*)

Tempo di marcia

Dmitri Shostakovich (Russia, 1906–1975)

Dmitri Shostakovich was one of the leading symphonic composers of the twentieth century. In addition to symphonies, operas, and chamber music, he wrote the keyboard work *Six Children's Pieces* for his daughter Galya.

German Dance No. 2

Franz Joseph Haydn (Austria, 1732–1809)

Oldest of the three leading composers of the Classical period (along with Mozart and Beethoven), Franz Joseph Haydn wrote 104 symphonies, 88 string quartets, and 52 piano sonatas as well as oratorios, choral music, operas, and other keyboard music. He was the court musician to Prince Esterházy, a position he held for decades.

Statement
(from *Little Piano Book,* Op. 60)

Allegro (il ritmo sempre molto preciso)

Vincent Persichetti (United States, 1915–1987)

American composer Vincent Persichetti is perhaps best known for his piano works and music for wind ensembles, but he also wrote nine symphonies and numerous orchestral works, concertos, choral works, chamber music pieces, organ pieces, and songs.

Bourrée
(from *Notenbuch für Wolfgang,* 1762)

Leopold Mozart (Austria, 1719–1787)

Perhaps best known as the father of the famed composer Wolfgang Amadeus Mozart, Leopold Mozart was himself a composer, pianist, and teacher. On his son's seventh birthday, Leopold gave him a personally selected collection of pieces entitled *Note Book for Wolfgang* that included *Bourrée* and a variety of music written by eighteenth-century composers.

A **bourrée** is a popular French dance of the Baroque period in quick duple meter with a short upbeat.

Für Elise
(excerpt)

Poco moto

Ludwig van Beethoven (Germany, 1770–1827)

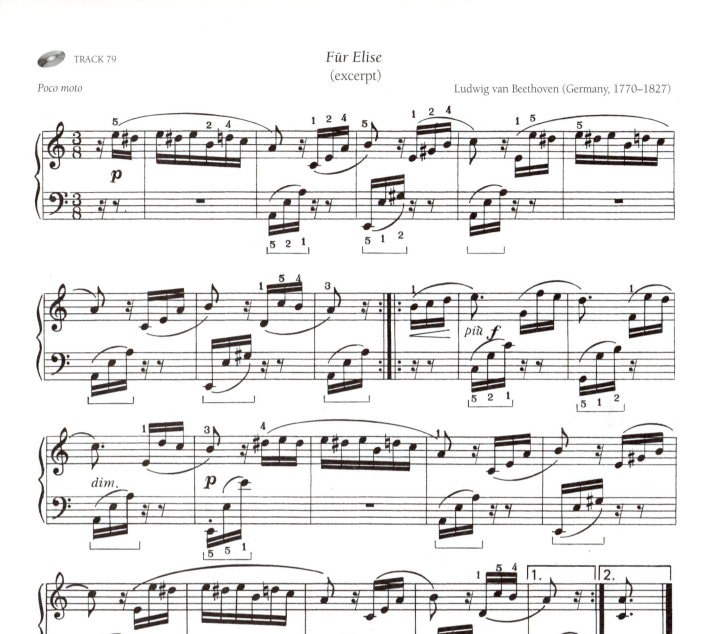

Beethoven was one of the most extraordinary composers of all time. His music represents the culmination of the Classical period and an important beginning to the Romantic period. He composed nine symphonies, string quartets, piano sonatas, an opera, five piano concertos, and chamber music.

Minuet in F, K. 2

Wolfgang Amadeus Mozart (Austria, 1756–1791)

Mozart wrote this minuet in 1762 at the age of six. His minuet, like others of the eighteenth century, is a dance in triple meter and is divided into three sections (A B A).

Op. 39, No. 5
(from *24 Little Pieces*)

Lively

Dmitri Kabalevsky (Russia, 1904–1987)

Kabalevsky, a Russian composer of note, wrote many pieces for beginning pianists. This piece, like other Kabalevsky selections in *PianoLab*, is from his *Twenty-Four Little Pieces*.

Minuet in G
(from *Notenbüchlein für Anna Magdalena Bach,* 1725)

Johann Sebastian Bach (Germany, 1685–1750)

Bach presented his wife, Anna Magdalena, with a music notebook, blank except for its initial entries—two of his keyboard suites. Throughout the years, Anna Magdalena selected pieces—some of them written by her children—and entered them in her notebook. "Minuet in G" is a selection from the notebook.

Theme from 6 Variations on
"Nel cor più non mi sento"

Andantino

Ludwig van Beethoven (Germany, 1770–1827)

Piano variations were very popular with composers of the Classical period. Beethoven wrote over twenty sets of piano variations on original or borrowed themes. "Nel cor più non mi sento" ("Why does my heart feel so dormant") is a theme borrowed from an aria by Giovanni Paisiello.

Pastorale

Herbert Bielawa (United States, b. 1930)

Herbert Bielawa, a composer and professor emeritus of theory and composition at San Francisco State University, has written numerous compositions, including electronic works, chamber music, keyboard works, and a variety of vocal and instrumental pieces.

TRACK 85

Stückchen
(from *Piano Pieces for the Young*, Op. 68)

Nicht schnell

Robert Schumann (Germany, 1810–1856)

Robert Schumann was one of the most important of the many pianist-composers of the nineteenth century. He wrote numerous songs and short piano pieces in addition to symphonies, concertos, and chamber music.

Minuet

Wilhelm Friedemann Bach (Germany, 1710–1784)

Wilhelm Friedemann Bach, the eldest of J. S. Bach's twenty children, was also a composer and keyboardist and wrote numerous keyboard, instrumental, and choral works.

III
(from *For Children*)

Béla Bartók (Hungary, 1881–1945)

Andante

Bartók, though distinguished as a composer of orchestral works, operas, string quartets, and so on, was dedicated to writing accessible music for beginning pianists. This piece is from a collection entitled *For Children*.

Prologue
(from *Little Piano Book,* Op. 60)

Adagio pesante

Vincent Persichetti (United States, 1915–1987)

© 1954, Elkan-Vogel, Inc. Reproduced by permission of the publsiher.

In addition to being a fine composer of music in all genres, Persichetti was a teacher at Juilliard School of Music and wrote the important book *Twentieth-Century Harmony.*

Mazurka No. 3
(from *24 Mazurkas*)

Maria Szymanowska (Poland, 1789–1831)

Maria Szymanowska was acclaimed as one of the greatest women pianists of the nineteenth century and was one of the first women composers of Poland. She composed mainly piano character pieces—that is, etudes, nocturnes, and mazurkas.

Shifting Shadows

Slowly (♪ = 108–116)

Nancy Van de Vate (United States, b. 1930)

Slightly faster (♩ = 63)

Founder of the International League of Women Composers (now part of the International Alliance for Women in Music), Nancy Van de Vate is an American composer of orchestral, chamber, vocal, and keyboard works. Performances of her music are heard around the world.

Prelude, Op. 28, No. 4

Largo

Frédéric Chopin (Poland, 1810–1849)

One of the foremost keyboard composers of the early Romantic period, Frédéric Chopin wrote many mazurkas, etudes, **preludes,** ballades, waltzes, polonaises, and fantasies, and two piano concertos.

TRACK 92

Slow-Walkin' Guy

With a steady, relaxed swing

Tony Caramia

© 1983 by Frances Clark and Louise Goss. From *Sound of Jazz,* Book 1
(Princeton, NJ: New School for Music Study Press, 1983). Used by permission.

Tony Caramia, professor of music at Eastman School of Music, is a contemporary composer and arranger and the coauthor of piano method books.

No Name Blues

Theresa McGlone

Theresa McGlone composed this blues piece while a student in a beginning piano course for nonmusic majors at San Francisco State University.

Just Struttin' Along

Martha Mier (United States, b. 1936)

Moderate blues swing

"Just Struttin' Along" from *Jazz, Rags 'n' Blues*, Book 1, by Martha Mier.
Copyright © 1993 by Alfred Publishing Co., Inc. Used with Permission of the Publisher.

Martha Mier is a piano teacher in Lake City, Florida. In addition to teaching, performing, and adjudicating, she composes and prepares collections of piano music for students of all ages. This piece is from her *Jazz, Rags 'n' Blues*, Book 1.

The Entertainer, A Ragtime Two-Step
(simplified)

Not too fast

Scott Joplin (United States, 1868–1917)

Scott Joplin, the composer, pianist, and undisputed "King of Classical Rag-time," wrote over fifty piano pieces, songs, a ragtime ballet, and two operas.

Blue, Blue, Blue

Matt Zlatunich

Matt Zlatunich composed this blues piece while a student in a beginning piano course for nonmusic majors at San Francisco State University.

Songs with Accompaniments

He's Got the Whole World in His Hands

African American Spiritual

He's got the whole world in his hands, He's got the whole world in his hands, He's got the whole world in his hands, He's got the whole world in his hands.

Kang Ding Ching Ge

Chinese Folk Song

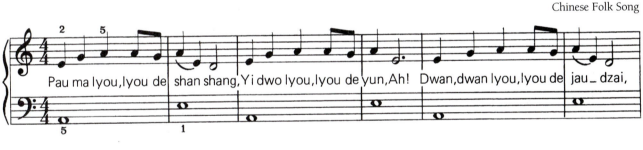

Pau ma lyou, lyou de shan shang, Yi dwo lyou, lyou de yun, Ah! Dwan, dwan lyou, lyou de jau_ dzai,

Kang Ding lyou, lyou de cheng, Ah! Ywe lyang, wan, wan, Kang Ding lyou, lyou de cheng, Ah!

© 1981, Patricia Hackett. Used by permission. (The *Melody Book,* 3rd ed. Englewood Cliffs, N.J.: Prentice-Hall, 1998).

Banks of the Ohio

American Ballad

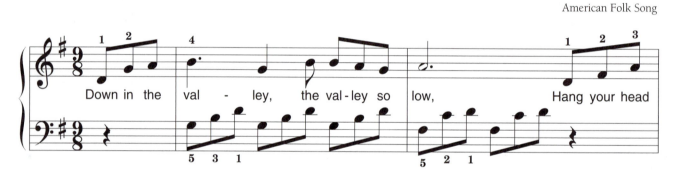

Down in the Valley

American Folk Song

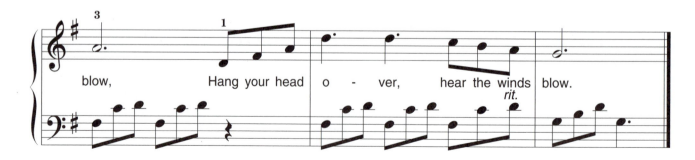

Give My Regards to Broadway

George M. Cohan (United States, 1878–1942)

Silent Night

Joseph Mohr (Austria, 1792–1848)
Franz Gruber (Austria, 1789–1863)

Si - lent night, ho - ly night. All is calm, all is bright,

Round yon vir - gin moth - er and child, Ho - ly in - fant so ten - der and mild,

Sleep in heav - en - ly peace,_____ Sleep__ in heav - en - ly peace.

Amen
(excerpt)

African American Spiritual

A - men, A - men, A - men, A - men, A - men.

We Shall Overcome

American Freedom Melody

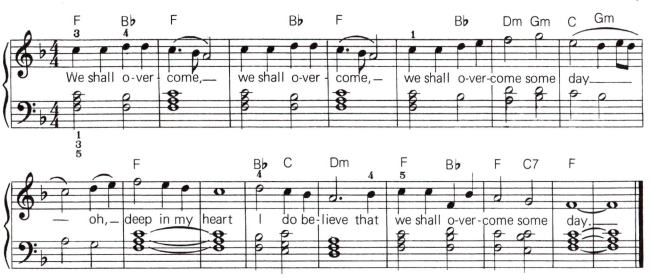

We shall o-ver-come,— we shall o-ver-come,— we shall o-ver-come some day.

— oh,— deep in my heart I do be-lieve that we shall o-ver-come some day.

Morning Has Broken

Eleanor Farjeon
Gaelic Melody

Morn-ing has bro-ken like the first morn-ing, Black-bird has

spo-ken like the first bird. Praise for the sing-ing! Praise for the

morn-ing! Praise for the spring-ing, Fresh from the word.

Take Me Out to the Ball Game

Jack Norworth
Albert von Tilzer (United States, 1873–1956)

America

Samuel F. Smith (United States, 1808–1895)
Henry Carey (England, 1685–1743)
Arranged by Alexander Post

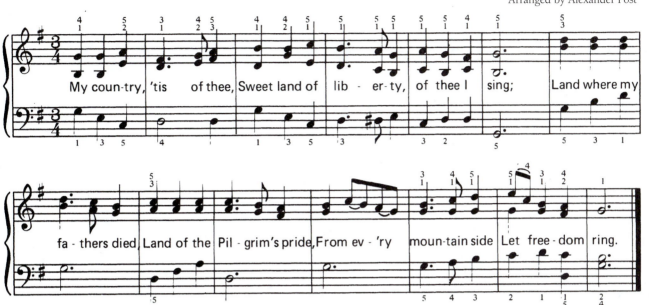

My coun-try, 'tis of thee, Sweet land of lib - er-ty, of thee I sing; Land where my fa - thers died, Land of the Pil - grim's pride, From ev - 'ry moun-tain side Let free - dom ring.

America the Beautiful

Katherine Lee Bates (United States, 1859–1929)
Samuel A. Ward (United States, 1847–1903)
Arranged by Alexander Post

O beau - ti - ful for spa - cious skies, For am - ber waves of grain, For pur - ple moun-tain maj - es-ties, A - bove the fruit - ed plain! A - mer - i - ca! A - mer - i - ca! God shed His grace on thee, And crown thy good with broth-er-hood From sea to shin-ing sea!

Memory
(excerpt rhythmically simplified)
from *Cats*

Trevor Nunn, after T. S. Eliot
Andrew Lloyd Webber (England, b. 1948)

Melodies

The following melodies do not have left-hand accompaniments notated. Rather, suggested chords (by letter-name symbol) appear above each melody. These symbols should serve as a guide for creating your own accompaniments. Refer to Appendix J for explanations of unfamiliar chord symbols.

Since the symbols indicate only the letter name and the chord quality, you may choose to use the root of the chord alone, any chord tone, the entire chord in root position, or the chord in one of the inversions studied earlier. You may also choose the accompaniment style in which to perform the chords. Appendix I has numerous accompaniment patterns to try.

Michael, Row the Boat Ashore

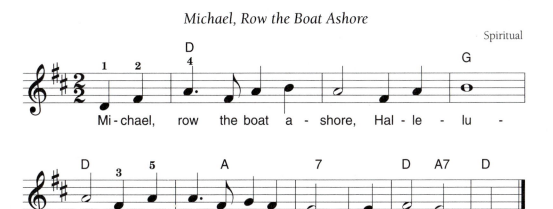

St. James Infirmary

Do, Lord

African American Spiritual

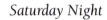

Do, Lord, O do, Lord, O do re-mem-ber me! Do, Lord, O do, Lord, O

do re-mem-ber me! Do, Lord, O do, Lord, O do re-mem-ber

me in the king-dom of Glo-ry to come. _____

Saturday Night

South African Folk Song

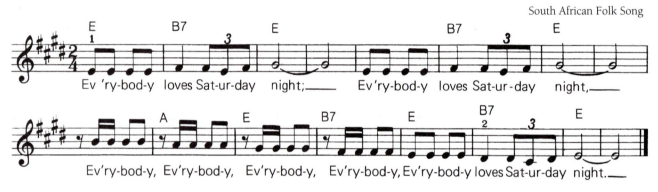

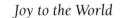

Ev 'ry-bod-y loves Sat-ur-day night;___ Ev'ry-bod-y loves Sat-ur-day night,___

Ev'ry-bod-y, Ev'ry-bod-y, Ev'ry-bod-y, Ev'ry-bod-y, Ev'ry-bod-y loves Sat-ur-day night.___

Joy to the World

Isaac Watts (England, 1674–1748)
George Frideric Handel (Germany, 1685–1759)

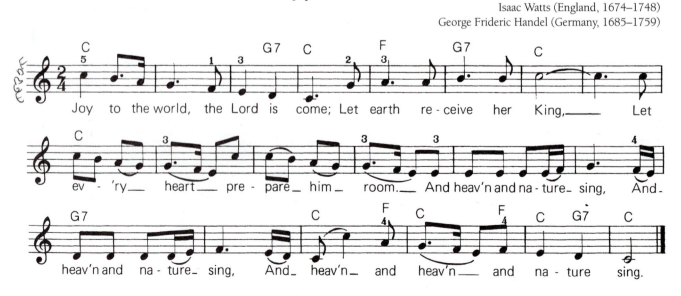

Joy to the world, the Lord is come; Let earth re-ceive her King,___ Let

ev - 'ry___ heart___ pre - pare___ him___ room.___ And heav'n and na - ture___ sing, And___

heav'n and na - ture___ sing, And___ heav'n___ and heav'n___ and na - ture sing.

St. Anthony Chorale

Franz Joseph Haydn (Austria, 1732–1809)

Hey, Lidee

American Folk Song

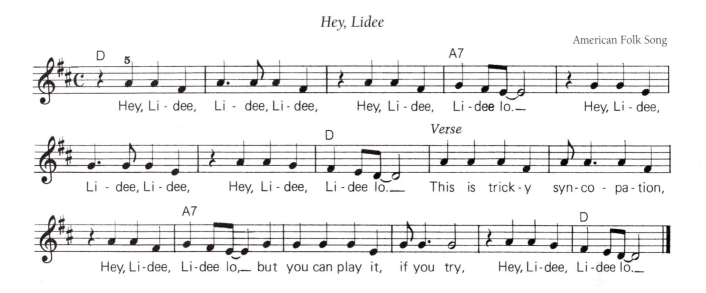

Hey, Li - dee, Li - dee, Li - dee, Hey, Li - dee, Li - dee lo.— Hey, Li - dee,

Li - dee, Li - dee, Hey, Li - dee, Li - dee lo.— This is trick - y syn - co - pa - tion,

Hey, Li - dee, Li - dee lo,— but you can play it, if you try, Hey, Li - dee, Li - dee lo.—

Capriccio in G Major
(excerpt)

Franz Joseph Haydn (Austria, 1732–1809)

Streets of Laredo

American Cowboy Song

As I _____ walked out in the streets of La - re - do, As I walked out in La - re - do one day; I spied a young cow - boy all dressed in his buck - skins, All dressed in his buck - skins and fit for the grave.

Worried Man Blues

American Folk Song

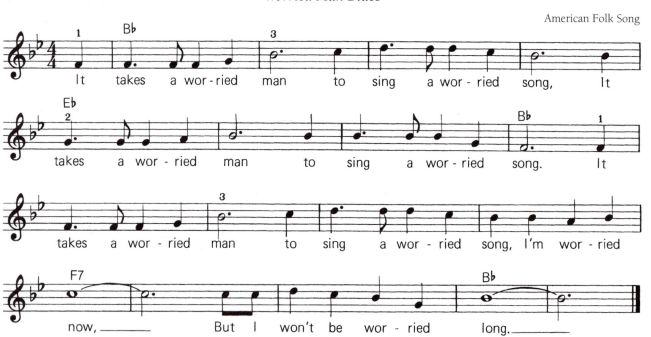

It takes a wor - ried man to sing a wor - ried song, It takes a wor - ried man to sing a wor - ried song. It takes a wor - ried man to sing a wor - ried song, I'm wor - ried now, _____ But I won't be wor - ried long. _____

John B.

Caribbean Folk Song

Oh, we sailed on the sloop, John B., my grand-fath-er and me. 'Round Nas-sau town we_ did roam.__ Drink-in' all night,__ we got in a fight.__ I feel so break-up I want to go home.__ So hoist up the John B. sails, and see how the main-s'l's set. Send for the cap-tain a - shore, lem-me go home,__ lem-me go home!__ Oh, lem-me go home!__ I feel so break-up, I want to go home.__

I Know Where I'm Going

American Folk Song

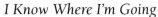

I know where I'm go - ing, And I know who's go - ing with me; I know who I love, ___ And my dear knows who I'll mar - ry. ___

De colores

Traditional Mexian Song
Arranged by Joan Baez

Lyrics line 1:
De __ co - lo - res, de co lo-res se vis-ten los cam-pos en la pri-ma-ve-ra __
Can __ ta el ga-llo, can-ta el ga-llo con el qui-ri qui-ri qui-ri qui-ri qui-ri, __

Lyrics line 2:
__ De __ co - lo-res, de co lo-res son las pa-ja-ri-tos, que vie-nen de a-
__ La __ ga - lli-na, la ga - lli-na con el ca-ra ca-ra ca-ra ca-ra

Lyrics line 3:
fue - ra, __ De. __ co - lo-res, de co-lo-res es el ar-co
ca - ra, __ Los __ po - llue-los, los po - llue-los con el pi-o

Lyrics line 4:
ir - is que ve-mos lu - cir, y por e-so-los gran-des a - mo-res de mu-chos co-
pi - o pi - o pi - o pi

Lyrics line 5:
lo - res me gus-tan a mí. Y por e-so-los gran-des a - mo-res de mu-chos co-

Lyrics line 6:
1. lo - res me gus-tan a mí.
2. lo - res me gus-tan a mí. __

You're a Grand Old Flag

George M. Cohan (United States, 1878–1942)

Aura Lee

American Folk Song

As the black-bird in the spring, 'Neath the wil - low tree,_____

Sat and piped, I heard him sing, Sing - ing Au - ra Lee.

Chorus

Au - ra Lee, Au - ra Lee, Maid of gol - den hair,

Sun - shine came a - long with thee, And swal - lows in the air.

Musical Terms and Signs

DYNAMIC TERMS AND SIGNS

pp   *pianissimo:* very soft

p   *piano:* soft

m p   *mezzo piano:* medium soft

mf   *mezzo forte:* medium loud

f   *forte:* loud

ff   *fortissimo:* very loud

 crescendo (*cresc.*): gradually louder

decrescendo (*decresc.*): gradually softer

diminuendo (*dim., dimin.*): gradually softer

COMMON TEMPO TERMS

largo: very slow

lento: very slow

adagio: slowly, leisurely

larghetto: slow

andante: moderately

andantino: slightly faster than andante

moderato: moderately

allegretto: moderately fast

allegro: fast, lively

vivace: animated, lively

presto: very rapidly

a tempo: return to original tempo

accelerando (*accel.*): gradually increasing tempo

rallentando (*rall.*): gradually becoming slower

ritardando (*rit.*): gradually slower and slower

ritenuto (*riten.*): immediately slowing in tempo

ADDITIONAL TERMS AND SIGNS

accent (>)

affettuoso: with affection, warmth

animato, animé: animated; with spirit

assai: very

calmado: calmly, tranquil

cantabile: in singing style

coda: a concluding section added to the end of a composition

commodo: conveniently, quietly, easily

con: with

con anima: with animation

con moto: with motion

con spirito: with spirit

D.C. (*da capo*): repeat from the beginning

D.C. al coda (*da capo al coda*): return to the beginning and play to the measure marked with coda sign (⊕), concluding with coda

D.C. al fine (*da capo al fine*): return to the beginning and conclude with the measure marked *fine*

D.S. (*dal segno*): repeat from the sign 𝄋

D.S. al coda (*dal segno al coda*): return to the sign 𝄋 and conclude with the coda

D.S. al fine (*dal segno al fine*): return to the sign 𝄋 and conclude with the measure marked *fine*

dolce: sweetly, softly

espressivo: with expression

Fermata (𝄐): hold or pause

fine: the end

giocoso: playfully, humorously

grazioso: gracefully

legato: smoothly, connected

leggiero: light, delicate

loco: place; play as written

lunga: prolonged pause

ma non troppo: but not too much

maestoso: majestically

marcia: in the style of a march

meno: less

molto: much

mosso: agitated

moto: motion; speed; movement

nicht schnell: not fast

ottava alta (8va ⁻ ⁻ ⌐): play an octave higher than written

ottava bassa (8va _ _ ⌐): play an octave lower than written

Pastorale: simple, tender, flowing

per: for, by, from, in

pesante: heavily

più: more

poco: little

preciso: precise

rinforzando (*rf., rfz.*): pronounced accent or stress

risoluto: resolute, bold

ritmo: rhythm

rubato: flexibility of tempo with slight ritards for musical expression

scherzando: playful

sempre: always, continually

sforzando (*sf., sfz.*): a strong accent

simile: in a similar manner

sostenuto: sustained

spirito: spirit, life

staccato (♪): short, detached

subito: suddenly, at once

tenuto (♩): sustain for full value

tranquillo: calm, quiet

très expressif: very expressive

tutti: all (singular: *tutto*)

un: one

valse: waltz

vivo: lively, spiritedly, briskly

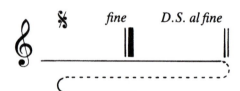

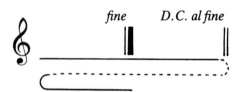

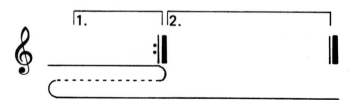

(First and Second Endings)

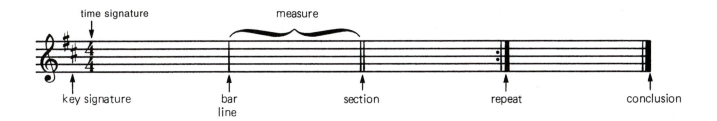

ACCIDENTALS

Accidentals are signs introduced before a note to change the pitch for one measure only. They are placed in the same space or on the same line as the notehead.

♯ (sharp): raises the pitch one half step

♭ (flat): lowers the pitch one half step

♮ (natural): cancels a preceding sharp or flat

✗ (double sharp): raises the pitch of a sharped note an additional half step

♭♭ (double flat): lowers the pitch of a flatted note an additional half step

METRONOME MARKINGS

Tempos are often indicated in *metronome markings*. A *metronome* is a mechanical device that ticks at a desired speed. Composers often specify metronome markings for a particular piece or for sections of a piece. For example, the metronome marking ♩ = 80 indicates that the metronome should be set at 80. The ♩ will be equal to 80 beats or ticks per minute on a metronome and is comparable to the *adagio* (moderately slow) tempo markings.

Sample Metronome Markings

Metronome Setting (no. of beats per min.)	Italian Term	English Term
about 60	*largo*	very slow
about 80	*adagio*	slowly
about 106	*andante*	moderately slow
about 132	*allegro*	fast, lively

Rhythm Notation

NOTES, RESTS, AND BEAMS

Notes

𝅝		whole note
𝅗𝅥		half note
𝅘𝅥		quarter note
𝅘𝅥𝅮		eighth note
𝅘𝅥𝅯		sixteenth note

Rests

▬	whole rest
▬	half rest
𝄾	quarter rest
𝄿	eighth rest
𝅀	sixteenth rest

Dotted Notes

𝅝·	dotted whole note
𝅗𝅥·	dotted half note
𝅘𝅥·	dotted quarter note
𝅘𝅥𝅮·	dotted eighth note
𝅘𝅥𝅯·	dotted sixteenth note

Dotted Rests

▬·	dotted whole rest
▬·	dotted half rest
𝄾·	dotted quarter rest
𝄿·	dotted eighth rest
𝅀·	dotted sixteenth rest

Beams

Single flags take single beams:

Multiple flags take multiple beams:

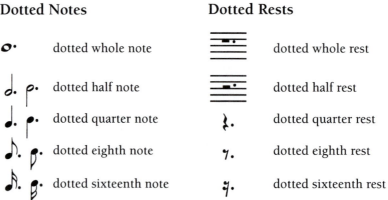

FREQUENTLY USED TIME SIGNATURES IN SIMPLE METER

Duple Meter: $\frac{2}{4}$ $\frac{2}{2}$ or ¢ (alla breve)

Triple Meter: $\frac{3}{8}$ $\frac{3}{4}$ $\frac{3}{2}$

Quadruple Meter: $\frac{4}{8}$ $\frac{4}{2}$ $\frac{4}{4}$ or **C** (common time)

FREQUENTLY USED TIME SIGNATURES IN COMPOUND METER

Compound Duple: $\frac{6}{8}$ $\frac{6}{4}$

Compound Triple: $\frac{9}{8}$ $\frac{9}{4}$

Compound Quadruple: $\frac{12}{8}$ $\frac{12}{4}$

FREQUENTLY USED TIME SIGNATURES IN ASYMMETRIC METER

$$\frac{7}{8} \qquad \frac{7}{4}$$

$$\frac{5}{8} \qquad \frac{5}{4}$$

Treble and Bass Clef Notation/ Octave Identification

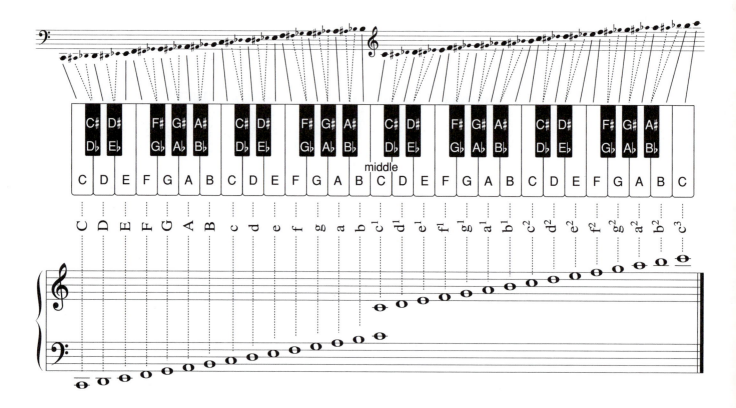

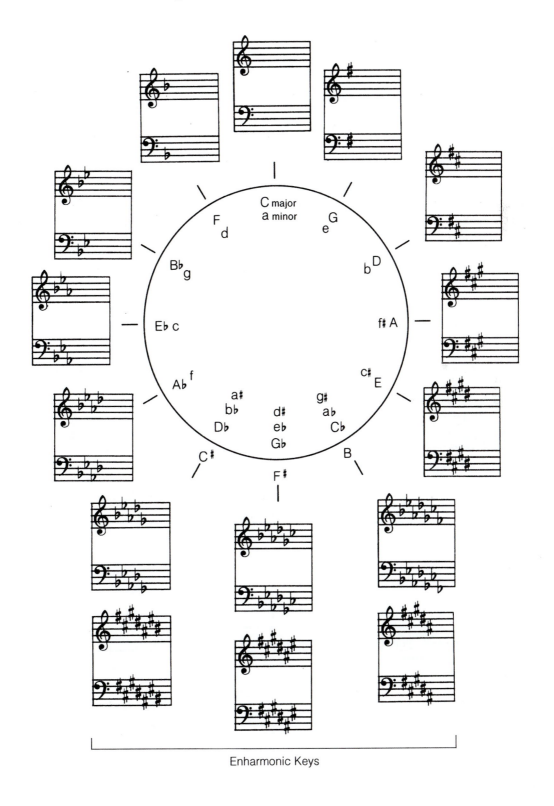

Circle of Fifths
(Major and Minor Keys)

Enharmonic Keys

Major Scales

MAJOR SCALE DEGREES

Number	Name
1	*Tonic*
2	*Supertonic* (one whole step above the tonic)
3	*Mediant* (between 1 and 5 and a third above the tonic)
4	*Subdominant* (a fifth below the tonic)
5	*Dominant* (a fifth above the tonic)
6	*Submediant* (a third below the tonic)
7	*Leading tone* (a half step below the tonic)

MAJOR SCALES (WITH PIANO FINGERINGS)

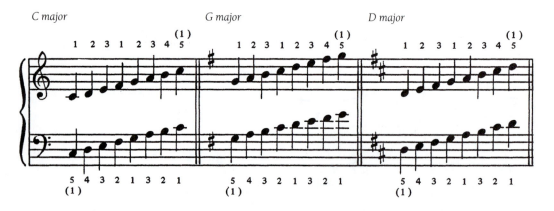

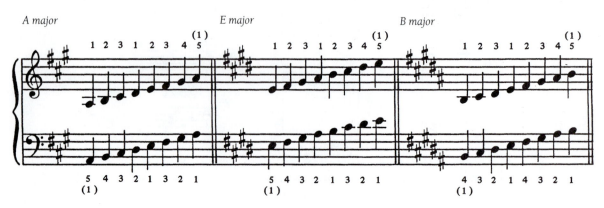

F# major   *C# major*

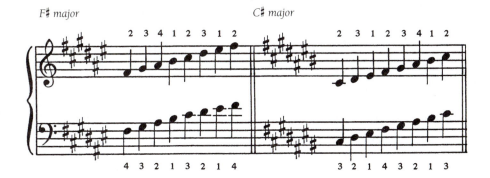

F major   (1)   *B♭ major*   *E♭ major*

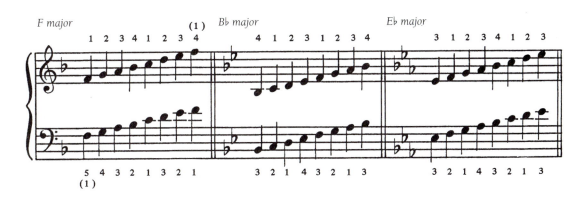

A♭ major   *D♭ major*

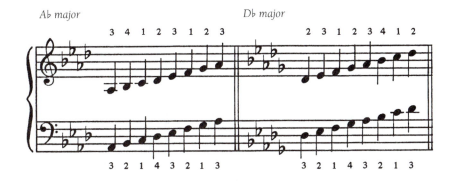

G♭ major   *C♭ major*

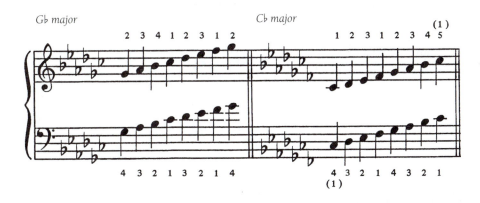

MAJOR SCALES (FINGERINGS FOR TWO-OCTAVE SCALES)

Scale		Fingering		
C major	RH	1 2 3 1 2 3 4	1 2 3 1 2 3 4 5	
	LH	5 4 3 2 1 3 2	1 4 3 2 1 3 2 1	
G major	RH	1 2 3 1 2 3 4̇	1 2 3 1 2 3 4̇ 5	
	LH	5 4 3 2 1 3 2̇	1 4 3 2 1 3 2̇ 1	
D major	RH	1 2 3̇ 1 2 3 4̇	1 2 3̇ 1 2 3 4̇ 5	
	LH	5 4 3̇ 2 1 3 2̇	1 4 3̇ 2 1 3 2̇ 1	
A major	RH	1 2 3̇ 1 2 3̇ 4̇	1 2 3̇ 1 2 3̇ 4̇ 5	
	LH	5 4 3̇ 2 1 3̇ 2̇	1 4 3̇ 2 1 3̇ 2̇ 1	
E major	RH	1 2̇ 3̇ 1 2 3̇ 4̇	1 2̇ 3̇ 1 2 3̇ 4̇ 5	
	LH	5 4̇ 3̇ 2 1 3̇ 2̇	1 4̇ 3̇ 2 1 3̇ 2̇ 1	
B major	RH	1 2̇ 3̇ 1 2̇ 3̇ 4	1 2̇ 3̇ 1 2̇ 3̇ 4 5	
	LH	4 3̇ 2̇ 1 4 3̇ 2̇	1 3̇ 2̇ 1 4 3̇ 2̇ 1	
F♯ major	RH	2̇ 3̇ 4̇ 1 2̇ 3̇ 1	2̇ 3̇ 4̇ 1 2̇ 3̇ 1 2̇	
	LH	4̇ 3̇ 2̇ 1 3̇ 2̇ 1	4̇ 3̇ 2̇ 1 3̇ 2̇ 1 4̇	
C♯ major	RH	2̇ 3̇ 1 2̇ 3̇ 4 1	2̇ 3̇ 1 2̇ 3̇ 4 1 2̇	
	LH	3̇ 2̇ 1 4̇ 3̇ 2̇ 1	3̇ 2̇ 1 4̇ 3̇ 2̇ 1 3̇	
F major	RH	1 2 3 4̇ 1 2 3	1 2 3 4̇ 1 2 3 4	
	LH	5 4 3 2̇ 1 3 2	1 4 3 2̇ 1 3 2 1	
B♭ major	RH	4̇ 1 2 3̇ 1 2 3	4̇ 1 2 3̇ 1 2 3 4̇	
	LH	3̇ 2 1 4̇ 3 2 1	3̇ 2 1 4̇ 3 2 1 3̇	
E♭ major	RH	3̇ 1 2 3̇ 4 1 2	3̇ 1 2 3̇ 4 1 2 3̇	
	LH	3̇ 2 1 4̇ 3 2 1	3̇ 2 1 4̇ 3 2 1 3̇	
A♭ major	RH	3̇ 4̇ 1 2̇ 3̇ 1 2	3̇ 4̇ 1 2̇ 3̇ 1 2 3̇	
	LH	3̇ 2̇ 1 4̇ 3 2 1	3̇ 2̇ 1 4̇ 3 2 1 3̇	
D♭ major	RH	2̇ 3̇ 1 2̇ 3̇ 4̇ 1	2̇ 3̇ 1 2̇ 3̇ 4̇ 1 2̇	
	LH	3̇ 2̇ 1 4̇ 3̇ 2̇ 1	3̇ 2̇ 1 4̇ 3̇ 2̇ 1 3̇	
G♭ major	RH	2̇ 3̇ 4̇ 1 2̇ 3̇ 1	2̇ 3̇ 4̇ 1 2̇ 3̇ 1 2̇	
	LH	4̇ 3̇ 2̇ 1 3̇ 2̇ 1	4̇ 3̇ 2̇ 1 3̇ 2̇ 1 4̇	
C♭ major	RH	1 2̇ 3̇ 1 2̇ 3̇ 4̇	1 2̇ 3̇ 1 2̇ 3̇ 4 5	
	LH	4 3̇ 2̇ 1 4 3̇ 2̇	1 3̇ 2̇ 1 4 3̇ 2̇ 1	

• = black key

Minor Scales

MINOR SCALE DEGREES

Number	Name
1	*Tonic*
2	*Supertonic* (one whole step above the tonic)
3	*Mediant* (between 1 and 5 and a third above the tonic)
4	*Subdominant* (a fifth below the tonic)
5	*Dominant* (a fifth above the tonic)
6	*Submediant* (a third below the tonic)
7	*Leading tone* (a half step below the tonic) or *Subtonic* (a whole step below the tonic)

SELECTED MINOR SCALES (WITH PIANO FINGERINGS)

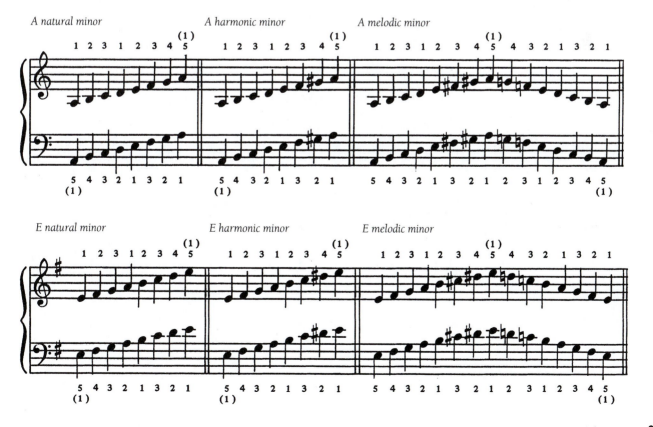

B natural minor

B harmonic minor

B melodic minor

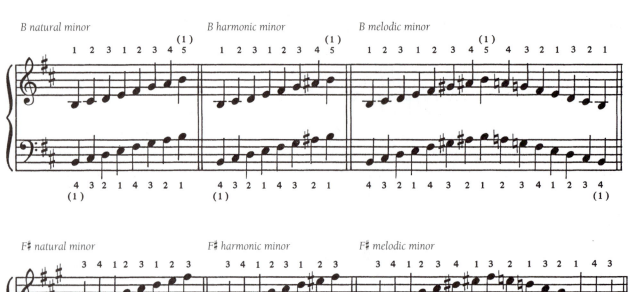

F# natural minor

F# harmonic minor

F# melodic minor

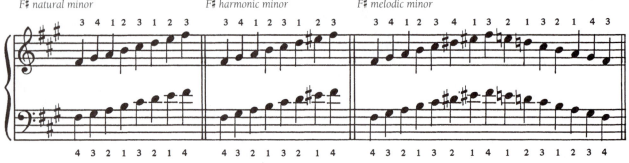

C# natural minor

C# harmonic minor

C# melodic minor

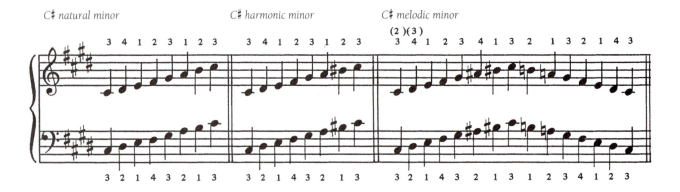

D natural minor

D harmonic minor

D melodic minor

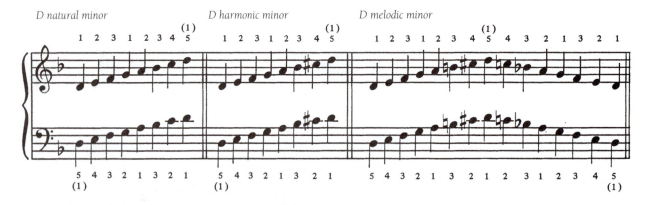

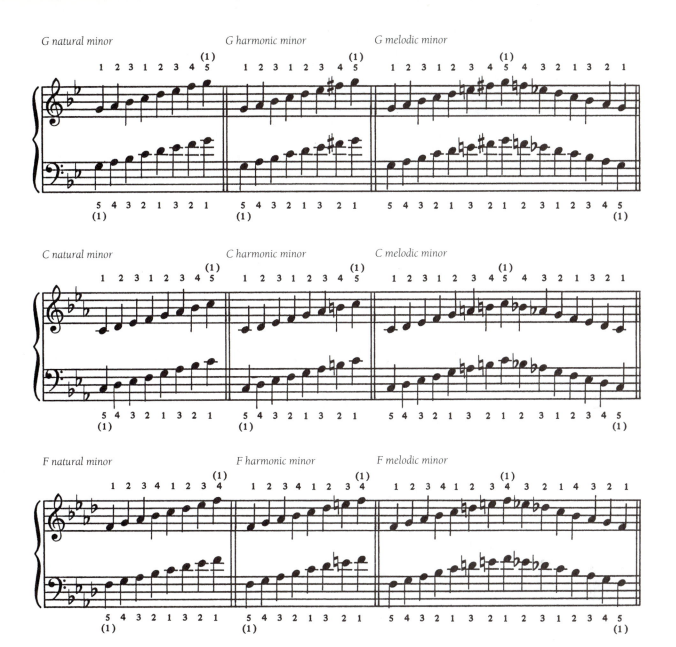

SELECTED HARMONIC MINOR SCALES
(FINGERINGS FOR TWO-OCTAVE SCALES)

Scale		Fingering	
A harmonic	RH	1 2 3 1 2 3 4̇	1 2 3 1 2 3 4̇ 5
	LH	5 4 3 2 1 3 2̇	1 4 3 2 1 3 2̇ 1
E harmonic	RH	1 2̇ 3 1 2 3 4̇	1 2̇ 3 1 2 3 4̇ 5
	LH	5 4̇ 3 2 1 3 2̇	1 4 3 2 1 3 2̇ 1
B harmonic	RH	1 2̇ 3 1 2̇ 3 4	1 2̇ 3 1 2 3 4̇ 5
	LH	4 3̇ 2 1 4̇ 3 2̇	1 3 2 1 4 3 2̇ 1
F♯ harmonic	RH	3̇ 4̇ 1 2 3̇ 1 2	3̇ 4̇ 1 2 3̇ 1 2 3̇
	LH	4̇ 3̇ 2 1 3̇ 2 1	4̇ 3̇ 2 1 3̇ 2 1 4̇
C♯ harmonic	RH	3̇ 4̇ 1 2̇ 3̇ 1 2	3̇ 4̇ 1 2̇ 3̇ 1 2 3̇
	LH	3̇ 2̇ 1 4̇ 3̇ 2 1	3̇ 2̇ 1 4̇ 3̇ 2 1 3̇
D harmonic	RH	1 2 3 1 2 3̇ 4̇	1 2 3 1 2 3̇ 4̇ 5
	LH	5 4 3 2 1 3̇ 2̇	1 4 3 2 1 3̇ 2̇ 1
G harmonic	RH	1 2 3̇ 1 2 3̇ 4	1 2 3̇ 1 2 3̇ 4̇ 5
	LH	5 4 3̇ 2 1 3̇ 2̇	1 4 3̇ 2 1 3̇ 2̇ 1
C harmonic	RH	1 2 3̇ 1 2 3̇ 4	1 2 3̇ 1 2 3̇ 4 5
	LH	5 4 3̇ 2 1 3̇ 2	1 4 3̇ 2 1 3̇ 2 1
F harmonic	RH	1 2 3̇ 4̇ 1 2̇ 3	1 2 3̇ 4̇ 1 2̇ 3 4
	LH	5 4 3̇ 2̇ 1 3̇ 2	1 4 3̇ 2̇ 1 3̇ 2 1

• = black key

Intervals and Chords

INTERVALS

An *interval* is the pitch distance between two tones. Intervals are identified by the number of steps they encompass and by quality. The five qualities are as follows: perfect (P), major (M), minor (m), diminished (d or °), and augmented (A or +).

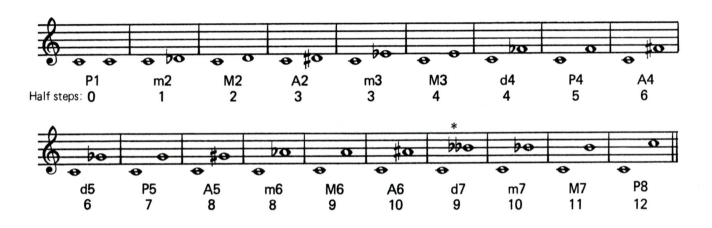

	P1	m2	M2	A2	m3	M3	d4	P4	A4
Half steps:	0	1	2	3	3	4	4	5	6

	d5	P5	A5	m6	M6	A6	d7	m7	M7	P8
	6	7	8	8	9	10	9	10	11	12

TRIADS

The four kinds of triads (three-note chords) are *major, minor, augmented,* and *diminished.*

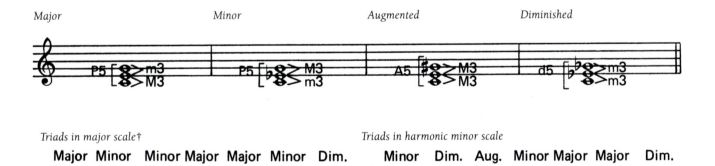

Major   Minor   Augmented   Diminished

Triads in major scale†

Major Minor Minor Major Major Minor Dim.

C: I ii iii IV V vi vii°

Triads in harmonic minor scale

Minor Dim. Aug. Minor Major Major Dim.

a: i ii° III+ iv V VI vii°

*♭♭ **(double flat)**. A double flat lowers a pitch one whole step.

†Chords built on steps 1, 4, and 5 of a major or a minor scale are primary chords. Chords built on steps 2, 3, 6, and 7 are **secondary chords.**

SEVENTH CHORDS

The seventh chord consists of four notes: a triad with an added third. There are five types of seventh chords: *major-minor, major-major, minor-minor, diminished-minor,* and *diminished-diminished.* Each seventh chord also has a common name, shown in the following chart. Use the terms recommended by your instructor. See also Appendix J.

Seventh Chord Type	Symbols	Common Name
Major-minor seventh	7 or Mm7	Dominant seventh
Major-major seventh	maj7 or MM7	Major seventh
Minor-minor seventh	m7 or mm7	Minor seventh
Diminished-minor seventh	half-dim7	Half-diminished seventh
Diminished-diminished seventh	dim7 or dd7	Diminished seventh

Major-minor (dominant) seventh chord

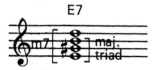

Major-major seventh chord

Minor-minor seventh chord

Half-diminished seventh chord

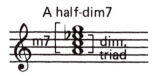

Diminished seventh chord

appendix H

Primary Chords in Selected Major and Minor Keys

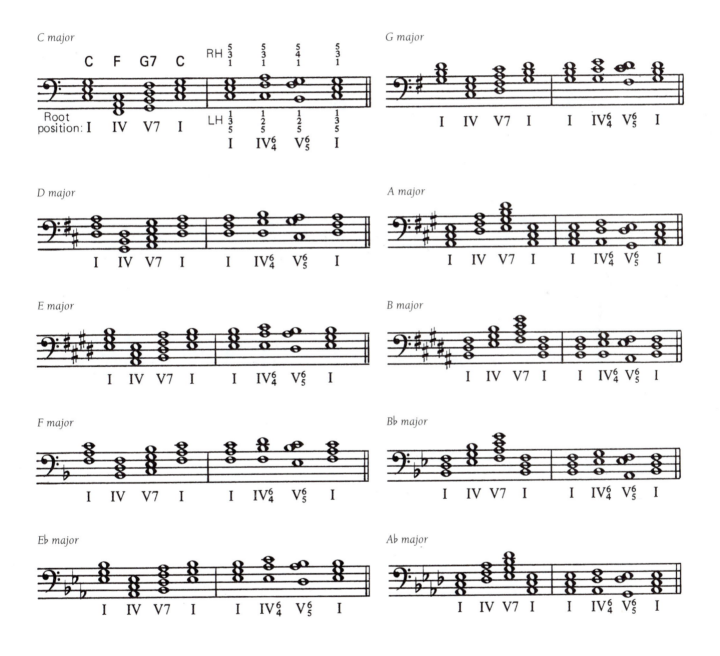

Db major

I IV V7 I   I IV⁶₄ V⁶₅ I

Gb major

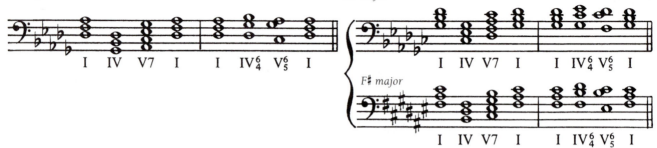

I IV V7 I   I IV⁶₄ V⁶₅ I

F♯ major

I IV V7 I   I IV⁶₄ V⁶₅ I

A harmonic minor

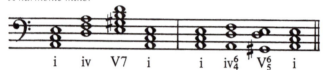

i iv V7 i   i iv⁶₄ V⁶₅ i

E harmonic minor

i iv V7 i   i iv⁶₄ V⁶₅ i

B harmonic minor

i iv V7 i   i iv⁶₄ V⁶₅ i

F♯ harmonic minor

i iv V7 i   i iv⁶₄ V⁶₅ i

C♯ harmonic minor

i iv V7 i   i iv⁶₄ V⁶₅ i

D harmonic minor

i iv V7 i   i iv⁶₄ V⁶₅ i

G harmonic minor

i iv V7 i   i iv⁶₄ V⁶₅ i

C harmonic minor

i iv V7 i   i iv⁶₄ V⁶₅ i

F harmonic minor

i iv V7 i   i iv⁶₄ V⁶₅ i

Accompaniment Patterns

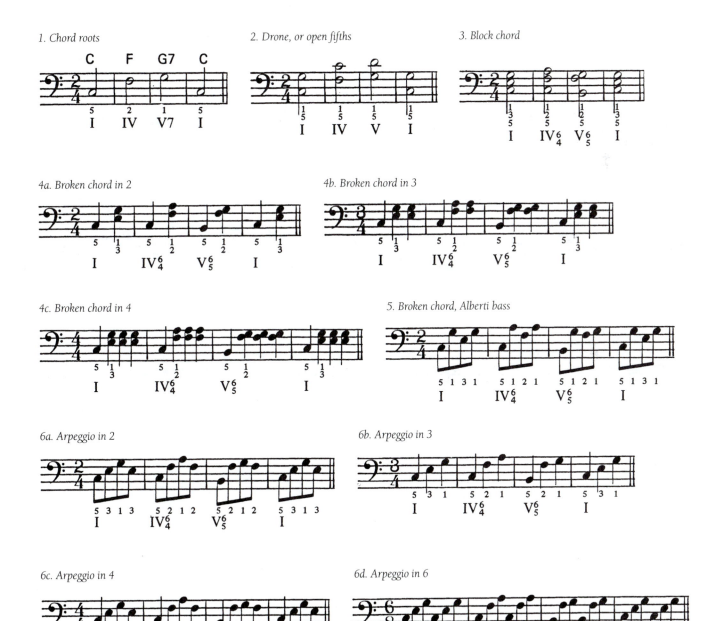

7. Arpeggiated, or rolled chords

I   IV⁶₄   V⁶₅   I

8a. Jump bass (easy stride)   *or*

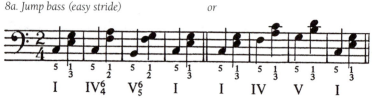

I IV⁶₄ V⁶₅ I   I IV V I

8b. Jump bass (full stride)   *or*

I   IV⁶₄   V⁶₅   I   I   IV   V7   I

9. Boogie bass

I   IV   V   I

10. Boogie-woogie walking bass

I7   IV7   V7   I7

11. Boogie-woogie barrel-house bass

I   IV   V   I

12. Rocking bass

13. Rock bass

14. Funk-rock bass

15. Blues bass

16. Western bass

17. Walking bass

18. Rock rhythm

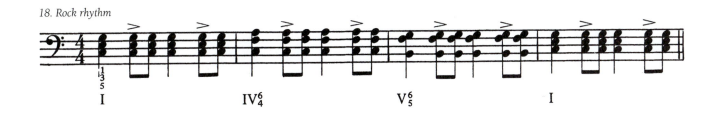

19. Rock ostinato

I   IV   V   IV

20. Habañera

Chords and Chord Symbols (Lead Sheet Notation)

KEY FOR CHORD SYMBOLS

1. A capital letter indicates a major triad.

2. A capital letter followed by a lowercase *m* indicates a minor triad.

3. A capital letter followed by *dim* or a small circle (°) indicates a diminished triad.

4. A capital letter followed by *aug* or a plus sign (+) indicates an augmented triad.

5. When any of the preceding letters and symbols are followed by the numeral 7, a seventh chord is indicated. (See also Appendix G.)

6. When any of the preceding letters and symbols are followed by a 6, a major sixth is added above the root.

*✗ **(double sharp)**. A double sharp raises a pitch one whole step.

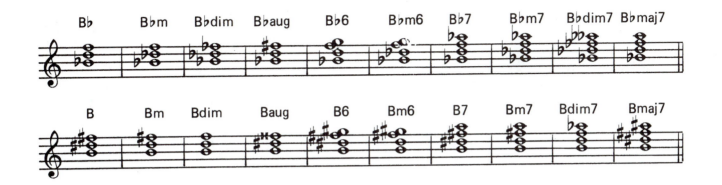

CHORDS OVER BASS NOTES

In jazz and popular music, chords are often superimposed over a bass note. In such cases, two capital letters, separated by a slash (/), are used—for example, C/G or Cm7/F. The first symbol indicates the chord to be played and the second symbol specifies the bass notes.

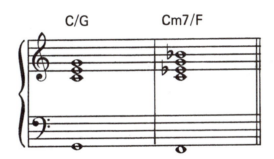

Timeline of Western Art Music and Keyboard Instruments

Musical Style Periods	Medieval ca. 500–ca. 1420	Renaissance ca. 1420–ca. 1600	Baroque ca. 1600–ca. 1750
Music Elements	*Melody:* moves mostly in steps; limited vocal range; uses church modes	*Melody:* moves mostly in steps; expanded vocal range	*Melody:* moves in steps and skips; sequential; use of ornamentation
	Harmony: monophonic; polyphonic for 2 to 4 voices; use of imitation in 14th c.	*Harmony:* 4 parts; use of imitation; dissonance (cadence points); text painting	*Harmony:* major-minor scales; polyphonic; homophonic; chord progressions I–IV–V
	Rhythm: moves in free chant rhythm; beat groupings of 3s in 13th c.; beat groupings of 2s in 14th c.	*Rhythm:* beat groupings of 2s; syncopation; more complex rhythms	*Rhythm:* free (recitative); steady, clear meters
	Form: free vocal chant forms; songs with verses, hymns; free and fixed poetic forms for secular music	*Form:* fixed poetic forms are replaced by imitation; songs with verses; hymns	*Form:* A B and A B A; fugue; development of multimovement compositions
	Tone color: small choirs (monophonic chants); soloists (polyphonic music); instrumental music (generally improvised)	*Tone color:* polyphonic; 5 or more voices in 16th c.; homophony; music for specific instruments; secular: soloists, small ensembles; sacred: small choirs, polyphony	*Tone color:* small choral groups; small orchestras—strings, winds, continuo; soloists
Types of Compositions	Mass; plainchant setting of parts of the Mass; motet (mostly secular); secular songs; instrumental dances	polyphonic settings of parts of Mass; motet; secular songs; instrumental dances; instrumental pieces	Mass and motet with instrumental accompaniment; opera; cantata; oratorio; sonata; concerto; fugue; suite
The Development of Keyboard Instruments	Organ (portative/positive)		Simplified church organ (pipe)
		Fretted clavichord	Unfretted clavichord
		Harpsichord	
		Virginal	

Classic ca. 1750–ca. 1820	Romantic ca. 1820–ca. 1900	Contemporary ca. 1900–
Melody: motivic; short phrases, 8-bar phrases	*Melody:* lyrical; phrases less regular; longer phrases	*Melody:* tone rows
Harmony: major-minor scales; use of modulation; change of key within a movement; homophony	*Harmony:* major-minor scales; expanded use of modulation and chromaticism; harmony; counterpoint	*Harmony:* major-minor scales; atonal; new methods of tonal harmony; homophony; counterpoint; polytonality
Rhythm: free (recitative), clear meters; rhythmic variety	*Rhythm:* variety of meters; varied rhythmic patterns; meter change within movements	*Rhythm:* variety of meters; varied rhythmic patterns; shifting meter, asymmetric meter
Form: sonata; rondo; theme and variations; A B and A B A; multimovement compositions	*Form:* multimovement works; classical forms are expanded	*Form:* forms of all previous periods are used, with extensive changes; freer forms developed
Tone color: instruments more prominent than voice; larger orchestras—without use of continuo	*Tone color:* growth of orchestra; large chorus; large bands; small ensembles	*Tone color:* same as previous period; large bands; emphasis on percussive sound
Mass; oratorio; opera; solo concerto; unaccompanied sonata; instrumental works: symphony, concerto, sonata, string quartet	classical forms are expanded; symphonic poem; solo song cycle; piano character piece	forms from all previous periods are used and expanded; impressionism; expressionism; electronic music; minimalism; new age music

Electronic (rotary-powered organ)

Pianoforte	Upright piano	Electronic piano
		Celesta
		Synthesizer Electronic keyboards
		Digital piano

Glossary

A B A musical form consisting of two sections, A and B, that contrast with each other (binary).

A B A A musical form consisting of three sections, A B A. Two are the same and the middle one is different (ternary).

accent A stress or emphasis given to certain tones. An accent sign is >.

accidental A sign introduced before a note of a composition that changes the pitch for one measure only: ♯ (sharp), ♭ (flat), ♮ (natural).

accompaniment Music that goes with or provides harmonic or rhythmic support for another musical part (usually a melody).

Alberti bass A left-hand accompaniment (named after the eighteenth-century keyboard composer Domenico Alberti) consisting of a figure of broken chords.

alla breve (¢) A term indicating two beats to a measure (duple meter); usually stands for $\frac{2}{2}$.

anacrusis An upbeat or unaccented note(s) found in the incomplete measure at the beginning of a phrase of music.

arpeggio, arpeggiated A pattern in which every tone of the chord is played separately, one after the other.

asymmetric meter Meter in which the beat groupings are irregular, as $\frac{5}{4}$ or $\frac{7}{8}$. Often created by combining two meters: $\frac{2}{4}$ and $\frac{3}{4} = \frac{5}{4}$.

atonal Describes twentieth-century music in which no tonic or key center is apparent.

augmented triad A three-note chord built with two major thirds.

authentic cadence A cadence in which the dominant chord (V) precedes the tonic (I).

bagatelle A short, light composition, usually for piano.

bar or **bar line** A vertical line through the staff to indicate a boundary for a measure of music.

Baroque period The period in music history spanning approximately the years 1600–1750.

bass clef The symbol 𝄢, which determines that the fourth line of the staff is F below middle C.

beat The underlying steady pulse present in most music; the rhythmic unit to which one responds in marching or dancing.

beat groupings *See* **meter.**

binary form A musical form consisting of two sections, A and B, that contrast with each other.

bitonality The use of two different scales/tonalities simultaneously.

blue notes Notes that are lowered—usually the third and the seventh tones of a major scale; often used in popular music and jazz.

blues Sorrow songs created by African Americans that influenced the development of jazz. Special characteristics include flatted third and seventh scale tones, the use of groups of twelve measures, seventh chords, syncopation, and improvisation.

blues scale A scale that can only be approximated in traditional notation or on the keyboard; a major scale with the third and the seventh pitches lowered a half step (the fifth is also lowered a half step in some bebop music).

boogie-woogie A jazz piano style (fast blues) in which the left hand repeats a fast-moving bass (generally moving through tonic, subdominant, and dominant harmonies) while the right hand improvises a melody part.

bourrée (BU-ray) A popular French dance of the Baroque period, in quick duple meter, with a short upbeat.

breve A note value that is equivalent to two whole notes, written as 𝄺 or 𝅜.

cadence A point of arrival that punctuates a musical phrase, section, and composition.

canon A musical form in which all parts have the same melody throughout but start at different times. A round is a type of canon.

celesta A percussion instrument in the form of a small upright piano; its tone is produced by the striking of steel bars with hammers connected to a keyboard by a simplified piano action.

chamber music Music played by small groups such as a piano trio or a string quartet.

chorale A hymn tune.

chord A combination of three or more pitches a third apart, sounded together.

chord progression A series of chords sounding in succession.

chord root The pitch on which a chord is constructed; the most important pitch in the chord.

chord tones The individual pitches within a chord.

chromatic scale A twelve-tone scale consisting entirely of half steps.

circle of fifths The key signatures of the major and minor keys arranged in a circular sequence of perfect fifths.

classical music A term for art music of Western European civilization, usually created by a trained composer.

Classical period The period in music history spanning approximately the years 1750–1820.

clavichord A stringed keyboard instrument used from the fifteenth through the eighteenth centuries; instead of hammers striking the strings as on a piano, tangents (upright metal wedges) strike the strings.

clef sign A symbol placed on a staff to designate a precise pitch that identifies the other pitches in the score.

compound meter A grouping of beats (meter) in which the beat is divided into three equal parts.

Contemporary period The period in music that is current.

continuo Abbreviation for basso continuo; the continuous bass part that was performed by the harpsichord or organ in works of the Baroque period and served as the basis for harmonies.

contour The shape of a melodic line.

contrary motion A type of motion in which two or more parts move in opposite directions.

damper pedal The piano pedal to the far right that, when pressed down, releases the dampers from the strings and allows the strings to vibrate freely, sustaining the sound; generally, used to produce a legato effect.

diatonic A seven-tone scale, consisting of five whole steps and two half steps, utilizing every pitch name. Major and minor scales are diatonic scales.

diminished triad A three-note chord built with two minor thirds.

dominant The fifth tone or chord of a major or minor scale.

dominant seventh chord A four-note chord constructed on the fifth degree of the scale with a minor seventh added above the root.

double flat A symbol that indicates that the written pitch is to be lowered two half steps: ♭♭.

double sharp A symbol that indicates that the written pitch is to be raised two half steps: ✗.

downbeat The first beat of a measure, usually accented.

drone An accompaniment created by sounding one or more tones (usually two, five notes apart) simultaneously and continuously throughout a composition or section of a composition; a special type of harmony.

duet A composition written for two performers.

duple meter A grouping of beats (meter) into two ($\frac{2}{4}$, $\frac{2}{2}$).

duration The length of time a musical tone sounds.

dynamics The degree and range of loudness of musical sounds.

écossaise A lively English country dance popular in the eighteenth and early nineteenth centuries.

electronic music Music made by creating, altering, and imitating sounds electronically.

enharmonic tones Tones sounding the same pitch or key on the keyboard but written differently, as E-flat and D-sharp.

etude French word meaning "study"; a technical study designed to facilitate technique.

expressionism A musical style of the early twentieth century in which irregular rhythms, jagged melody lines, and dissonances were used to express strong subjective feelings.

F clef *See* **bass clef.**

fermata A musical sign indicating that the designated note, chord, or rest is to be held beyond its normal duration: ⌒.

figured bass A system of arabic numerals used in the Baroque period to indicate specific chord inversions.

flat A symbol that indicates that the written pitch is to be lowered a half step: ♭.

folk song A song having no known composer, usually transmitted orally, and reflecting the musical consensus of a cultural group.

form The plan, order, or design in which a piece of music is organized, incorporating repetition and contrast.

G clef *See* **treble clef.**

gavotte A French dance in moderately quick duple meter, often with an upbeat of two quarter notes.

glissando A very rapid sliding passage up or down the white and black keys.

grace note A short note, printed in small type, that ornaments the note that follows it. A grace note is not counted in the rhythm of the measure.

grand or **great staff** Treble and bass clef staves joined together by a vertical line and a bracket.

half step An interval comprising two adjacent pitches, as C to C♯.

harmonic minor scale A minor scale in which the pattern of whole and half steps is: whole, half, whole, whole, half, whole & half, half.

harmony A simultaneous sounding of two or more tones.

harpsichord A keyboard instrument, popular in the Renaissance and Baroque periods; instead of hammers striking the strings as on a piano, the strings are plucked by quills.

homophonic A musical texture in which all parts move in the same rhythm but use different pitches, as in hymns; also, a melody supported by chords.

hymn A religious song; usually a metric poem to be sung by a congregation.

imitation The restatement of a theme in different voices (parts).

impressionism A musical style of the late nineteenth and early twentieth centuries, in which musical textures and timbres were used to convey impressions (hint) rather than make precise "statements."

improvisation Music performed extemporaneously, often within a framework determined by the musical style.

indeterminate music "Chance" music emphasizing improvisation within limitations set by the composer.

interval The distance between two tones, named by counting all pitch names involved; a harmonic interval occurs when two pitches are sounded simultaneously, and a melodic interval occurs when two pitches are sounded successively.

inversion The rearrangement of the pitches of a chord, for example, CEG becomes GCE; performing a melody by turning the contour upside down.

jazz A style that originated with African Americans in the early twentieth century, characterized by improvisation and syncopated rhythms.

key The scale and tonality of a composition.

key signature The sharps or the flats at the beginning of the staff, after the clef sign, indicating in which key or on what scale the composition is written.

leading tone The seventh tone or triad of a major or a harmonic or melodic minor scale.

leger or **ledger lines** (LEH-jer) Short lines above or below the five-line staff on which higher or lower pitches may be indicated.

major interval An interval a half step larger than the corresponding minor interval.

major scale A scale in which the pattern of whole and half steps is: whole, whole, half, whole, whole, whole, half.

major triad A three-note chord with a major third and a minor third.

march A composition written in duple meter with a strong, vigorous rhythm and regular phrases.

mazurka A Polish dance in quick triple meter with strong emphasis on beat 2 or 3.

measure A unit of beats delineated by bar lines; informally called a "bar."

mediant The third tone or triad of a major or minor scale.

Medieval period Also called Middle Ages; the earliest period in Western music history, spanning approximately the years 500–1420.

melodic minor scale A minor scale in which the ascending pattern of whole and half steps is: whole, half, whole, whole, whole, whole, half, whereas the descending pattern is identical with the natural minor scale.

melodic rhythm Durations of pitches used in a melody.

melody A succession of sounds (pitches) and silences moving one at a time through time.

meter The grouping of beats in music.

meter signature Two numerals that show the number of beats grouped in a measure and the basic beat: $\frac{3}{4}$.

middle C The C midway between the treble and bass clefs; approximately midway on the piano keyboard.

minimalism A twentieth-century musical style in which the musical elements are subjected to a minimal amount of development; an attempt to simplify music by using the fewest of means.

minor interval An interval a half step smaller than the corresponding major interval.

minor scale A scale in which one characteristic feature is a half step between the second and third tones. There are three forms of the minor scale: natural, harmonic, and melodic.

minor triad A three-note chord that includes a minor third and a major third.

minuet A dance in triple meter with an elegant, graceful quality of movement; of French origin.

modes Scales (each with seven notes) consisting of various patterns of whole and half steps. The seven possible modes—Ionian, Dorian, Phrygian, Lydian, Mixolydian, Aeolian, and Locrian—were used in the Medieval and Renaissance periods and served as the basis from which major and minor scales emerged.

modulation The change from one key to another within a composition.

monophonic A musical texture created when a single melody is heard without accompaniment.

motive A brief rhythmic or melodic figure that recurs throughout a composition as a unifying element.

musical style The characteristic manner in which the musical elements—melody, rhythm, harmony, and form—are treated in a piece of music.

natural A sign that cancels a sharp or a flat: ♮. A note that is neither sharp nor flat, as C, D, E, F, G, A, B on the piano keyboard.

natural minor scale A minor scale in which the pattern of whole and half steps is: whole, half, whole, whole, half, whole, whole.

neighboring tones Tones placed a step above (upper neighbor) or a step below (lower neighbor) two repeated pitches.

notes Symbols used to represent durational sounds.

oblique motion A type of motion in which one part remains stationary while the other parts move.

octave The interval in which two pitches share the same letter name (C-C) and are eight steps apart (eight lines and spaces from one note to the next); one pitch with twice the frequency of the other.

opus (op.) A composition or group of compositions with designated numbers that indicate the chronological position of the composition(s) in the composer's total output.

organ A keyboard wind instrument consisting of a series of pipes standing on a wind chest; features one or more keyboards, operated by a player's hands and feet. The portative organ was a small portable organ of the late Middle Ages; the positive organ was a self-contained, medium-sized organ also used in the Middle Ages.

ostinato A continuous repetition of a melodic or rhythmic pattern.

parallel keys The major and minor scales that share the same tonic but have different key signatures.

parallel motion A type of motion in which two or more parts move in the same direction.

passing tones Tones placed stepwise between chord tones.

pattern *See* **motive.**

pedals Levers operated by the feet on pianos and organs; pianos have a damper pedal, a sostenuto pedal, and an una corda pedal.

pentatonic scale A five-tone scale often identified with the pattern of the black keys of the piano. Many other five-tone arrangements are possible.

phrase A musical segment with a clear beginning and ending, comparable to a simple sentence or a clause in speech.

plagal cadence A cadence in which the subdominant chord (IV) precedes the tonic (I).

polyphonic A musical texture created when two or more melodies sound simultaneously.

polytonal Music that employs two or more tonalities (or keys) simultaneously.

prelude An introductory piece for a larger composition or drama, usually written for a solo instrument; in the nineteenth century, "prelude" was used as the title for piano character pieces.

primary chords The three chords built on the first degree (I), the fourth degree (IV), and the fifth degree (V) of any major or harmonic or melodic minor scale.

progression *See* **chord progression.**

quadruple meter A grouping of beats into four ($\frac{4}{4}$, $\frac{4}{8}$, $\frac{4}{2}$).

ragtime Piano music, developed at the turn of the century, that features a syncopated melody against a steady "oom PAH" bass; piano "rags" are usually divided into three or four different sections—each symmetrical in length.

relative keys The major and minor scales that share the same key signature but different tonics.

Renaissance period The period in Western music history spanning approximately the years 1420–1600.

repeat sign (‖:) A symbol that indicates that a passage of music is to be repeated from the beginning. Two repeat signs (‖: and :‖) indicate that the passage between the two signs is to be repeated.

rest A symbol designating silence.

retrograde Backward motion; beginning with the last note of a melody and ending with the first.

rhythm All of the durations or lengths of sounds and silences that occur in music; the organization of sounds and silences in time.

rhythm of the melody *See* **melodic rhythm.**

rhythm pattern Any grouping, generally brief, of long and short sounds and silences.

Romantic period The period in Western music history spanning approximately the years 1820–1900.

rondo A musical form consisting of a recurring section with two or more contrasting sections, as A B A C A.

root The tone on which a chord is built. A chord using C as its root is labeled a C chord.

round A melody performed by two or more groups entering at stated and different times; also called "canon."

scale A pattern of pitches arranged in ascending or descending order. Scales are identified by their specific arrangement of whole and half steps. *See also* **major scale; minor scale; chromatic scale; pentatonic scale; whole-tone scale.**

schwaebisch A rustic dance.

secondary chords The four chords built on the second degree (II), the third degree (III), the sixth degree (VI), and the seventh degree (VII) of any major or harmonic or melodic minor scale.

section A distinct portion of a composition; one of a number of parts that together make a composition. A section consists of several phrases.

serial music Music that uses a set sequence of pitches as the basis for a composition, such as arranging the twelve pitches of the chromatic scale into a series and then manipulating that series.

seventh chord A four-note chord built in thirds.

sharp A symbol that raises the pitch a half step (♯).

shifting meter The changing of beat groupings in music, as from twos to threes.

simple meter A grouping of beats (meter) in which the beat is divided into two equal parts.

skip A melodic interval exceeding a second or whole step.

slur A curved line, above or below a number of notes, that indicates that these pitches should be connected (legato).

soft pedal *See* **una corda pedal.**

sonata An extended composition in several movements for one to two instruments.

sonata form The most important form of the Classical period; includes a main theme and a subsidiary theme presented in the *exposition,* followed by a *development* of the themes, and concludes with a restatement, or *recapitulation,* of the themes.

sostenuto pedal The piano pedal in the middle that, when depressed, sustains only those tones whose dampers are already raised by the action of the keys.

step An interval of a second, as A to B.

subdominant The fourth tone or triad of a major or minor scale.

submediant The sixth tone or triad of a major or minor scale.

subtonic The seventh tone of a natural minor scale.

supertonic The second tone or triad of a major or minor scale.

syncopation Placement of emphasis on normally weak beats or weak parts of beats.

tempo The rate of speed of music.

ternary form A musical form consisting of three sections, A B A; two are the same and the middle one is different.

tetrachord Four successive scale tones.

theme A distinctive melodic statement, usually part of a long movement.

theme and variations A composition in which each section is a modified version of the original musical theme.

tie A curved line that connects two identical pitches and indicates that they should be performed as a single note; to perform, play the first note only and hold through the time value of the second:

timbre The quality or color of sound; the characteristic sound of an instrument. Synonyms: tone color, tone quality.

time Commonly used in place of more precise terms—namely, meter, rhythm, tempo, duration.

time signature *See* **meter signature.**

tonality The relationship of tones in a scale to the tonic.

tonal music Music that is centered on a particular tonic or key center.

tone cluster The simultaneous sounding of a group of adjacent tones, usually dissonant in sound.

tone row A series of twelve tones (the tones of a chromatic scale), arranged in a specific order, that forms the basis for a musical composition.

tonic The central tone or chord of the key and the first note or chord of a major or minor scale.

transposition Changing a piece of music from one key (scale/tonality) to another.

treble clef The symbol 𝄞, which determines the second line of the staff as G above middle C.

triad A three-note chord with pitches a third apart.

triple meter A grouping of beats (meter) into threes ($\frac{3}{4}$, $\frac{3}{8}$, $\frac{3}{2}$).

triplet A musical sign (♪♪♪) indicating three notes of equal value within a beat that normally divides into two (♪♪).

twelve-tone row *See* **tone row.**

una corda pedal The piano pedal to the far left that, when depressed, shifts the grand piano keyboard so that each hammer strikes only two of the three strings in the upper register and only one in the lower; the same effect of reducing the volume is achieved by different means on an upright piano.

upbeat *See* **anacrusis.**

virginal A small type of harpsichord with one set of strings and jacks and one keyboard; the earliest forms were shaped like a rectangular box and placed on a table or held in the performer's lap.

Western art music Art music of Western European civilization, usually created by a trained composer.

whole step An interval comprising two consecutive half steps, as C to D.

whole-tone scale A scale of six different tones, each a whole step apart.

Classified Indexes

Solo Repertoire
(alphabetized by composer)

Bach, Carl Philipp Emanuel (Germany, 1714–1788)
  Minuet (from *Notenbuch für Wolfgang*), 258
Bach, Johann Christoph Friedrich (Germany, 1732–1795)
  Schwaebisch, 258
Bach, Johann Sebastian (Germany, 1685–1750)
  Minuet in G (from *Notenbüchlein für Anna Magdalena Bach*), 268
Bach, Wilhelm Friedemann (Germany, 1710–1784)
  Minuet, 272
Bartók, Béla (Hungary, 1881–1945)
  (from *First Term at the Piano*)
  Dialogue, 237
  Duet, A, No. 2, 132
  Folk Song, No. 7, 251
  Morning Song, No. 5, 156
  Round Dance, 220
  Study: Changing Hand Position, 88
  Unison Melody, No. 1, 37
  III (from *For Children*), 273
Beethoven, Ludwig van (Germany, 1770–1827)
  Für Elise (excerpt), 265
  Russian Folk Song, Op. 107, No. 3, 158
  Theme from Six Variations on "Nel cor più non mi sento," 269
Beyer, Ferdinand (Germany, 1803–1863)
  Etude No. 12, 38
  Etude No. 13, 38
  Etude No. 14, 50
Bielawa, Herbert (United States, b. 1930)
  Pastorale, 270
  Promenade, 186
Biggs, John (United States, b. 1932)
  Etude No. 9, 246

Caramia, Tony
  Slow-Walkin' Guy, 280
Chopin, Frédéric (Poland, 1810–1849),
  Prelude, Op. 28, No. 4, 278

Czerny, Carl (Austria, 1791–1851),
  Study from Op. 823, 223

Diabelli, Anton (Austria, 1781–1858)
  Bagatelle, 256
  Melody, 185
Diemer, Emma Lou (United States, b. 1927)
  Growing, 259

Finney, Ross Lee (United States, 1906–1997) (from *32 Piano Games*)
  IV, Three White-Note Clusters, 245
  X, Two-Handed Duet, 239

Gurlitt, Cornelius (Germany, 1820–1901)
  Joy, 244
  Op. 117, No. 5, 61
  Op. 117, No. 10, 126
  Study for Two, 132

Haydn, Franz Joseph (Austria, 1732–1809)
  German Dance, No. 2, 262

Johnson, Tom (United States, b. 1939)
  Doodling, 11
Joplin, Scott (United States, 1868–1917)
  The Entertainer, A Ragtime Two-Step (simplified), 284

Kabalevsky, Dmitri (Russia, 1904–1987)
  Funny Dialogue, 133
  (from *24 Little Pieces*)
    Little Dance, A, Op. 39, No. 9, 186
    Melody, Op. 39, No. 1, 85
    Melody, Op. 39, No. 3, 195
    Op. 39, No. 4, 219
    Op. 39, No. 5, 267
    Op. 39, No. 8, 245
Konowitz, Bert
  Feelings, 157
Künz, Konrad Max (Germany, 1812–1875)
  Canon, 108
  Canon, 203

McGlone, Theresa
  No Name Blues, 281

Mier, Martha (United States, b. 1936)
  Just Struttin' Along, 282
Mozart, Leopold (Austria, 1719–1787)
  Bourrée (from *Notenbuch für Wolfgang*), 264
  Minuet (D minor), 220
  Minuet (F major from *Nannerl Notenbuch*), 17, 246
Mozart, Wolfgang Amadeus (Austria, 1756–1791)
  Minuet in F, K. 2, 266
  Minuet in G, K. 1, 256
  12 Variations (excerpts) on "Ah, vous dirai-je, Maman," K. 265, 214–216
Müller, August Eberhard (Germany, 1767–1817)
  Andante, 130

Olson, Lynn Freeman (United States, 1938–1987)
  Chimes, 155
  Seeds, 86
  Swing Tune, 60

Persichetti, Vincent (United States, 1915–1987)
  (from *Little Piano Book,* Op. 60)
  Prologue, 274
  Statement, 263

Rameau, Jean-Philippe (France, 1683–1764)
  Minuet, 260
Rebikov, Vladimir (Russia, 1886–1920)
  The Bear, 233
Reinagle, Alexander (England, 1756-1809)
  Minuet, 131
Rollin, Catherine (United States, b. 1952)
  jazz around the clock, 152

Schubert, Franz (Austria, 1797–1828)
  Écossaise, 257
Schumann, Robert (Germany, 1810–1856)
  (from *Piano Pieces for the Young,* Op. 68)
  Ein Choral, 248
  Stückchen, 271

337

Ensemble Pieces

Technique Exercises

Composing Projects

General Index

Ellington, Duke, 15
Enharmonics, 15
Evans, Lee, 51
Extension fingering, 110, 187, 221, 247

Fermata, 146
Figured bass, 166–167
Finger numbers, 9
Fingering
    arpeggio, 80, 104, 176, 188, 206, 321
    changing fingers, 248
    chromatic scale, 22
    contraction, 222
    extension, 110, 187, 221, 247
    major scale, 117, 119, 310–312
    minor scale, 196, 200–201
    thumb-under, 133, 134
Finney, Ross Lee, 239
Five-finger pattern, 22
    major, 22
    minor, 93
Flags, 26, 306
Flat, 15, 32, 305
    double flat, 305
Form, 5
    binary, 245, 331
    defined, 5
    phrases, 69, 84–85
    rondo, 255, 334
    ternary, 240, 331
    theme and variations, 214, 219, 269

Gavotte, 199
Glissando, 332
Grace note, 332
Grand staff, 32, 308
Gurlitt, Cornelius, 61

Half steps, 22
Hand position, 9
Hanon, Charles Louis, 187
Harmonic interval, 48
Harmonic minor scale, 199
    one-hand fingering, 200
Harmonization, 179–184
Harmony, 5
Harpsichord, 1, 328, 332
Haydn, Franz Joseph, 262

Impressionism, 232, 333
Improvisation, 17
    black key, 17
    blues, 145
    boogie-woogie, 17
    descriptive miniature, 18
    indeterminate music, 11
    modal, 231
    pentatonic, 229
    whole-tone scale, 233
Indeterminacy, 11
Interval reading, 48–50

Intervals, 48, 63, 95–96, 109, 116, 135, 317
    augmented, 317
    defined, 22
    diminished, 317
    half steps, 22
    numerical identification, 317
    quality identification, 317
    whole steps, 22
Inversions, 78, 166–167
Invertible counterpoint, 107

Johnson, Tom, 12
Joplin, Scott, 285
Jump bass, 322

Kabalevsky, Dmitri, 85, 267
Key, 121, 197
Key signatures, 32, 34, 120–121,
      197–198, 309
    determining major key, 121
    determining minor key, 197
    major, 120, 197
    minor, 197
Keyboard, 10
    black keys, 15, 16
    finger numbers, 9
    landmarks, 12
    playing position, 8
    white keys, 12
Keyboard, electronic, 4–5
    basic, 4
    digital pianos, 4–5
    synthesizers, 5
Konowitz, Bert, 157

Lead sheet notation, 55, 325–327
Legato pedaling, 159, 248
Legato touch, 23, 37, 39
Leger (ledger) lines, 31–32
Lydian mode, 230

Major five-finger pattern, 22
Major key signatures, 120–122, 309
    determining major key, 121
Major scale, 114
    defined, 114
    degrees, 115
    fingerings, 117, 119, 310–312
    key signatures, 120–122, 309
    syllables, 115
Major triads, 78, 317
Major-major seventh chords, 318
Major-minor seventh chords, 164, 318
Manone, Wingy, 143
Mazurka, 333
Measure, 27
    incomplete, 74
Medieval period, 328
Melodic interval, 48
Melodic minor scale, 201
    fingering, 201

Melody, 5
Memorizing, 91
Meter, 26
    asymmetric, 241–243
    bar lines, 27
    compound, 171, 307
    counting compound meters, 172
    counting simple meters, 7
    duple, 26–27, 172, 307
    quadruple, 26–27, 172, 307
    shifting, 239–241
    simple, 27
    time signatures, 27, 307
    triple, 26–27, 172, 307
Meter signatures, see Time Signatures.
Metronome, 305
Middle C, 12, 32
MIDI, 4
Mier, Martha, 283
Minimalism, 333
Minor five-finger pattern, 93
Minor key signatures, 197–198, 309
    determining minor key, 197
Minor scales, 194, 313–316
    degrees, 201
    fingerings, 196, 200–201
    harmonic, 199
    melodic, 201
    natural, 194
    syllables, 202
Minor-minor seventh chords, 318
Minor triads, 102–103, 317
Minuet, 266
Mixolydian mode, 230
Modes, 229–232
Motive, 133
Mozart, Leopold, 17, 221, 264
Mozart, Wolfgang Amadeus, 256

Natural minor scale, 194
    fingering, 196
Natural sign, 305
Neighboring tones, 180
New age music, 254
Nonchord tones, 180
    neighboring, 180
    passing, 180
Notation
    pitch, 31–32
    rhythm, 26–27
Notes, 26, 68, 306
    beams, 26, 306
    defined, 25
    flags, 26, 306
    parts of notes, 26, 306
    relative note duration, 26

Octave, 64
Octave identification, 308
Olson, Lynn Freeman, 61
Opus (op.), 334

Organ, 328, 334
Ostinato, 17

Parallel majors and minors, 213
Parallel motion, 37, 109
Parallel phrases, 70, 83–84
Passing tones, 180
Pedaling, 10
    legato/syncopated, 159, 248
Pedals, 3, 10, 159
Pentatonic scale, 227–229
Persichetti, Vincent, 263, 274
Phrases, 70, 83–85
    contrasting, 70, 84–85
    parallel, 70, 83–84
Piano
    acoustic, 3
    electronic, 4–5
    grand, 2–3
    history, 1–3
    instrument parts, 3
    pedals, 3, 10
    upright, 2–3
Pickup notes, 74
Plagal cadence, 142
Polyphonic, 334
Polytonal, 334
Portative organ, 328
Position at the keyboard, 8
Positive organ, 328
Practice Journal, 46
Practice Plan, 44
Practice Tips, 191–192
Practice Worksheet, 45
Prelude, 334
Primary chords, 142, 173–175, 204–205,
    319–320

Quadruple meter, 26–27, 172, 307

Ragtime, 334
Rameau, Jean-Phillippe, 260
Rebikov, Vladimir, 233
Reinagle, Alexander, 131
Relative major and minor keys, 197, 212
Renaissance period, 328
Repeat signs, 16
Rests, 26, 306
Retrograde, 238
Rhythm, 25, 149

Rolled chord, 322
Rollin, Catherine, 153
Romantic period, 329
Rondo, 255, 334
Root, 55

Scale degrees
    major, 115
    minor, 201
Scales
    blues, 234
    chromatic, 22
    defined, 114
    harmonic minor, 199
    major, 114
    melodic minor, 201
    natural minor, 194
    pentatonic, 227–229
    whole tone, 232–233
Schubert, Franz, 210
Schumann, Robert, 271
Schwaebisch, 258
Secondary chords, 317
Sequencing, 4
Serial music, 238
Seventh chords, 164, 318
    diminished-diminished, 318
    diminished-minor, 318
    dominant, 164
    figures, 166–167
    major-major, 318
    major-minor, 164, 318
    minor-minor, 318
Sharp, 15, 32, 305
    double sharp, 305
Shifting meter, 239–241
Shostakovich, Dmitri, 261
Sight-reading, 140
Simple meter, 27, 307
Slur, 334
Soft pedal, 3, 10
Sol-fa syllables, 115, 202, 229–232
Sonata, 334
Sonata form, 335
Sostenuto pedal, 3, 10
Staccato, 126, 134
Staff, 30
    bass clef, 31
    grand, 32
    treble clef, 31

Stravinsky, Igor, 241
Subdominant, 142
Syllable names (sol-fa)
    major, 115
    minor, 202
    modes, 229–232
Syncopation, 149
Synthesizers, 5
Szymanowska, Maria, 275

Tempo, 6
    tempo terms, 303–304
Ternary form, 240, 331
Tetrachord, 114
Theme and variation form, 214, 219, 269
Thumb-under technique, 133–134
Ties, 77
Timbre, 6
Time signatures, 27, 172, 307
Tone clusters, 243, 245
Tone color, 6
Tone row, 238–239
Tonic, 23, 81, 104
Transposition, 51–53
Treble clef, 31–32, 308
Triad, 78
    augmented, 317
    diminished, 317
    figures, 167
    inversions, 78
    major, 78, 317
    minor, 102, 317
    symbols, 55, 325–327
Triple meter, 26–27, 172, 307
Triplet, 152, 256
Türk, Daniel Gottlob, 62
Twelve-bar blues, 14, 144–145
Twelve-tone row, 238–239

Una corda pedal, 3
Upbeat, 74

Van de Vate, Nancy, 107, 227
Virginal, 328, 335

Western art music, 328–329
Whole steps, 22
Whole-tone scale, 232–233

Yeager, Jeanine, 254

Title Index

CD Acknowledgments

The *PianoLab* CD Repertoire